HOW THE
Brain Learns
THIRD EDITION

David A. Sousa

 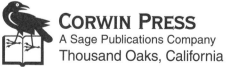

CORWIN PRESS
A Sage Publications Company
Thousand Oaks, California

For information:

Corwin Press
A Sage Publications Company
2455 Teller Road
Thousand Oaks, California 91320
www.corwinpress.com

Sage Publications Ltd
1 Oliver's Yard
55 City Road
London EC1Y 1SP
United Kingdom

Sage Publications India Pvt. Ltd.
B-42, Panchsheel Enclave
Post Box 4109
New Delhi 110 017 India

Printed in the United States of America on acid-free paper

Library of Congress Cataloging-in-Publication Data

Sousa, David A.
How the brain learns / David A. Sousa.— 3rd ed.
        p. cm.
Includes bibliographical references and index.
ISBN 1-4129-3660-8 (cloth) — ISBN 1-4129-3661-6 (pbk.)
    1. Learning, Psychology of. 2. Learning—Physiological aspects. 3. Brain. I. Title.
LB1057.S65 2006
370.15'23—dc22

                                          2005029776

05 06 07 08 10 9 8 7 6 5 4 3 2 1

Acquisitions editor: Robert D. Clouse
Editorial assistant: Jingle Vea
Production editor: Sanford Robinson
Typesetter: C&M Digitals (P) Ltd.
Cover designer: Tracy Miller
Production artist: Lisa Miller

Contents

List of Practitioner's Corners

About the Author

David A. Sousa, Ed.D., is an international educational consultant. He has made presentations at national conventions of educational organizations and has conducted workshops on brain research and science education in hundreds of school districts and at several colleges and universities across the United States, Canada, Europe, and Asia.

Dr. Sousa has a bachelor of science degree in chemistry from Massachusetts State College at Bridgewater, a master of arts in teaching degree in science from Harvard University, and a doctorate from Rutgers University. His teaching experience covers all levels. He has taught junior and senior high school science, served as a K–12 director of science, and was Supervisor of Instruction for the West Orange, New Jersey, schools. He then became superintendent of the New Providence, New Jersey, public schools. He has been an adjunct professor of education at Seton Hall University, and a visiting lecturer at Rutgers University. He was president of the National Staff Development Council in 1992.

Dr. Sousa has edited science books and published numerous books and articles in leading educational journals on staff development, science education, and brain research. He has received awards from professional associations and school districts for his commitment and contributions to research, staff development, and science education. He received the Distinguished Alumni Award and an honorary doctorate in education from Bridgewater (Mass.) State College.

He has appeared on the NBC Today show and on National Public Radio to discuss his work with schools using brain research. He makes his home in south Florida.

Who dares to teach
must never cease to learn.

—*John Cotton Dana*

Preface to the Third Edition

Since the publication of the second edition of this book, neuroscientists have continued to make remarkable discoveries about how the human brain grows, develops, and learns. Scanning technologies are more sophisticated and are able to track brain activity faster and more accurately than ever before. Perhaps the greatest discovery of neuroscientists that has bene-fitted many children has been the improved understanding of how the brain acquires language and learns to read. These research insights have allowed scientists to design educational interventions that are amazingly successful in actually rewiring the brains of young struggling readers so that their reading skills improve dramatically. Can you imagine that? We can now rewire young brains!

For this third edition, I have made some changes in the text as a result of new knowledge about the brain. Specifically, I have

- Updated the Information Processing Model to reflect newer terminology and understandings about memory systems
- Updated the exciting research about language acquisition and how the brain learns to read
- Expanded the chapter on thinking skills and included the recently revised version of Bloom's Taxonomy
- Added more examples of how emotions influence learning and memory
- Added two Practitioner's Corners
- Added a section on resources that includes additional books and Internet sites
- Included more primary sources for those who wish to review the actual research studies

When the first edition of this book was published over a decade ago, not too many educators were familiar with the growing knowledge base in cognitive neuroscience. Today, most educators are very familiar with the explosion of current research on the brain. There is little doubt that some of the findings of this exciting research have implications for what we do in schools and classrooms. But there is also a lot of hype about the brain these days and not all of it is accurate. Educators must avoid the hype and use caution when deciding whether new knowledge can improve our practice.

I firmly believe that science will continue to reveal deeper understandings about how the brain learns. As educators become more familiar with these revelations, I also believe they will ensure that brain-compatible schools provide opportunities for all learners to succeed.

—David A. Sousa

Acknowledgments

Corwin Press gratefully acknowledges the contribution of the following people:

Elizabeth F. Day
Teacher of the Year
Mechanicville Middle School
Mechanicville, NY

Janice Ferguson
Professor, Exceptional Education
Department of Special Instruction Programs
Western Kentucky University
Bowling Green, KY

Janet Steck
Part-Time Faculty
Department of Early Childhood,
Physical and Special Education
The University of Toledo
Toledo, OH

Nicola Salvatico
Teacher of the Year
General Wayne Elementary School
Malvern, PA

Randy J. Wormald
Teacher of the Year
Belmont High School
Belmont, NH

Carrie Jane Carpenter
Teacher of the Year
Hugh Hartman Middle School
Redmond, OR

Jensi Kellogg-Andrus
Teacher of the Year
Watertown High School
Watertown, SD

Marguerite Lawler-Rohner
Teacher of the Year
Westcott Junior High School
Portland, ME

Introduction

*You start out as a single cell derived from the coupling
of a sperm and egg; this divides into two, then four,
then eight, and so on, and at a certain stage there
emerges a single cell which will have as all its prog-
eny the human brain. The mere existence of that cell
should be one of the great astonishments of the earth.*
                                    —Lewis Thomas,
                          The Medusa and the Snail

The human brain is an amazing structure—a universe of infinite possibilities and mystery. It
constantly shapes and reshapes itself as a result of experience, yet it can take off on its own
without input from the outside world. How does it form a human mind, capture experience,
or stop time in memory? Although it does not generate enough energy to light a simple bulb, its
capabilities make it the most powerful force on Earth.

For thousands of years, humans have been delving into this mysterious universe and trying to
determine how it accomplishes its amazing feats. How fast does it grow? What impact does the
environment have on its growth? What is intelligence? How does it learn language? How does it
learn to read?

Just how the brain learns has been of particular interest to teachers for centuries. Now, in the
21st century, there is new hope that our understanding of this remarkable process called teaching and
learning will improve dramatically. A major source of that understanding is coming from the sophisticated medical instruments that allow scientists to peer inside the living—and learning—brain.

LOOKING INSIDE THE BRAIN

New technologies for looking inside and seeing the workings of the living brain have advanced
faster than scientists predicted just 10 years ago. The more we learn about the brain, the more
remarkable it seems. Hardly a week goes by when some major news story about the brain appears
in the press or on television. Consequently, most of us have heard about the imaging technologies,

and some readers may have even experienced a brain scan. Because we will be mentioning brain scans throughout this book, here is a brief review of the more common scanning instruments that have contributed to our understanding of brain structure and function.

Types of Brain Imaging

The imaging technologies fall into two major categories: those that look at brain *structure* and those that look at brain *function*. When aimed at the brain, computerized axial tomography (CAT) and magnetic resonance imaging (MRI) are very useful diagnostic tools that produce computer images of the brain's internal structure. For example, they can detect tumors, malformations, and the damage caused by cerebral hemorrhages.

Different technologies, however, are required to look at how the brain works. An alphabet soup describes the five most common procedures that can be used to isolate and identify the areas of the brain where distinct levels of activity are occurring. The scanning technologies for looking at brain function are the following:

- Electroencephalography (EEG)
- Magnetoencephalography (MEG)
- Positron Emission Tomography (PET)
- Functional Magnetic Resonance Imaging (fMRI)
- Functional Magnetic Resonance Spectroscopy (fMRS)

Here is a brief explanation of how each one works. A summary chart follows.

- **Electroencephalography (EEG) and Magnetoencephalography (MEG).** These two techniques are helpful in determining how quickly something occurs in the brain. To do that, they measure electrical and magnetic activity occurring in the brain during mental processing. In an EEG, anywhere from 19 to 128 electrodes are attached to various positions on the scalp with a conductive gel so electrical signals can be recorded in a computer. In a MEG, about 100 magnetic detectors are placed around the head to record magnetic activity. EEGs and MEGs can record changes in brain activity that occur as rapidly as one millisecond (one-thousandth of a second), typical times when the brain is processing language. When a group of neurons responds to a specific event (like a word), they activate and their electrical and magnetic activity can be detected above the noise of the nonactivated neurons. This response is called an *Event-Related Potential* or ERP. ERP evidence has provided information about the time needed for the brain to do mathematical calculations or process reading. EEG and MEG do not expose the subject to radiation and are not considered hazardous.

- **Positron Emission Tomography (PET).** The first technology to observe brain functions, it involves injecting the subject with a radioactive solution that circulates to the brain. Brain regions of higher activity accumulate more of the radiation, which is picked up by a ring of detectors around the subject's head. A computer displays the concentration of radiation as a picture of blood flow in a cross-sectional slice of the brain regions that are aligned with the detectors. The picture is in color, with the more active areas in reds and yellows, the quieter areas in blues and greens. Two major drawbacks to PET scans are the invasive nature of the injection and the use of radioactive materials. Consequently, this technique is not used with normal children because the radioactive risk is too high.

- **Functional Magnetic Resonance Imaging (fMRI).** This newer technology is rapidly replacing PET scans because it is painless, noninvasive, and does not use radiation. The technology helps to pinpoint the brain areas of greater and lesser activity. Its operation is based on the fact that when any part of the brain becomes more active, the need for oxygen and nutrients increases. Oxygen is carried to the brain cells by hemoglobin. Hemoglobin contains iron, which is magnetic. The fMRI uses a large magnet to compare the amount of oxygenated hemoglobin entering brain cells with the amount of deoxygenated hemoglobin leaving the cells. The computer colors in the brain regions receiving more oxygenated blood and can locate the activated brain region to within one centimeter (less than a half-inch).

- **Functional Magnetic Resonance Spectroscopy (fMRS).** This technology involves the same equipment as fMRI but uses different computer software to record levels of various chemicals in the brain while the subject is thinking. Like the fMRI, fMRS can precisely pinpoint the area of activity, but it can also identify whether certain key chemicals are also present at the activation site. fMRS has been used to study language function in the brain by mapping the change in specific chemicals, such as lactate, that respond to brain activation during tasks involving language.

Researchers are also learning much more about several dozen brain chemicals called *neurotransmitters*. These substances bathe the brain cells and either permit signals to pass between them or inhibit them. Wide fluctuations in the concentration of neurotransmitters in certain brain areas can change our mood, affect our movement, diminish or enhance our alertness, and interfere with our ability to learn.

To determine which parts of the brain control various functions, neurosurgeons use tiny electrodes to stimulate individual nerve cells and record their reactions. Besides the information collected by these techniques, the growing body of case studies of individuals recovering from various types of brain damage is giving us new evidence about and insights into how the brain develops, changes, learns, remembers, and recovers from injury.

IMPLICATIONS FOR TEACHING

As we examine the clues that this research is yielding about learning, we recognize its importance to the teaching profession. Every day teachers enter their classrooms with lesson plans, experience, and the hope that what they are about to present will be understood, remembered, and useful to their students. The extent that this hope is realized depends largely on the knowledge base that these teachers use in designing those plans and, perhaps more important, on the instructional techniques they select during the lessons. Teachers try to change the human brain every day. The more they know about how it learns, the more successful they can be.

Techniques for Mapping Brain Functions		
Technique	**What It Measures**	**How It Works**
Electroencephalography (EEG) Magnetoencephalography (MEG)	The electrical and magnetic activity occurring in the brain during mental processing. The spikes of activity are called Event-Related Potentials (ERP).	In EEG, multiple electrodes are attached to the scalp to record electrical signals in a computer. In MEG, magnetic detectors are placed around the head to record magnetic activity. EEGs and MEGs record changes in brain activity that occur as rapidly as one millisecond. When a group of neurons responds to a specific event, they activate and their electrical and magnetic activity can be detected. This response is called an Event-Related Potential or ERP.
Positron Emission Tomography (PET)	Amount of radiation present in brain regions	The subject is injected with a radioactive solution that circulates to the brain. Brain regions of higher activity accumulate more radiation, which is picked up by a ring of detectors. A computer displays the concentration of radiation in a cross-sectional slice of the brain regions aligned with the detectors. The picture shows the more active areas in reds and yellows, the quieter areas in blues and greens.
Functional Magnetic Resonance Imaging (fMRI)	Levels of deoxygenated hemoglobin in brain cells	Any part of the brain that is thinking requires more oxygen, which is carried to the brain cells by hemoglobin. The fMRI uses a large magnet to compare the amount of oxygenated hemoglobin entering brain cells with the amount of deoxygenated hemoglobin leaving the cells. The computer colors in the brain regions receiving more oxygenated blood and locates the activated brain region to within one centimeter (half-inch).
Functional Magnetic Resonance Spectroscopy (fMRS)	Levels of specific chemicals present during brain activity	This technology involves the same equipment as fMRI but uses different computer software to record levels of various chemicals in the brain while the subject is thinking. fMRS can precisely pinpoint the area of activity, but it can also identify whether certain key chemicals are also present at the activation site.

Educators in recent years have become much more aware that neuroscience is finding out a lot about how the brain works, and that some of the discoveries have implications for what happens in schools and classrooms. There is a growing interest among educators in the biology of learning and how much an individual's environment can affect

> *Teachers try to change the human brain every day. The more they know about how it learns, the more successful they can be.*

the growth and development of the brain. Teacher training institutions are beginning to incorporate brain research into their courses. Staff development programs are devoting more time to this area, more books about the brain are available, brain-compatible teaching units are sprouting up, and the journals of most major educational organizations have devoted special issues to the topic. These are all good signs. I believe this focus on recent brain research can improve the quality of our profession's performance and its success in helping others learn.

Some Important Findings

As research continues to provide a deeper understanding of the workings of the human brain, educators need to be cautious about how they apply these findings to practice. There are critics who believe that brain research should not be used at this time in schools and classrooms. Some critics say it will be years before this has any application to educational practice. Others fear that unsubstantiated claims are being made, and that educators are not sufficiently trained to tell scientific fact from hype. The concerns are understandable but should not prevent educators from learning what they need to know to decide whether a research study has applications to their practice. For those who wonder how recent discoveries about the brain can affect teaching and learning, we can tell them that this research has:

- Reaffirmed that the human brain continually reorganizes itself on the basis of input. This process, called *neuroplasticity*, continues throughout our life but is exceptionally rapid in the early years. Thus, the experiences the young brain has in the home and at school help shape the neural circuits that will determine how and what that brain learns in school and later.
- Revealed more about how the brain acquires spoken language.
- Developed scientifically based computer programs that dramatically help young children with reading problems.
- Shown how emotions affect learning, memory, and recall.
- Suggested that movement and exercise improve mood, increase brain mass, and enhance cognitive processing.
- Tracked the growth and development of the teenage brain to better understand the unpredictability of adolescent behavior.
- Developed a deeper understanding of circadian cycles to explain why teaching and learning can be more difficult at certain times of day.
- Studied the effects of sleep deprivation and stress on learning and memory.
- Recognized that intelligence and creativity are separate abilities, and that both can be modified by the environment and schooling.

Other researchers strongly disagree with the critics and support the increased attention that educators are giving to neuroscience. Several universities here and abroad have established dedicated research centers to examine how discoveries in neuroscience can affect educational practice. As a result, educational theory and practice will become much more research-based, similar to the medical model.

There is, of course, no panacea that will make teaching and learning a perfect process—and that includes brain research. It is a long leap from making a research finding in a laboratory to the changing of schools and practice because of that finding. These are exciting times for educators, but we must ensure that we don't let the excitement cloud our common sense.

WHY THIS BOOK CAN HELP IMPROVE TEACHING AND LEARNING

What I have tried to do here is report on research (from neuroscience as well as the behavioral and cognitive sciences) that is sufficiently reliable that it can inform educational practice. This is hardly a novel idea. Madeline Hunter in the late 1960s introduced the notion of teachers using what science was learning about learning and modifying traditional classroom procedures and instructional techniques accordingly. Her program at the UCLA School of Education came to be called "Instructional Theory Into Practice," or ITIP. Readers familiar with that model will recognize some of Dr. Hunter's work here, especially in the areas of transfer and practice. I had the privilege of working periodically with her for nine years, and I firmly believe that she was the major force that awakened educators to the importance of continually updating their knowledge base and focusing on research-based strategies and the developing science of learning.

This book will help answer questions such as:

- When do students remember best in a learning episode?
- How can I help students understand and remember more of what I teach?
- Why is focus so important, and why is it so difficult to get?
- How can I teach motor skills effectively?
- How can humor and music help the teaching-learning process?
- How can I get students to find meaning in what they are learning?
- Why is transfer such a powerful principle of learning, and how can it destroy a lesson without my realizing it?
- What classroom strategies are more likely to appeal to the brain of today's student?
- What important questions should I be asking myself as I plan daily and unit lessons?

Chapter Contents

Chapter 1. Basic Brain Facts and Brain Development. Because we are going to talk a lot about the brain, we should be familiar with some of its anatomy. This chapter discusses some of the majors structures of the human brain and their functions. It explores how the young brain grows and develops, focusing on those important windows of opportunity for learning in the early years. There is an explanation of how students' brains today are very different from those of just a few years ago, especially in what they expect from their school experiences.

Chapter 2. How the Brain Processes Information. Trying to develop a simple model to describe the complex process of learning is not easy. The model at the heart of this chapter outlines what cognitive researchers believe are the critical steps involved in the brain's acquisition and processing of information. The components of the model are discussed in detail and updated from previous editions. Also included is an instrument to help you determine your sensory preferences.

Chapter 3. Memory, Retention, and Learning. Teachers want their students to remember forever what they are taught, but that does not happen too often. The third chapter focuses on the different types of memory systems and how they work. Those factors that affect retention of learning are discussed here along with ideas of how to plan lessons that result in greater remembering.

Chapter 4. The Power of Transfer. Transfer is one of the most powerful and least understood principles of learning. Yet a major goal of education is to enable students to transfer what they learn in school to solve future problems. The nature and power of transfer are examined in this chapter, including how to use past knowledge to enhance present and future learning.

Chapter 5. Brain Specialization and Learning. This chapter explores how areas of the brain are specialized to perform certain tasks. It examines hemispheric specialization and debunks some myths that have obscured the value of this work. You will be able to determine whether you have a hemispheric preference and what that means about how you think, learn, and teach. The chapter also examines the latest research on how we learn to speak and read, and the implications of this research for classroom instruction and for the curriculum and structure of schools.

Chapter 6. The Brain and the Arts. Despite strong evidence that the arts enhance cognitive development, they run the risk of being abandoned so more time can be devoted to preparing for mandated high stakes testing. Public support for keeping the arts is growing. This chapter presents the latest evidence of how the arts in themselves contribute to the growth of neural networks as well as enhance the skills needed for mastering other academic subjects.

Chapter 7. Thinking Skills and Learning. Are we challenging our students enough to do higher-level thinking? This chapter discusses some of the characteristics and dimensions of human thinking. It focuses on the recent revision of Bloom's Taxonomy, notes its continuing compatibility with current research on higher-order thinking, and explains the taxonomy's critically important relationship to difficulty, complexity, and intelligence.

Chapter 8. Putting It All Together. So how do we use these important findings in daily practice? This chapter emphasizes how to use the research presented in this book to plan lessons. It discusses different types of teaching methods, and suggests guidelines and a format for lesson design. Because neuroscience continues to reveal new information about learning, the chapter describes support systems to help educators maintain expertise in brain-compatible techniques and move toward continuous professional growth.

At the end of each chapter are the **Practitioner's Corners.** Some include activities that check for understanding of the major concepts and research presented in the chapter. Others offer my interpretation of how this research might translate into effective classroom strategies that improve the teaching-learning process. Readers are invited to critically review my suggestions and rationale to determine if they have any value for their work.

Main thoughts are highlighted in boxes throughout the book. At the very end of each chapter, you will find a page called **Key Points to Ponder**, an organizing tool to help you remember important ideas, strategies, and resources you may wish to consider later.

Where appropriate, I have explained some of the chemical and biological processes occurring within the brain. However, I have intentionally omitted complex chemical formulas and reactions, and have avoided side issues that would distract from the main purpose of this book. My intent is to present just enough science to help the average reader understand the research and the rationale for any suggestions I offer.

Who Should Use This Book?

This book will be useful to **classroom teachers** because it presents a research-based rationale for why and when certain instructional strategies should be considered. It focuses on the brain as the organ of thinking and learning, and takes the approach that the more teachers know about how the brain learns, the more instructional options become available. Increasing the options that teachers have during the dynamic process of instruction also increases the likelihood that successful learning will occur.

The book should also help **staff developers** who continually need to update their own knowledge base and include research and research-based strategies and support systems as part of their repertoire. Chapter 8 offers some suggestions to help staff developers implement and maintain the knowledge and strategies suggested here.

Principals and Head Teachers should find here a substantial source of topics for discussion at faculty meetings, which should include, after all, instructional as well as informational items. In doing so, they support the attitude that professional growth is an ongoing school responsibility and not an occasional event. More important, being familiar with these topics enhances the principal's credibility as the school's instructional leader and promotes the notion that the school is a learning organization for *all* its occupants.

> **This book can help teachers, staff developers, principals, college instructors, and parents.**

College and university instructors should also find merit in the research and applications presented here, as both suggestions to improve their own teaching as well as information to be passed on to prospective teachers.

Some of the information in this book will be useful to **parents**, who are, after all, the child's first teachers.

Indeed, the ideas in this book provide the research support for a variety of initiatives, such as cooperative learning groups, differentiated instruction, integrated thematic units, and the interdisciplinary approach to curriculum. Those who are familiar with constructivism will recognize many similarities in the ideas presented here. The research is yielding more evidence that knowledge is not only transmitted from the teacher to the learners but is transformed in the learner's mind as a result of cultural and social mediation. Much of this occurs through elaborative rehearsal and transfer and is discussed in several chapters.

Try It Yourself—Do Action Research

Benefits of Action Research

One of the best ways to assess the value of the strategies suggested in this book is to try them out in your own classroom or in any other location where you are teaching. Conducting this action research allows you to gather data to determine the effectiveness of new strategies and affirm those you already use, to acclaim and enhance the use of research in our profession, and to further your own professional development.

Other benefits of action research are that it provides teachers with consistent feedback for self-evaluation, it introduces alternative forms of student assessment, and its results may lead to important changes in curriculum. Action research can be the work of just one teacher, but its value grows immensely when it is the consistent effort of a teacher team, department, school staff, or even an entire district. Incorporating action research as a regular part of the K–12 academic scene not only provides useful data but also enhances the integrity of the profession and gains much-needed respect from the broad community that schools serve.

> *Using action research provides valuable data, affirms best practices, and enhances the integrity of the profession.*

Teachers are often hesitant to engage in action research, concerned that it may take too much time or that it represents another accountability measure in an already test-saturated environment. Yet, with all the programs and strategies emerging today in the name of reform, we need data to help determine their validity. The valuable results of cognitive neuroscience will continue to be ignored in schools unless there is reliable evidence to support their use. Action research is a cost-effective means of assessing the effectiveness of brain-compatible strategies that are likely to result in greater student learning.

The Outcomes of Action Research

The classroom is a laboratory in which the teaching and learning processes meet and interact. Action research can provide continual feedback on the success of that interaction. Using a solution-oriented approach, action research includes identifying the problem, systematically collecting data, analyzing the data, taking action based on the data, evaluating and reflecting on the results of those actions, and, if needed, redefining the problem (Figure I.1). The teacher is always in control of the type of data collected, the pace of assessment, and the analysis of the results. This process encourages teachers to reflect on their practices, to refine their skills as a practitioner, and to direct their

The Action Research Cycle

Identify or Redefine the Problem → Collect Appropriate Data → Analyze Data → Report Results → Take Action Based on Results of Data → Evaluate and Reflect →

Figure I.1 The diagram illustrates the six steps in the action research cycle.

own professional development. This is a new view of the profession, with the teacher as the main agent of change.

Building administrators have a special obligation to encourage action research among their teachers. With so much responsibility and accountability being placed on schools and teachers, action research can quickly assess the effectiveness of instructional strategies. By supporting such a program, principals demonstrate by action that they are truly instructional leaders and not just building managers. See the **Practitioner's Corner** at the end of this chapter on page 13 for specific suggestions on using action research in the classroom.

Finally, this third edition of the book reflects what more I have gathered about the brain and learning at the time of publication. Because this is now an area of intense research and scrutiny, educators need to constantly read about new discoveries and adjust their understandings accordingly. As we discover more about how the brain learns, we can devise strategies that can make the teaching-learning process more efficient, effective, and enjoyable.

What's Coming Up?

As neuroscience advances, educators are realizing that some basic information about the brain must now become part of their knowledge base. Educators are not neuroscientists, but they are members of the *only* profession whose job is to change the human brain every day. Therefore, the more they know about how it works, the more likely they are to be successful at changing it. To that end, the next chapter will take the reader through a painless and easy-to-read explanation of some major brain structures and their functions as well as a peek at the brain of today's students.

> *Educators are in the only profession whose job is to change the human brain every day.*

PRACTITIONER'S CORNER

What Do You Already Know?

The value of this book can be measured in part by how it enhances your understanding of the brain and the way it learns. Take the following true-false test to assess your current knowledge of the brain. Decide whether the statements are generally true or false and circle T or F. Explanations for the answers are identified throughout the book in special boxes.

1. T F The structures responsible for deciding what gets stored in long-term memory are located in the brain's rational system.

2. T F Learners who can perform a new learning task well are likely to retain it.

3. T F Reviewing material just before a test is a good practice to determine how much has been retained.

4. T F Increased time on task increases retention of new learning.

5. T F Two very similar concepts or motor skills should be taught at the same time.

6. T F The rate at which a learner retrieves information from memory is closely related to intelligence.

7. T F The amount of information a learner can deal with at one time is genetically linked.

8. T F It is usually not possible to increase the amount of information that the working (temporary) memory can deal with at one time.

9. T F Most of the time, the transfer of information from long-term storage is under the conscious control of the learner.

10. T F Bloom's Taxonomy has not changed over the years.

PRACTITIONER'S CORNER

How Brain Compatible Is
My Teaching/School/District?

Directions: On a scale of 1 (lowest) to 5 (highest), circle the number that indicates the degree to which your teaching/school/district does the following. Connect the circles to see a profile.

1. I/We adapt the curriculum to recognize the windows of opportunity students have during their cognitive growth. 1——2——3——4——5

2. I/We are trained to provoke strong, positive emotions in students during the learning process. 1——2——3——4——5

3. I/We are trained to help students adjust their self-concept to be more successful in different learning situations. 1——2——3——4——5

4. I/We provide an enriched and varied learning environment. 1——2——3——4——5

5. I/We search constantly for opportunities to integrate curriculum concepts between and among subject areas. 1——2——3——4——5

6. Students have frequent opportunities during class to talk about what they are learning, while they are learning. 1——2——3——4——5

7. I/We do not use lecture as the main mode of instruction. 1——2——3——4——5

8. One of the main criteria I/we use to decide on classroom activities and curriculum is relevancy to students. 1——2——3——4——5

9. I/We understand the power of chunking and use it in the design of curriculum and in daily instruction. 1——2——3——4——5

10. I/We understand the primacy-recency effect and use it regularly in the classroom to enhance retention of learning. 1——2——3——4——5

PRACTITIONER'S CORNER

Using Action Research

Basic Guidelines

Action research helps teachers assess systematically the effectiveness of their own educational practices using the techniques of research. Because data collection is essential to this process, teachers need to identify the elements of the research question that can be measured.

- **Select the Research Question.** Because you need to collect data, choose a research question that involves elements which can be easily measured quantitatively or qualitatively. Some examples:

  1. How does the chunking of material affect the learner's retention? This can be measured by a short oral or written quiz.

  2. How does teaching material at the beginning or middle of a lesson affect learner retention? This can be measured by quizzes.

  3. How does changing the length of wait time affect student participation? This can be measured by comparing the length of the wait time to the number of subsequent student responses.

  4. Does using humor or music increase student focus? Can either be measured by number of students who are on/off task with or without humor or music.

  5. Does teaching two very similar concepts at different times improve student understanding and retention of them? This can be measured by oral questioning or quizzes after teaching each concept.

- **Collect the Data.** Remember that you need baseline data before you try the research strategy to provide a comparison. Plan carefully the methods you will use to measure and collect the data. Try not to use paper-and-pencil tests exclusively. You will collect pretrial and posttrial data.

  Pretrial. Select a control group, which is usually the same group of students that will be used with the research strategy. Collect test data without using the research strategy.
  Posttrial. Use the strategy (e.g., chunking, prime-time-1, wait time, humor) and then collect the appropriate data.

- **Analyze the Data.** Use simple analytical techniques, such as comparing the average group test scores before and after using the research strategy. What changes did you notice in the two sets of data? Did the research strategy produce the desired result? If not, why not? Was there an unexpected consequence (positive or negative) of using the strategy?

- **Share the Data.** Sharing the data with colleagues is an important component of the action research process. Too often, teachers work in isolation, with few or no opportunities to interact continuously with colleagues to design and discuss their lessons.

- **Implement the Change.** If the research strategy produced the desired results, decide how you will make it part of your teaching repertoire. If you did not get the desired results, decide whether you need to change some aspect of the strategy or perhaps use a different measure.

- **Try New Practices.** Repeat the above steps with other strategies so that action research becomes part of your ongoing professional development.

Chapter 1

Basic Brain Facts

With our new knowledge of the brain, we are just dimly beginning to realize that we can now understand humans, including ourselves, as never before, and that this is the greatest advance of the century, and quite possibly the most significant in all human history.

—Leslie A. Hart,
Human Brain and Human Learning

Chapter Highlights: This chapter introduces some of the basic structures of the human brain and their functions. It explores the growth of the young brain and some of the environmental factors that influence its development into adolescence. Whether the brain of today's student is compatible with today's schools is also discussed.

The adult human brain is a wet, fragile mass that weighs a little over three pounds. It is about the size of a small grapefruit, is shaped like a walnut, and can fit in the palm of your hand. Cradled in the skull and surrounded by protective membranes, it is poised at the top of the spinal column. The brain works ceaselessly, even when we are asleep. Although it represents only about 2 percent of our body weight, it consumes nearly 20 percent of our calories! The more we think, the more calories we burn. Perhaps this can be a new diet fad, and we could modify Descartes' famous quotation from "I think, therefore I am" to "I think, therefore I'm thin"!

Through the centuries, surveyors of the brain have examined every cerebral feature, sprinkling the landscape with Latin and Greek names to describe what they saw. They analyzed structures and

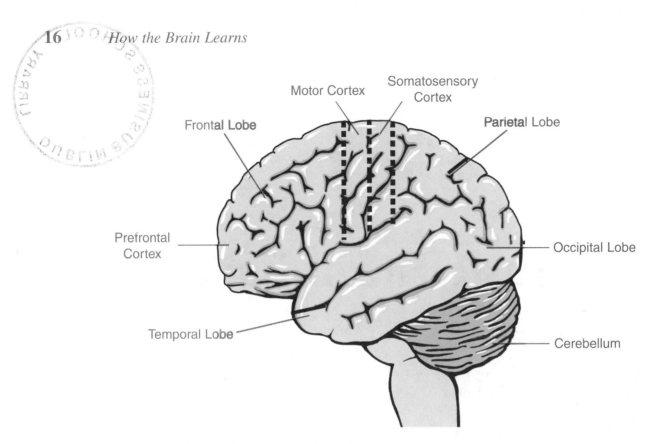

Figure 1.1 The major exterior regions of the brain.

functions and sought concepts to explain their observations. One early concept divided the brain by location—forebrain, midbrain, and hindbrain. Another, proposed by Paul MacLean in the 1960s, described the triune brain according to three stages of evolution: reptilian (brain stem), paleo-mammalian (limbic area), and mammalian (frontal lobes).

For our purposes, we will take a look at major parts of the outside of the brain (Figure 1.1). We will then look at the inside of the brain and divide it into three parts on the basis of their general functions: the brainstem, limbic system, and cerebrum (Figure 1.2). We will also examine the structure of the brain's nerve cells, called *neurons*.

SOME EXTERIOR PARTS OF THE BRAIN

Lobes of the Brain

Although the minor wrinkles are unique in each brain, several major wrinkles and folds are common to all brains. These folds form a set of four lobes in each hemisphere. Each lobe tends to specialize for certain functions.

Frontal Lobes. At the front of the brain are the *frontal lobes*, and the part lying just behind the forehead is called the *prefrontal cortex*. These lobes deal with planning and thinking. They comprise the rational and executive control center of the brain, monitoring higher-order thinking, directing problem solving, and regulating the excesses of the emotional system. The frontal lobe

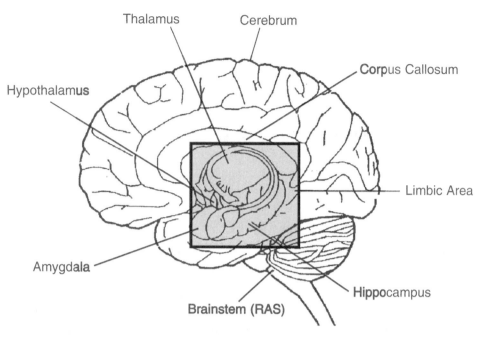

Figure 1.2   A cross section of the human brain.

also contains our self-will area—what some might call our personality. Trauma to the frontal lobe can cause dramatic—and sometimes permanent—behavior and personality changes. Because most of the working memory is located here, it is the area where focus occurs (Smith & Jonides, 1999). The frontal lobe matures slowly. MRI studies of post-adolescents reveal that the frontal lobe continues to mature into early adulthood. Thus, the capability of the frontal lobe to control the excesses of the emotional system is not fully operational during adolescence (Sowell, Thompson, Holmes, Jernigan, & Toga, 1999; Goldberg, 2001). This is one important reason why adolescents are more likely than adults to submit to their emotions and resort to high-risk behavior.

> *Because the rational system matures slowly in adolescents, they are more likely to submit to their emotions.*

Temporal Lobes. Above the ears rest the *temporal lobes*, which deal with sound, music, face and object recognition, and some parts of long-term memory. They also house the speech centers, although this is usually on the left side only.

Occipital Lobes. At the back are the paired *occipital lobes*, which are used almost exclusively for visual processing.

Parietal Lobes. Near the top are the *parietal lobes*, which deal mainly with spatial orientation, calculation, and certain types of recognition.

Motor Cortex and Somatosensory Cortex

Between the parietal and frontal lobes are two bands across the top of the brain from ear to ear. The band closer to the front is the *motor cortex*. This strip controls body movement and, as we will learn later, works with the cerebellum to coordinate the learning of motor skills. Just behind the motor cortex, at the beginning of the parietal lobe, is the *somatosensory cortex,* which processes touch signals received from various parts of the body.

SOME INTERIOR PARTS OF THE BRAIN

Brainstem

The brainstem is the oldest and deepest area of the brain. It is often referred to as the reptilian brain because it resembles the entire brain of a reptile. Of the 12 body nerves that go to the brain, 11 end in the brainstem (the olfactory nerve—for smell—goes directly to the limbic system, an evolutionary artifact). Here is where vital body functions, such as heartbeat, respiration, body temperature, and digestion, are monitored and controlled. The brainstem also houses the reticular activating system (RAS), responsible for the brain's alertness and about which more will be explained in the next chapter.

The Limbic System

Nestled above the brainstem and below the cerebrum lies a collection of structures commonly referred to as the limbic system and sometimes called the old mammalian brain. Many researchers now caution that viewing the limbic system as a separate functional entity is outdated because all of its components interact with many other areas of the brain.

Most of the structures in the limbic system are duplicated in each hemisphere of the brain. These structures carry out a number of different functions including the generation of emotions and processing emotional memories. Its placement between the cerebrum and the brainstem permits the interplay of emotion and reason.

Four parts of the limbic system are important to learning and memory. They are:

The Thalamus. All incoming sensory information (except smell) goes first to the thalamus (Greek for "inner chamber"). From here it is directed to other parts of the brain for additional processing. The cerebrum and cerebellum also send signals to the thalamus, thus involving it in many cognitive activities.

The Hypothalamus. Nestled just below the thalamus is the hypothalamus. While the thalamus monitors information coming in from the outside, the hypothalamus monitors the internal systems to maintain the normal state of the body (called *homeostasis*). By controlling the release of a variety of hormones, it moderates numerous body functions, including sleep, food intake, and liquid intake. If body systems slip out of balance, it is difficult for the individual to concentrate on cognitive processing of curriculum material.

The Hippocampus. Located near the base of the limbic area is the hippocampus (the Greek word for "seahorse," because of its shape). It plays a major role in consolidating learning and in converting information from working memory via electrical signals to the long-term storage regions, a process that may take days to months. It constantly checks information relayed to working memory and compares it to stored experiences. This process is essential for the creation of meaning.

Its role was first revealed by patients whose hippocampus was damaged or removed because of disease. These patients could remember everything that happened before the operation, but not afterward. If they were introduced to you today, you would be a stranger to them tomorrow. Because they can remember information for only a few minutes, they can read the same article repeatedly and believe on each occasion that it is the first time they have read it. Brain scans have confirmed the role of the hippocampus in permanent memory storage. Alzheimer's disease progressively destroys neurons in the hippocampus, resulting in memory loss.

Recent studies of brain-damaged patients have revealed that although the hippocampus plays an important role in the recall of facts, objects, and places, it does not seem to play much of a role in the recall of long-term personal memories (Lieberman, 2005).

The Amygdala. Attached to the end of the hippocampus is the amygdala (Greek for "almond"). This structure plays an important role in emotions, especially fear. It regulates the individual's interactions with the environment than can affect survival, such as whether to attack, escape, mate, or eat.

Because of its proximity to the hippocampus and its activity on PET scans, researchers believe that the amygdala encodes an emotional message, if one is present, whenever a memory is tagged for long-term storage. It is not known at this time whether the emotional memories themselves are actually stored in the amygdala. One possibility is that the emotional component of a memory is stored in the amygdala while other cognitive components (names, dates, etc.) are stored elsewhere (Squire & Kandel, 1999). The emotional component is recalled whenever the memory is recalled. This explains why people recalling a strong emotional memory will often experience those emotions again. The interactions between the amygdala and the hippocampus ensure that we remember for a long time those events that are important and emotional.

Teachers, of course, hope that their students will permanently remember what was taught. Therefore, it is intriguing to realize that the two structures in the brain mainly responsible for long-term remembering are located in the *emotional* area of the brain. Understanding the connection between emotions and cognitive learning and memory will be discussed in later chapters.

Test Question No. 1: The structures responsible for deciding what gets stored in long-term memory are located in the brain's rational system.

Answer: False. These structures are located in the emotional (limbic) system.

Cerebrum

A soft jellylike mass, the cerebrum is the largest area, representing nearly 80 percent of the brain by weight. Its surface is pale gray, wrinkled, and marked by furrows called fissures. One large fissure runs from front to back and divides the cerebrum into two halves, called the *cerebral hemispheres*. For some still unexplained reason, the nerves from the left side of the body cross over to the right hemisphere, and those from the right side of the body cross to the left hemisphere. The two hemispheres are connected by a thick cable of over 250 million nerve fibers called the *corpus callosum* (Latin for "large body"). The hemispheres use this bridge to communicate with each other and coordinate activities.

The hemispheres are covered by a thin but tough laminated *cortex* (meaning "tree bark"), rich in cells, that is about 1/10th of an inch thick and, because of its folds, has a surface area of about two square feet. That is about the size of a large dinner napkin. The cortex is composed of six layers of cells meshed in about 10,000 miles of connecting fibers per cubic inch! Here is where most of the action takes place. Thinking, memory, speech, and muscular movement are controlled by areas in the cerebrum. The cortex is often referred to as the brain's gray matter.

The neurons in the thin cortex form columns whose branches extend down through the cortical layer into a dense web below known as the white matter. Here, neurons connect with each other to form vast arrays of neural networks that carry out specific functions.

Cerebellum

The cerebellum (Latin for "little brain") is a two-hemisphere structure located just below the rear part of the cerebrum, right behind the brainstem. Representing about 11 percent of the brain's weight, it is a deeply folded and highly organized structure containing more neurons than all of the rest of the brain put together. The surface area of the entire cerebellum is about the same as that of one of the cerebral hemispheres.

This area coordinates movement. Because the cerebellum monitors impulses from nerve endings in the muscles, it is important in the performance and timing of complex motor tasks. It modifies and coordinates commands to swing a golf club, smooth a dancer's footsteps, and allow a hand to bring a cup to the lips without spilling its contents. The cerebellum may also store the memory of automated movements, such as touch-typing and tying a shoelace. Through such automation, performance can be improved as the sequences of movements can be made with greater speed, greater accuracy, and less effort. The cerebellum also is known to be involved in the mental rehearsal of motor tasks, which also can improve performance and make it more skilled. A person whose cerebellum is damaged slows down and simplifies movement, and would have difficulty with finely-tuned motion, such as catching a ball, or completing a handshake.

Recent studies indicate that the role of the cerebellum has been underestimated. Researchers now believe that it also acts as a support structure in cognitive processing by coordinating and fine-tuning our thoughts, emotions, senses (especially touch), and memories. Because the cerebellum is connected also to regions of the brain that perform mental and sensory tasks, it can perform these skills automatically, without conscious attention to detail. This allows the conscious part of the

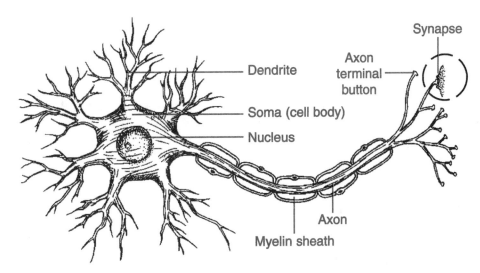

Figure 1.3 Neurons transmit signals along an axon and across the synapse (in dashed circle) to the dendrites of a neighboring cell. The myelin sheath protects the axon and increases the speed of transmission.

brain the freedom to attend to other mental activities, thus enlarging its cognitive scope. Such enlargement of human capabilities is attributable in no small part to the cerebellum and its contribution to the automation of numerous mental activities.

Brain Cells

The brain is composed of a trillion cells of at least two known types, nerve cells and glial cells. The nerve cells are called *neurons* and represent about one-tenth of the total—roughly 100 billion. Most of the cells are *glial* (Greek for "glue") cells that hold the neurons together and act as filters to keep harmful substances out of the neurons. Very recent studies indicate that some glial cells, called *astrocytes*, have a role in regulating the rate of neuron signaling. By attaching themselves to blood vessels, astrocytes also serve to form the blood-brain barrier, which plays an important role in protecting brain cells from blood-borne substances that could disrupt cellular activity.

The neurons are the functioning core for the brain and the entire nervous system. Neurons come in different sizes, but the body of each brain neuron is about 1/100th the size of the period at the end of this sentence. Unlike other cells, the neuron (see Figure 1.3) has tens of thousands of branches emerging from its core, called *dendrites* (from the Greek word for "tree"). The dendrites receive electrical impulses from other neurons and transmit them along a long fiber, called the *axon* (Greek for "axis"). There is normally only one axon per neuron. A layer called the *myelin sheath* surrounds each axon. The sheath insulates the axon from the other cells and increases the speed of impulse transmission. This impulse travels along the neurons through an electrochemical process and can move through the entire length of a 6-foot adult in 2/10ths of a second. A neuron can transmit between 250 and 2,500 impulses per second.

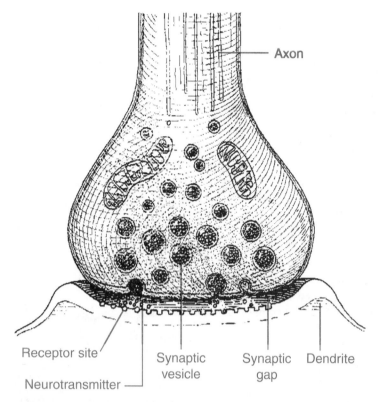

Axon

Receptor site

Neurotransmitter

Synaptic
vesicle

Synaptic
gap

Dendrite

Figure 1.4   The neural impulse is carried across the synapse by chemicals called neurotransmitters that lie within the synaptic vesicles.

Neurons have no direct contact with each other. Between each dendrite and axon is a small gap of about a millionth of an inch called a *synapse* (from the Greek, meaning "to join together"). A typical neuron collects signals from others through the dendrites, which are covered at the synapse with thousands of tiny bumps, called *spines*. The neuron sends out spikes of electrical activity (impulses) through the axon to the synapse where the activity releases chemicals stored in sacs (called *synaptic vesicles*) at the end of the axon (Figure 1.4). These chemicals, called *neurotransmitters*, either excite or inhibit the neighboring neuron. More than 50 different neurotransmitters have been discovered so far. Some of the common neurotransmitters are acetylcholine, epinephrine, serotonin, and dopamine. Learning occurs by changing the synapses so that the influence of one neuron on another also changes.

A direct connection seems to exist between the physical world of the brain and the work of the brain's owner. Recent studies of neurons in people of different occupations (e.g., professional musicians) show that the more complex the skills demanded of the occupation, the more dendrites were found on the neurons. This increase in dendrites allows for more connections between neurons resulting in more sites in which to store learnings.

There are about 100 billion neurons in the adult human brain—about 16 times as many neurons as people on this planet and about the number of stars in the Milky Way. Each neuron can have up to 10 thousand dendrite branches. This means that it is possible to have up to one quadrillion (that's a one followed by 15 zeros) synaptic connections in one brain. This inconceivably large number allows the brain to process the data coming continuously from the senses; to store decades of memories, faces, and places; to learn languages; and to combine information in a way that no other individual on this planet has ever thought of before. This is a remarkable achievement for just three pounds of soft tissue!

Believe it or not, the number of potential synaptic connections in just one human brain is about 1,000,000,000,000,000.

Conventional wisdom has been that neurons were the only body cells that never regenerate. However, researchers have discovered that the adult human brain does generate neurons in at least one site—the hippocampus. This discovery raises the question of whether neurons regenerate in other parts of the brain and, if so, if it might be possible to stimulate them to repair and heal damaged brains, especially for the growing number of people with Alzheimer's disease. Research into Alzheimer's disease is exploring ways to stop the deadly mechanisms that trigger the destruction of neurons.

Mirror Neurons

Scientists using fMRI technology recently discovered clusters of neurons in the premotor cortex (the area in front of the motor cortex that plans movements) firing just before a person carries out a planned movement. Curiously, these neurons also fired when a person saw someone else perform the movement. For example, the firing pattern of these neurons that preceded the subject grasping a cup of coffee, was identical to the pattern when the subject saw someone else do that. Thus, similar brain areas process both the production and perception of movement. Neuroscientists believe these *mirror neurons* may help an individual to decode the intentions and predict the behavior of others. They allow us to re-create the experience of others within ourselves, and to understand others' emotions and empathize. Seeing the look of disgust or joy on other people's faces cause mirror neurons to trigger similar emotions in us. We start to feel their actions and sensations as though we were doing them.

Mirror neurons probably explain the mimicry we see in young children when they imitate our smile and many of our other movements. We have all experienced this phenomenon when we attempted to stifle a yawn after seeing someone else yawning. Neuroscientists believe that mirror neurons may explain a lot about mental behaviors that have remained a mystery. For instance, there is experimental evidence that children with autism may have a deficit in their mirror-neuron system. That would explain why they have difficulty inferring the intentions and mental state of others (Oberman et al., 2005). Researchers also suspect that mirror neurons may play a role in our ability to develop articulate speech.

Brain Fuel

Brain cells consume oxygen and glucose (a form of sugar) for fuel. The more challenging the brain's task, the more fuel it consumes. Therefore, it is important to have adequate amounts of these substances in the brain for optimum functioning. Low amounts of oxygen and glucose in the blood can produce lethargy and sleepiness. Eating a moderate portion of food containing glucose (fruits are an excellent source) can boost the performance and accuracy of working memory, attention, and motor function (Korol & Gold, 1998; Scholey, Moss, Neave, & Wesnes, 1999).

> *Many students (and their teachers) do not eat a breakfast with sufficient glucose, nor drink enough water during the day for healthy brain function.*

Water, also essential for healthy brain activity, is required to move neuron signals through the brain. Low concentrations of water diminish the rate and efficiency of these signals. Moreover, water keeps the lungs sufficiently moist to allow for the efficient transfer of oxygen into the bloodstream.

Many students (and their teachers, too) do not eat a breakfast that contains sufficient glucose, nor do they drink enough water during the day to maintain healthy brain function. Schools should have breakfast programs and educate students on the need to have sufficient blood levels of glucose during the day. Schools should also provide frequent opportunities for students and staff to drink plenty of water. The current recommended amount is one eight-ounce glass of water a day for each 25 pounds of body weight.

NEURON DEVELOPMENT IN CHILDREN

Neuron development starts in the embryo shortly after conception and proceeds at an astonishing rate. In the first four months of gestation, about 200 billion neurons are formed, but about half will die off during the fifth month because they fail to connect with any areas of the growing embryo. This purposeful destruction of neurons (called *apoptosis*) is genetically programmed to ensure that only those neurons that have made connections are preserved, and to prevent the brain from being overcrowded with unconnected cells. Any drugs or alcohol that the mother takes during this time can interfere with the growing brain cells, increasing the risk of fetal addiction and mental defects.

The neurons of a newborn are immature; many of their axons lack the protective myelin layer and there are few connections between them. Thus, most regions of the cerebral cortex are quiet. Understandably, the most active areas are the brainstem (body functions) and the cerebellum (movement).

The neurons in a child's brain make many more connections than those in adults. A newborn's brain makes connections at an incredible pace as the child absorbs its environment. Information is entering the brain through "windows" that emerge and taper off at various times. The richer the environment, the greater the number of interconnections that are made. Consequently, learning can take place faster and with greater meaning.

As the child approaches puberty, the pace slackens and two other processes begin: Connections the brain finds useful become permanent; those not useful are eliminated (apoptosis) as the brain selectively strengthens and prunes connections based on experience. This process continues throughout our lives, but it appears to be most intense between the ages of three and 12. Thus, at an early age, experiences are already shaping the brain and designing the unique neural architecture that will influence how it handles future experiences in school, work, and other places.

Windows of Opportunity

Windows of opportunity represent important periods in which the young brain responds to certain types of input to create or consolidate neural networks. Some windows are critical, and are called *critical periods* by pediatric researchers. For example, if even a perfect brain doesn't receive visual stimuli by the age of two, the child will be forever blind, and if it doesn't hear words by the age of 12, the person will most likely never learn a language. When these critical windows close, the brain cells assigned to those tasks may be pruned or recruited for other tasks (Diamond & Hopson, 1998).

Other windows are more plastic, but still significant. It is important to remember that learning can occur in each of the areas for the rest of our lives, even after a window tapers off. However, the

Windows of Opportunity as a Child's Brain Matures

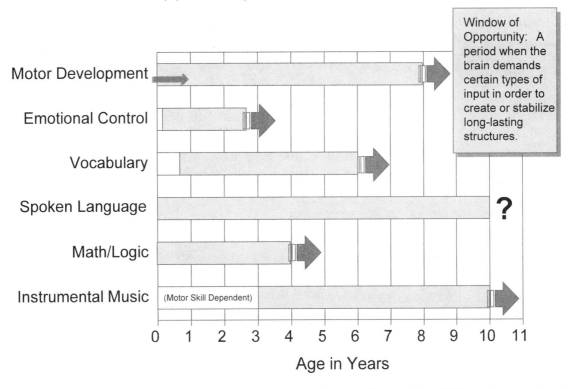

Figure 1.5 The chart shows some of the sensitive periods for learning during childhood, according to current research. Future studies may modify the ranges shown in the chart. It is important to remember that learning occurs throughout our entire life.

skill level probably will not be as high. This ability of the brain to continually change during our lifetime in subtle ways as a result of experience is referred to as *plasticity.*

An intriguing question is why the windows taper off so early in life, especially since the average life span is now over 75 years of age. One possible explanation is that these developmental spurts are genetically determined and were set in place many thousands of years ago when our life span was closer to 20 years. Figure 1.5 shows just a few of the windows which we will examine to understand their importance.

Motor Development

This window opens during fetal development. Those who have borne children remember all too well the movement of the fetus during the third trimester as motor connections and systems are consolidating. The child's ability to learn motor skills appears to be most pronounced in the first eight years. Such seemingly simple tasks as crawling and walking require complicated associations of neural networks, including integrating information from the balance sensors in the inner ear and output signals to the leg and arm muscles. Of course, a person can learn motor skills after

> *What is learned while a window of opportunity is opened will most likely be learned masterfully.*

the window tapers off. However, what is learned while it is open will most likely be learned masterfully. For example, most concert virtuosos, Olympic medalists, and professional players of individual sports (e.g., tennis and golf) began practicing their skills by the age of eight.

Emotional Control

The window for developing emotional control seems to be from two to 30 months. During that time, the limbic (emotional) system and the frontal lobe's rational system are evaluating each other's ability to get its owner what it wants. It is hardly a fair match. Studies of human brain growth suggest that the emotional (and older) system develops faster than the frontal lobes (Figure 1.6) (Beatty, 2001; Goldberg, 2001; Gazzaniga, Ivry, & Mangun, 2002; Luciana, Conklin, Hooper, & Yarger, 2005; Paus, 2005; Restak, 2001; Steinberg, 2005). Consequently, the emotional system is more likely to win the tug-of-war for control. If tantrums almost always get the child satisfaction when the window is open, then that is likely the method the child will use when the window tapers off. This constant emotional-rational battle is one of the major contributors to the "terrible twos." Certainly, one can learn to control emotions after that age. But what the child learned during that open window period will be difficult to change, and it will strongly influence what is learned after the window tapers off.

> **The struggle between the emotional and rational systems is a major contributor to the "terrible twos."**

In an astonishing example of how nurturing can influence nature, there is considerable evidence confirming that how parents respond to their children emotionally during this time frame can encourage or stifle genetic tendencies. Biology is not destiny, so gene expression is not necessarily inevitable. To produce their effects, genes must be turned on. The cells on the tip of your nose contain the same genetic code as those in your stomach lining. But the gene that codes for producing stomach acid is activated in your stomach, yet idled on your nose. For example, shyness is a trait that seems to be partially hereditary. If parents are overprotective of their bashful young daughter, the toddler is likely to remain shy. On the other hand, if they encourage her to interact with other toddlers, she may overcome it. Thus, genetic tendencies toward intelligence, sociability, or schizophrenia and aggression can be ignited or moderated by parental response and other environmental influences (Reiss, Neiderheiser, Hetherington, & Plomin, 2000).

Development of the Brain's Limbic Area and Frontal Lobes

— Limbic Area
– – Frontal Lobes

Figure 1.6   Based on research studies, this chart suggests the possible degree of development of the brain's limbic area and frontal lobes. The 10- to 12-year lag in the full development of the frontal lobes (the brain's rational system) explains why so many adolescents and young adults get involved in risky situations.

Vocabulary

Because the human brain is genetically predisposed for language, babies start uttering sounds and babble nonsense phrases as early as the age of two months. By the age of eight months, infants begin to try out simple words like "mama" and "dada." The language areas of the brain become really active at 18 to 20 months. A toddler can learn 10 or more words per day, yielding a vocabulary of about 900 words at age three, increasing to 2,500 to 3,000 words by the age of five.

Here's testimony to the power of talk: Researchers have shown that babies whose mothers talked to them more had significantly larger vocabularies. Knowing a word is not the same as understanding its meaning. So it is crucial for parents to encourage their children to use new words in a context that demonstrates they know what the words mean. Children who know the meaning of most of the words in their large vocabulary will start school with a greater likelihood that learning to read will be easier and quicker.

Language Acquisition

The newborn's brain is not the *tabula rasa* (blank slate) we once thought. Certain areas are specialized for specific stimuli, including spoken language. The window for acquiring spoken language opens soon after birth and tapers off around the ages of 10 to 12 years. Beyond that age, learning any language becomes more difficult. The genetic impulse to learn language is so strong that children found in feral environments often make up their own language. There is also evidence that the human ability to acquire grammar may have a specific window of opportunity in the early years (Diamond & Hopson, 1998). Knowing this, it seems illogical that many schools still wait to *start* new language instruction in middle school or high school rather than in the primary grades. Chapter 5 deals in greater detail with how the brain acquires spoken language.

Mathematics and Logic

How and when the young brain understands numbers is uncertain, but there is mounting evidence that infants have a rudimentary number sense which is wired into certain brain sites at birth (Butterworth, 1999). The purpose of these sites is to categorize the world in terms of the "number of things" in a collection, that is, they can tell the difference between two of something and three of something. We drive along a road and see horses in a field. While we are noticing that they are brown and black, we cannot help but see that there are four of them. Researchers have also found that toddlers as young as two recognize the relationships between numbers as large as 4 and 5, even though they are not able to verbally label them. This research shows that fully functioning language ability is not needed to support numerical thinking (Brannon & van der Walle, 2001).

Instrumental Music

All cultures create music, so we can assume that it is an important part of being human. Babies respond to music as early as two to three months of age. A window for creating music may be open

> *School districts should communicate with the parents of newborns and offer their services and resources to help parents succeed as the first teachers of their children.*

at birth, but obviously neither the baby's vocal chords nor motor skills are adequate to sing or to play an instrument. Around the age of three years, most toddlers have sufficient manual dexterity to play a piano (Mozart was playing the harpsichord and composing at age four). Several studies have shown that children ages three to four years who received piano lessons scored significantly higher in spatial-temporal tasks than a group who did not get the instrumental music training. Further, the increase was long-term. Brain imaging reveals that creating instrumental music excites the same regions of the left frontal lobe responsible for mathematics and logic. See Chapter 6 for more on the effects of music on the brain and learning.

Research on how the young brain develops suggests that an enriched home and preschool environment during the early years can help children build neural connections and make full use of their mental abilities. Because of the importance of early years, I believe school districts should communicate with the parents of newborns and offer their services and resources to help parents succeed as the first teachers of their children. Such programs are already in place on a statewide basis in Michigan, Missouri, and Kentucky, and similar programs sponsored by local school districts are springing up elsewhere. But we need to work faster toward achieving this important goal.

THE BRAIN AS A NOVELTY SEEKER

Part of our success as a species can be attributed to the brain's persistent interest in novelty, that is, changes occurring in the environment. The brain is constantly scanning its environment for stimuli. When an unexpected stimulus arises—such as a loud noise from an empty room—a rush of adrenalin closes down all unnecessary activity and focuses the brain's attention so it can spring into action. Conversely, an environment that contains mainly predictable or repeated stimuli (like some classrooms?) lowers the brain's interest in the outside world and tempts it to turn within for novel sensations.

Environmental Factors That Enhance Novelty

We often hear teachers remark that students are more different today in the way they learn than ever before. They seem to have shorter attention spans and bore easily. Why is that? Is there something happening in the environment of learners that alters the way they approach the learning process?

The Environment of the Past

The home environment for many children several decades ago was quite different from that of today. For example,

- The home was quieter—some might say boring compared to today.
- Parents and children did a lot of talking and reading.
- The family unit was more stable and ate together, and the dinner hour was an opportunity for parents to discuss their children's activities as well as reaffirm their love and support.
- If the home had a television, it was in a common area and controlled by adults. What children watched could be carefully monitored.
- School was an interesting place because it had television, films, field trips, and guest speakers. Because there were few other distractions, school was an important influence in a child's life and the primary source of information.
- The neighborhood was also an important part of growing up. Children played together, developing their motor skills as well as learning the social skills needed to interact successfully with other children in the neighborhood.

The Environment of Today

In recent years, children have been growing up in a very different environment.

- Family units are not as stable as they once were. Single-parent families are more common, and children have fewer opportunities to talk with the adults who care for them. Their dietary habits are changing as home cooking is becoming a lost art.
- They are surrounded by media: cell phones, multiple televisions, movies, computers, video games, e-mail, and the Internet. Teens spend nearly 17 hours a week on the Internet and nearly 14 hours a week watching television (Guterl, 2003).
- Many 10- to 18-year olds can now watch television and play with other technology in their own bedrooms, leading to sleep deprivation. Furthermore, with no adult present, what kind of moral compass is evolving in the impressionable pre-adolescent mind as a result of watching programs containing violence and sex on television and the Internet?
- They get information from many different sources beside school.
- The multi-media environment divides their attention. Even newscasts are different. In the past, only the reporter's face was on the screen. Now, the TV screen I am looking at is loaded with information. Three people are reporting in from different corners of the world. Additional non-related news is scrolling across the bottom, and the stock market averages are changing in the lower right-hand corner just below the local time and temperature. For me, these tidbits are distracting and are forcing me to split my attention into several components. I find myself missing a reporter's comment because a scrolling item caught my attention. Yet, children have become accustomed to these information-rich and rapidly changing messages.

They can pay attention to several things at once, but they do not go into any one thing in depth.

- They spend much more time indoors with their technology, thereby missing outdoor opportunities to develop gross motor skills and socialization skills necessary to communicate and act personally with others. One unintended consequence of spending so much time indoors is the rapid rise in the number of overweight children and adolescents, now more than 15 percent of 6- to 19-year olds.

- Young brains have responded to the technology by changing their functioning and organization to accommodate the large amount of stimulation occurring in the environment. By acclimating itself to these changes, brains respond more than ever to the unique and different—what is called *novelty*. There is a dark side to this increased novelty-seeking behavior. Some adolescents who perceive little novelty in their environment may turn to mind-altering drugs, such as ecstasy and amphetamines, for stimulation. This drug dependence can further enhance the brain's demand for novelty to the point that it becomes unbalanced and resorts to extremely risky behavior.

- Their diet contains increasing amounts of substances that can affect brain and body functions. Caffeine is a strong brain stimulant, considered safe for most adults in small quantities. But caffeine is found in many of the foods and drinks that teens consume daily. Too much caffeine causes insomnia, anxiety, and nausea. Some teens can also develop allergies to aspartame (an artificial sugar found in children's vitamins and many "lite" foods) and other food additives. Possible symptoms of these allergic reactions include hyperactivity, difficulty concentrating, and headaches (Bateman, et al., 2004; Millichap & Yee, 2003).

When we add to this mix the changes in family lifestyles and the temptations of alcohol and drugs, we can realize how very different the environment of today's child is from that of just 15 years ago.

Have Schools Changed With the Environment?

Many educators are recognizing the characteristics of the new brain, but they do not always agree on what to do about it. Granted, teaching methodologies are changing, new technologies are being used, and teachers are even introducing pop music and culture to supplement traditional classroom materials. But schools and teaching are not changing fast enough. In high schools, lecturing continues to be the main method of instruction, primarily because of the vast amount of required curriculum material and the pressure of increased accountability and testing. Students remark that school is a dull, nonengaging environment that is much less interesting than what is available outside school.

Despite the recent efforts of educators to deal with this new brain, many high school students still do not feel challenged. In a 2004 survey of 90,000 high school students in 26 states, 55 percent of students said they devoted three hours a week or less to classroom preparation, but 65 percent

> *As we continue to develop a more scientifically based understanding about today's novel brain, we must decide how this new knowledge should change what we do in schools and classrooms.*

reported getting grades of A or B. Survey administrators reported that many students said they did not feel challenged to do their best work and thus were more likely to spend time doing personal reading online than doing assigned reading for their classes (HSSSE, 2005).

In another survey of 10,500 high school students, conducted by the National Governors Association, more than one-third of the students said their school had not done a good job challenging them to think critically and analyze problems. About 11 percent said they were thinking of dropping out of school. Over one-third of this group said they were leaving because they were "not learning anything" (NGA, 2005).

The Gallup Poll asked nearly 800 students ages 13 to 17 in an online survey to select three adjectives that best described how they felt about school. Half the students chose "bored" and 42 percent chose "tired" (Gallup, 2004a).

Clearly, we educators have to rethink now, more than ever, how we must adjust schools to accommodate and maintain the interest of this new brain. As we continue to develop a more scientifically based understanding about today's novel brain and how it learns, we must decide how this new knowledge should change what we do in schools and classrooms.

What's Coming Up?

Now that we have reviewed some basic parts of the brain, and discussed how the brain of today's student has become acclimated to novelty, the next step is to look at a model of how the brain processes new information. Why do students remember so little and forget so much? How does the brain decide what to retain and what to discard? The answers to these and other important questions about brain processing will be found in the next chapter.

PRACTITIONER'S CORNER

Fist for a Brain

This activity shows how you can use your fists to represent the human brain. Metaphors are excellent learning and remembering tools. When you are comfortable with the activity, share it with your students. They are often very interested in knowing how their brain is constructed and how it works. This is a good example of novelty.

1. Extend both arms with palms open and facing down and lock your thumbs.

2. Curl your fingers to make two fists.

3. Turn your fists inward until the knuckles touch.

4. While the fists are touching, pull both toward your chest until you are looking down on your knuckles. This is the approximate size of your brain! Not as big as you thought? Remember, it's not the size of the brain that matters; it's the number of connections between the neurons. Those connections form when stimuli result in learning. The thumbs are the front and are crossed to remind us that the left side of the brain controls the right side of the body, and the right side of the brain controls the left side of the body. The knuckles and outside part of the hands represent the **cerebrum** or thinking part of the brain.

5. Spread your palms apart while keeping the knuckles touching. Look at the tips of your fingers, which represent the **limbic** or emotional area. Note how this area is buried deep within the brain, and how the fingers are mirror-imaged. This reminds us that most of the structures of the limbic system are duplicated in each hemisphere.

6. The wrists are the **brainstem** where vital body functions (such as body temperature, heart beat, blood pressure) are controlled. Rotating your hands shows how the brain can move on top of the spinal column, which is represented by your forearms.

PRACTITIONER'S CORNER

Review of Brain Area Functions

Here is an opportunity to assess your understanding of the major brain areas. Write in the table below your own key words and phrases to describe the functions of each of the eight brain areas. Then draw an arrow to each brain area on the diagram below and label it.

Cerebrum:	
Frontal Lobe:	
Thalamus:	
Hypothalamus:	
Hippocampus:	
Amygdala:	
Cerebellum:	
Brainstem:	

PRACTITIONER'S CORNER

Using Novelty in Lessons

Using novelty does *not* mean that the teacher needs to be a stand-up comic or the classroom a three-ring circus. It simply means using a varied teaching approach that involves more student activity. Here are a few suggestions for incorporating novelty in your lessons.

- **Humor.** There are many positive benefits that come from using humor in the classroom at *all* grade levels. See the **Practitioner's Corner** in Chapter 2 (p. 63) which suggests guidelines and beneficial reasons for using humor.

- **Movement.** When we sit for more than twenty minutes, our blood pools in our seat and in our feet. By getting up and moving, we recirculate that blood. Within a minute, there is about 15 percent more blood in our brain. We do think better on our feet than on our seat! Students sit too much in classrooms, especially in secondary schools. Look for ways to get students up and moving, especially when they are verbally rehearsing what they have learned.

- **Multi-Sensory Instruction.** Today's students are acclimated to a multi-sensory environment. They are more likely to give attention if there are interesting, colorful visuals and if they can walk around and talk about their learning.

- **Quiz Games.** Have students develop a quiz game or other similar activity to test each other on their knowledge of the concepts taught. This is a common strategy in elementary classrooms, but underutilized in secondary schools. Besides being fun, it has the added value of making students rehearse and understand the concepts in order to create the quiz questions and answers.

- **Music.** Although the research is inconclusive, there are some benefits of playing music in the classroom at certain times during the learning episode. See the **Practitioner's Corner** in Chapter 6 (p. 235) on the use of music.

PRACTITIONER'S CORNER

Preparing the Brain for Taking a Test

Taking a test can be a stressful event. Chances are your students will perform better on a test of cognitive or physical performance if you prepare the brain by doing the following:

- **Exercise.** Get the students up to do some exercise for just two minutes. Jumping jacks are good because the students stay in place. Students who may not want to jump up and down can do five brisk round trip walks along the longest wall of the classroom. The purpose here is to get the blood oxygenated and moving faster.

- **Fruit.** Besides oxygen, brain cells also need glucose for fuel. Fruit is an excellent source of glucose. Students should eat about 2 ounces (over 50 grams) of fruit. Dried fruit, such as raisins, is convenient. Avoid fruit drinks as they often contain just fructose, a fruit sugar that does not provide immediate energy to cells. The chart below shows how just 50 grams of glucose increased long-term memory recall in a group of young adults by 35 percent and recall from working memory by over 20 percent (Korol & Gold, 1998).

Mean Percent Change in Cognitive Performance
(Young Adults - 50g Glucose)

- **Water.** Wash down the fruit with an 8-ounce glass of water. The water gets the sugar into the bloodstream faster and hydrates the brain.

Wait about five minutes after these steps before giving the test. That should be enough time for the added glucose to fire up the brain cells. The effect lasts for only about 30 minutes, so the steps need to be repeated periodically for longer tests.

Chapter 1—Basic Brain Facts

Key Points to Ponder

Jot down on this page key points, ideas, strategies, and resources you want to consider later. This sheet is your personal journal summary and will help to jog your memory.

_____

_____

_____

_____

_____

_____

_____

_____

_____

Chapter 2

How the Brain Processes Information

There are probably more differences in human brains than in any other animal partly because the human brain does most of its developing in the outside world.

—Robert Ornstein and Richard Thompson,
The Amazing Brain

Chapter Highlights*:* This chapter presents a modern dynamic model of how the brain deals with information from the senses. It covers the behavior of the two temporary memories, the criteria for long-term storage, and the impact of the self-concept on learning.

Although the brain remains largely a mystery beyond its own understanding, we are slowly uncovering more about its baffling processes. Using scanning technologies, researchers can display in vivid color the differences in brain cell metabolism that occur in response to different types of brain work. A computer constructs a color-coded map indicating what different areas are doing during such activities as learning new words, analyzing tones, doing mathematical calculations, or responding to images. One thing is clear: The brain calls selected areas into play depending on what the individual is doing at the moment. This knowledge encourages us to construct models that explain data and behavior, but models are useful only when they contain some predictability about specific operations. In choosing a model, it is necessary to select those specific operations that can be meaningfully depicted and represented in a way that is consistent with more recent research findings.

THE INFORMATION PROCESSING MODEL

Several models exist to explain brain behavior. In designing a model for this book, I needed one that would accurately represent the complex research of neuroscientists in such a way as to be understood by educational practitioners. I recognize that a model is just one person's view of reality, and I readily admit that this particular information processing model comes closest to *my* view of how the brain learns. It differs from other models in that it escapes the limits of the computer metaphor and recognizes that learning, storing, and remembering are dynamic and interactive processes. Beyond that, the model incorporates much of the recent findings of research and is sufficiently flexible to adjust to new findings as they are revealed. I have already made several changes in this model since I began working with it nearly 25 years ago. A few additional changes are the result of new information learned since the second edition of this book was published. My hope is that classroom teachers will be encouraged to reflect on their methodology and decide if there are new insights here that could affect their instruction and improve learning.

Origins of the Model

The precursor of this model was developed by Robert Stahl (1985) of Arizona State University in the early 1980s. Stahl's more complex model synthesized the research in the 1960s and 1970s on cognitive processing and learning. His goal was to convince teacher educators that they should use his model to help prospective teachers understand how and why learning occurs. He also used the model to develop an elaborate and fascinating learning taxonomy designed to promote higher-order thinking skills. Certain components of the model needed to be altered as a result of subsequent discoveries in neuroscience.

Usefulness of the Model

The model discussed here (Figure 2.1) has been updated so that it can be used by the widest range of teacher educators and practitioners. It uses common objects to represent various stages in the process. Even this revised model does not pretend to include all the ways that researchers believe the human brain deals with information, thought, and behavior. It limits its scope to the major cerebral operations that deal with the collecting, evaluating, storing, and retrieving of information—the parts most useful to educators.

The model starts with information from our environment and shows how the senses reject or accept it for further processing. It then explains the two temporary memories, how they operate, and

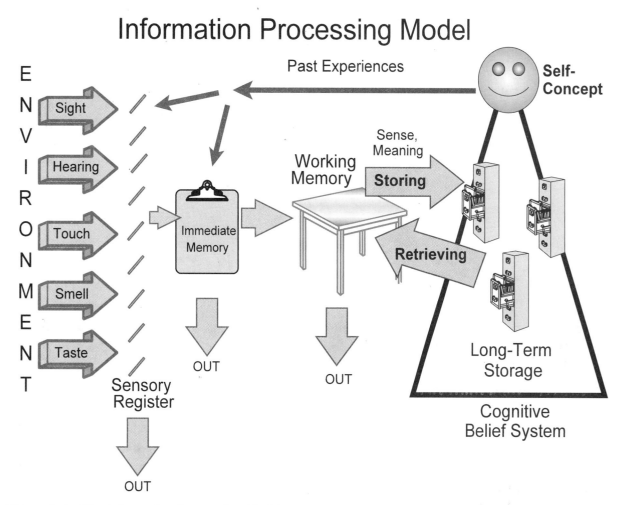

Figure 2.1 The Information Processing Model represents a simplified explanation of how the brain deals with information from the environment. Information from the senses passes through the sensory register to immediate memory and then on to working memory for conscious processing. If the learner attaches sense and meaning to the learning, it is likely to be stored. The self-concept often determines how much attention the learner will give to new information.

the factors that determine if a learning is likely to be stored. Finally, it shows the inescapable impact that experiences and self-concept have on future learning. The model is simple, but the processes are extraordinarily complex. Knowing how the human brain seems to process information and learn can help teachers plan lessons that students are more likely to understand and remember.

Limitations of the Model

Although the explanation of the model will follow items going through the processing system, it is important to note that this linear approach is used solely for simplicity and clarity. Much of the recent evidence on memory supports a model of parallel processing. That is, many items are processed quickly and simultaneously (within limits), taking different paths through and out of the

> **The brain changes its own properties as a result of experience.**

system. Memories are dynamic and dispersed, and the brain has the capacity to change its own properties as the result of experience. Even though the model may seem to represent learning and remembering as a mechanistic process, it must be remembered that we are describing a *biological process*. Nonetheless, I have avoided a detailed discussion of the biochemical changes that occur within and between neurons. That would not contribute to the understanding necessary to convert the fruits of research and this model into successful classroom practice, which is, after all, our goal.

Inadequacy of the Computer Model

The rapid proliferation of computers has encouraged the use of the computer model to explain brain functions. This is indeed tempting, especially as computers become more complex. Using the analogy of input, processing, and output seems so natural, but there are serious problems with such a model. Certainly, the smallest hand-held calculator can out-tally the human brain in solving complex mathematical operations. Larger computers can play chess, translate one language into another, and correct massive manuscripts for most spelling and grammatical errors in just seconds. The brain performs more slowly because of the time it takes for a nerve impulse to travel along the axon, synaptic delays, and because the capacity of its working memory is limited. But computers cannot exercise judgment with the ease of the human brain. Even the most sophisticated computers are closed linear systems limited to binary code, the 0s and 1s in linear sequences that are the language of computer operations.

The human brain has no such limitations. It is an open, parallel-processing system continually interacting with the physical and social worlds outside. It analyzes, integrates, and synthesizes information and abstracts generalities from it. Each neuron is alive and altered by its experiences and its environment. As you read these words, neurons are interacting with each other, reforming and dissolving storage sites, and establishing different electrical patterns that correspond to your new learning.

> **As you read these words, neurons in your brain are interacting with each other in patterns that correspond to your new learning.**

How the brain stores information is also very different from a computer. The brain stores sequences of patterns, and recalling just one piece of a pattern can activate the whole. We can also identify the same thing in different forms, such as recognizing our best friend from behind or by her walk or voice. Computers cannot deal well with such variations (Hawkins & Blakeslee, 2004). Moreover, emotions play an important role in human processing and creativity. And the ideas generated by the human brain often come from images, not from logical propositions. For these and many other reasons, the computer model is, in my opinion, inadequate and misleading.

At first glance, the model may seem to perpetuate the traditional approach to teaching and learning—that students repeat newly learned information in quizzes, tests, and reports. On the contrary, the new research is revealing that students are more likely to gain greater understanding of and derive greater pleasure from learning when allowed to *transform* the learning into creative thoughts and products. This model emphasizes the power of transfer during learning and the importance of moving students through higher levels of complexity of thought. This will be explained further in Chapters 4 and 5.

The Senses

Our brain takes in more information from our environment in a single day than the largest computer does in a year. That information is detected by our five senses. (Note: Apart from the five classical senses of sight, hearing, smell, touch, and taste, our body has special sensory receptors that detect internal signals. For example, we have receptors inside the ear and body muscles that detect the body's movement and position in space; sensory hairs in the ear that detect balance and gravity; stretch receptors in muscles to help the brain coordinate muscular contraction; and pain receptors throughout the body. For the purposes of the model, however, I have focused on the classical senses because they are the major receptors of *external* stimuli.)

All sensory stimuli enter the brain as a stream of electrical impulses that result from neurons firing in sequence along the specific sensory pathways. The brain sits in a black box (the skull) and does not see light waves or hear sound waves. Rather, certain specialized modules of neurons process the electrical impulses created by the light and sound waves into what the brain *perceives* as vision and sound.

The senses do not all contribute equally to our learning. Over the course of our lives, sight, hearing, and touch (including kinesthetic experiences) contribute the most. Our senses constantly collect tens of thousands of bits of information from the environment every second, even while we sleep. That number may seem very high, but think about it. The nerve endings on your skin are detecting the clothes you are wearing. Your ears pick up sounds around you, the rods and cones in your eyes are reacting to this print as they move across the page, you may still be tasting recent food or drink, and your nose may be detecting an odor. Put these data together and you see how they can add up. Of course, the stimuli must be strong enough for the senses to detect and record them.

Sensory Register

Imagine if the brain had to give its full attention to all those bits of data at once. We would blow the cerebral equivalent of a fuse! Fortunately, the brain has evolved a system for screening all these data to determine their importance to the individual. This system involves the *thalamus* (located in the limbic system) and a portion of the brain stem known as the *reticular activation system* (RAS). This system, which is also referred to as the *sensory register*, is drawn in the model as the side view of Venetian blind slats (see the slashes in Figure 2.1). Like the blinds, the sensory register filters incoming information to determine how important it is.

All incoming sensory information (except smell) is sent first to the thalamus, which briefly monitors the strength and nature of the sensory impulses for survival content and, in just milliseconds (a millisecond is 1/1,000th of a second), uses the individual's past experiences to determine the data's degree of importance. Most of the data signals are unimportant, so the sensory register allows them to drop out of the processing system. Have you ever noticed how you can be in a room studying while there is construction noise outside? Eventually, it seems that you no longer hear the noise. Your sensory register is blocking these repetitive stimuli, allowing your conscious brain to focus on more important things. This process is called *perceptual* or *sensory filtering*, and, to a large degree, we are consciously unaware of it.

The sensory register does hold sensory information for a very brief period of time (seconds). This is referred to as *sensory memory*. Let's say you are intently watching a football game during the final minutes of play. Your spouse comes in and starts talking about an important matter. After a few minutes, your spouse says, "You're not listening to me!" Without batting an eye you say, "Yes, I am," and then proceed to repeat your spouse's last sentence word for word. Fortunately, you captured this sensory memory trace just before it decayed, and nipped a potential argument in the bud.

Short-Term Memory

As researchers gain greater insight into the brain's memory processes, they have had to devise and revise terms that describe the various stages of memory. *Short-term memory* is used by cognitive neuroscientists to include all of the early steps of temporary memory that will lead to stable long-term memory. Short-term memory primarily includes *immediate memory* and *working memory* (Gazzaniga, et al., 2002; Squire & Kandel, 1999).

Immediate Memory

Sensory data that are not lost move from the thalamus to the sensory processing areas of the cortex and through the first of two temporary memories, now called *immediate memory*. The idea that we seem to have two temporary memories is a way of explaining how the brain deals with large amounts of sensory data, and how we can continue to process these stimuli subconsciously for many seconds beyond the sensory register's time limits. Indeed, some neuroscientists equate sensory memory and immediate memory, arguing that separating them is more a convenience rather than a biological necessity.

For our purposes, we will represent immediate memory in the model as a clipboard, a place where we put information briefly until we make a decision on how to dispose of it. Immediate memory operates subconsciously or consciously and holds data for up to about 30 seconds. (Note: The numbers used in this chapter are averages over time. There are always exceptions to these values as a result of human variations or pathologies.) The individual's experiences determine its importance. If the item is of little or no importance within this time frame, it drops out of the system. For example, when you look up the telephone number of the local pizza parlor, you usually can remember it just long enough to make the call. After that, the number is of no further importance and drops out of

> *You cannot recall information that your brain does not retain.*

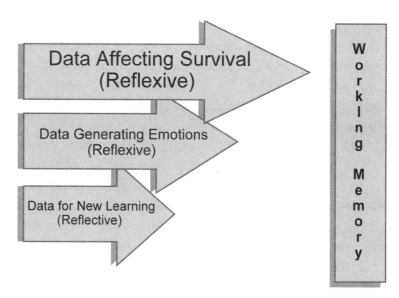

Figure 2.2 Data affecting survival and data generating emotions are processed ahead of data for new learning, which in school is called curriculum.

immediate memory. Later on, you will have little success in remembering the entire number because you cannot recall information that your brain does not retain.

Examples of Immediate Memory at Work. Here are two other examples to understand how the processing occurs up to this point. Suppose you decide to wear a new pair of shoes to work today. They are snug, so when you put them on, the receptors in your skin send pain impulses to the sensory register. For a short time you feel discomfort. After a while, however, as you get involved with work, you do not notice the discomfort signals anymore. The sensory register is now blocking the impulses from reaching your consciousness. Should you move your foot in a way that causes the shoe to pinch, however, the sensory register will pass this pain stimulus along to your consciousness and you become aware of it.

Another example: You are sitting in a classroom and a police car with its siren wailing passes by. Experience reminds you that a siren is an important sound. Signals from the sensory register pass the auditory stimuli over to immediate memory. If over the next few seconds the sound of the siren gets fainter, experience signals the immediate memory that the sound is of no further importance and the auditory data are blocked and dropped from the system. All this is happening subconsciously while your attention is focused on something else. If asked about the sound 15 minutes later, you will not remember it. You cannot recall what you have not stored.

Suppose, on the other hand, that the siren sound gets louder and suddenly stops, followed by another siren that gets louder and stops. Experience will now signal that the sounds are important because they are nearby, may affect your survival, and therefore require your attention. At this point, the now-important auditory data move rapidly into working memory for conscious processing so that you can decide what action to take.

Threats and Emotions Affect Memory Processing. This last example illustrates another characteristic of brain processing: There is a hierarchy of response to sensory input (Figure 2.2). Any input that is of higher priority diminishes the processing of data of lower priority. The brain's main job is to help its owner survive. Thus, data interpreted as posing a threat to the survival of the individual, such as a burning odor, a snarling dog, or someone threatening bodily injury, are processed immediately. Upon receiving the stimulus, the reticular activating system sends a rush of adrenaline throughout the brain. This reflexive response shuts down all unnecessary activity and directs the brain's attention to the source of the stimulus.

Emotional data also take high priority. When an individual responds emotionally to a situation, the older limbic system (stimulated by the amygdala) takes a major role and the complex cerebral processes are suspended. We have all had experiences when anger, fear of the unknown, or joy quickly overcame our rational thoughts. This reflexive override of conscious thought can be strong enough to cause temporary inability to talk ("I was dumbfounded") or move ("I froze"). This happens because the hippocampus is susceptible to stress hormones that can inhibit cognitive functioning and long-term memory.

> **Students must feel physically safe and emotionally secure before they can focus on the curriculum.**

Under certain conditions, emotions can enhance memory by causing the release of hormones that stimulate the amygdala to signal brain regions to strengthen memory. Strong emotions can shut down conscious processing during the event while enhancing our memory of it. Emotion is a powerful and misunderstood force in learning and memory. Another way of stating the hierarchy illustrated in Figure 2.2 is that before students will turn their attention to cognitive learning (the curriculum), they must feel physically safe and emotionally secure.

Over the years, most teacher-training classes have told prospective teachers to focus on reason, cover the curriculum, and avoid emotions in their lessons. Now, we need to enlighten educators about how emotions consistently affect attention and learning. Districts must ensure that schools are free of weapons and violence. Teachers can then promote emotional security in the classroom by establishing a positive climate that encourages students to take appropriate risks. Students must sense that the teacher wants to help them be right rather than catch them being wrong.

> **How a person "feels" about a learning situation determines the amount of attention devoted to it.**

Moreover, superintendents and board members need to examine their actions, which set the emotional climate of a district. Is it a place where people want to come to work? Does the district reward or frown on appropriate risk taking?

How a person "feels" about a learning situation determines the amount of attention devoted to it. Emotions interact with reason to support or inhibit learning. To be successful learners and productive citizens, we need to know how to use our emotions intelligently. Thus, we need to explore what and how we teach students about their emotions. For example, we could teach about controlling impulses, delaying gratification, expressing feelings, managing relationships, and reducing stress. Students should recognize that they can manage their emotions for greater productivity and can develop emotional skills for greater success in life.

Working Memory

Working memory is also a temporary memory and the place where conscious, rather than subconscious, processing occurs. The information processing model represents working memory as a work table, a place of limited capacity where we can build, take apart, or rework ideas for eventual storage somewhere else. When something is in working memory, it generally captures our focus and demands our attention. Information in working memory can come from the sensory/immediate memories or be retrieved from long-term memory. Brain imaging studies show that most of working memory's activity occurs in the frontal lobes, although other parts of the brain are often called into action.

In recent years, researchers have compiled studies suggesting that the functioning of working memory can be explained by a three-part system (Figure 2.3) containing a *central control* (executive) *mechanism* and two subordinate components involved in rehearsal (Baddeley, 1995; Gazzaniga et al., 2002). The central control mechanism manages the interactions between the two subordinate systems and long-term memory. The *phonological loop* is the mechanism that uses auditory signals to code information into working memory, such as when we are talking about what we are learning. The *visuospatial sketchpad* allows for encoding information into working memory in solely visual or as a combination of visual and spatial (visuospatial) codes. This three-part model suggests that auditory and visual rehearsal *occurring during learning* increase working memory's interactions with long-term memory, raising the probability it will be stored.

There is also experimental evidence that when working memory is processing new information, the visuospatial component can become so activated that it has difficulty filtering out non-related images (de Fockert, Rees, Frith, & Lavie, 2001). This finding could have implications for cellular phone use in cars. If the phone conversation requires sufficient thought processing, it may sufficiently stimulate working memory so that the driver becomes distracted by irrelevant sights along the road.

Figure 2.3 This model represents the three-part system that comprises working memory. The central control mechanism manages the phonological loop and the visuospatial sketchpad (Baddeley, 1995).

Capacity of Working Memory. Miller (1956) discovered years ago that working memory can handle only a few items at once. This functional capacity changes with age. Table 2.1 shows how the capacity of working memory increases as one passes through the major growth spurts in cognitive development. Preschool infants can deal with about two items of information at once. Preadolescents can handle three to seven items, with an average of five. Through adolescence, further cognitive expansion occurs and the capacity increases to a range of five to nine, with an average of seven. For most people, that number remains constant throughout life.

More recent research has raised questions about the exact capacity limit of working memory. Some studies suggest that it now may be as low as four items for adults. A few others say it is difficult to state an actual number because variables such as interest, mental time delays, and distractions

Table 2.1 Changes in Capacity of Working Memory With Age			
Approximate Age Range in Years	**Capacity of Working Memory in Number of Chunks**		
	Minimum	**Maximum**	**Average**
Younger Than 5	1	3	2
Between 5 and 14	3	7	5
14 and Older	5	9	7

may undermine and invalidate experimental attempts to find a capacity limit (Cowan, 2001). Nonetheless, most of the research evidence to date supports the notion that working memory has a functional limit, and the number seven continues to be accepted as a workable guideline for adolescents and adults.

Let's test this notion. Get a pencil and a piece of paper. When ready, stare at the number below for seven seconds, then look away and write it down. Ready? Go.

9217053

Check the number you wrote down. Chances are you got it right. Let's try it again with the same rules. Stare at the number below for seven seconds, then look away and write it down. Ready? Go.

4915082637

Again, check the number you wrote down. Did you get all 10 of the digits in the correct sequence? Probably not. Because the digits were random, you had to treat each digit as a single item, and your working memory just ran out of functional capacity.

This limited capacity explains why we have to memorize a song or a poem in stages. We start with the first group of lines by repeating them frequently (a process called *rehearsal*). Then we memorize the next lines and repeat them with the first group, and so on. It is possible to increase the number of items within the functional capacity of working memory through a process called *chunking*. This process will be explained in the next chapter.

Keep the number of items in a lesson objective within the capacity limits of students and they are likely to remember more of what they learned. Less is more!

Why would such a sophisticated structure like the human brain exhibit such severe limitations in working memory capacity? No one knows for sure. One possible explanation is that it is unlikely during the development of the brain thousands of years ago that our ancestors had to process or identify more than one thing at a time. It is also unlikely that they had to make several split-second decisions at the same time. Even in fight-or-flight situations, there probably was only one enemy or predator at a time. Today, however, people are often trying to do several things at once during their workday, making the memory's capacity limits more obvious.

Implications for Teaching. Can you see the implication this functional capacity has on lesson planning? It means that the elementary teacher who expects students to remember in one lesson the eight rules for using the comma is already in trouble. So is the high school or college teacher who wants students to learn in one lesson the names and locations of the 10 most important rivers in the world. Keeping the number of items in a lesson objective within the appropriate capacity limit increases the likelihood that students will remember more of what they learned. Less is more!

Time Limits of Working Memory. Working memory is temporary and can deal with items for only a limited time. How long is that time? This intriguing question has been clinically investigated for over a century, starting with the work of Hermann Ebbinghaus (1850-1909) during the 1880s. He concluded that we can process items intently in working memory (he called it short-term memory) for up to 45 minutes before becoming fatigued. Because Ebbinghaus mainly used himself as the subject to measure retention in laboratory conditions, the results are not readily transferable to the average high school classroom.

Any discussion of time limits for processing new information has to include motivation. People who are intensely motivated about a subject can spend hours reading and processing it. They are not likely to quit until they are physically tired. That is because motivation is essentially an emotional response, and we already know that emotions play an important part in attention and learning. Students are not equally motivated in all subjects. Therefore, these time limits are more likely to apply to students who are in learning episodes that they do not find motivating.

Peter Russell (1979) shows this time span to be much shorter and age dependent. Although his work was done nearly 30 years ago, the time limits for the novelty-seeking brain of today are very similar. For preadolescents, it is 5 to 10 minutes, and for adolescents and adults, 10 to 20 minutes. These are average times, and it is important to understand what the numbers mean. An adolescent (or adult) normally can process an item in working memory *intently* for 10 to 20 minutes before mental fatigue (as opposed to physical fatigue) or boredom with that item occurs and the individual's focus drifts. For focus to continue, there must be some change in the way the individual is dealing with the item. For example, the person may switch from thinking about it to physically using it, or making different connections to other learnings. If something else is not done with the item, it is likely to fade from working memory.

This is not to say that some items cannot remain in working memory for hours, or perhaps days. Sometimes, we have an item that remains unresolved—a question whose answer we seek or a troublesome family or work decision that must be made. These items can remain in working memory, continually commanding some attention and, if of sufficient importance, interfere with our accurate processing of other information.

Implications for Teaching. These time limits suggest that packaging lessons into 15- to 20-minute components are likely to result in maintaining greater student interest than one 40-minute lesson. It seems that, with many lessons, shorter is better! We'll talk more about lesson length and memory in Chapter 3.

Criteria for Long-Term Storage

Now comes the most important decision of all: Should the items in working memory be encoded to long-term storage for future recall, or should they drop out of the system? This is an important decision because we cannot recall what we have not stored. Yet teachers teach with the hope that students will retain the learning objective for future use. So, if the learner is ever to recall this information in the future, it has to be stored.

What criteria does the working memory use to make that decision? Figure 2.2 can help us here. Information that has survival value is quickly stored. You don't want to have to learn every day that walking in front of a moving bus or touching a hot stove can injure you. Strong emotional experiences also have a high likelihood of being permanently stored. We tend to remember the best and worst things that happened to us.

> **Information is most likely to get stored if it makes sense and has meaning.**

But in classrooms, where the survival and emotional elements are minimal or absent, other factors come into play. It seems that the working memory connects with the learner's past experiences and asks just two questions to determine whether an item is saved or rejected. They are: "Does this make *sense*?" and "Does this have *meaning*?" Imagine the many hours that go into planning and teaching lessons, and it all comes down to these two questions! Let's review them.

- **"Does this make sense?"** This question refers to whether the learner can understand the item on the basis of experience. Does it "fit" into what the learner knows about how the world works? When a student says, "I don't understand," it means the student is having a problem making sense of the learning.
- **"Does it have meaning?"** This question refers to whether the item is *relevant* to the learner. For what purpose should the learner remember it? Meaning, of course, is a very personal thing and is greatly influenced by that person's experiences. The same item can have great meaning for one student and none for another. Questions like "Why do I have to know this?" or "When will I ever use this?" indicate that the student has not, for whatever reason, accepted this learning as relevant.

Here are two examples to explain the difference between sense and meaning. Suppose I tell a 15-year-old student that the minimum age for getting a driver's license in his state is age 16, but it is 17 in a neighboring state. He can understand this information, so it satisfies the sense criterion. But the age in his own state is much more relevant to him, because this is where he will apply for his license. Chances are high that he will remember his own state's minimum age (it has both sense *and* meaning) but will forget that of the neighboring state (it has sense but lacks meaning).

Suppose you are a teacher and you read in the newspaper that the average salary for dock workers last year was $60,000, whereas the average for teachers was $42,000. Both numbers make sense to you, but the average teacher's salary has more meaning because you are in that profession.

Whenever the learner's working memory decides that an item does not make sense or have meaning, the probability of it being stored is extremely low (see Figure 2.4). If either sense or meaning is

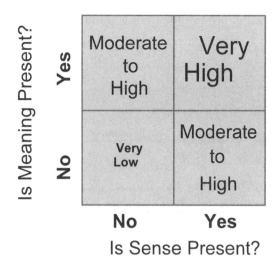

Figure 2.4 The probability of storing information varies with the degree of sense and meaning that are present.

present, the probability of storage increases significantly (assuming, of course, no survival or emotional component). If both sense *and* meaning are present, the likelihood of long-term storage is very high.

Relationship of Sense to Meaning

Sense and meaning are independent of each other. Thus, it is possible to remember an item because it makes sense but has no meaning. If you have ever played *Trivial Pursuit* or similar games, you may have been surprised at some of the answers you knew. If another player asked how you knew that answer, you may have replied, "I don't know. It was just there!" This happens to all of us. During our lifetime, we pick up bits of information that made sense at the time and, although they were trivial and had no meaning, they made their way into our long-term memory.

It is also possible to remember an item that makes no sense but has meaning. My sixth-grade teacher once asked the class to memorize Lewis Carroll's nonsense poem "Jabberwocky." It begins, *Twas brillig, and the slithy toves did gyre and gimble in the wabe.* The poem made no sense to us sixth graders, but when the teacher said that she would call on each of us the next day to recite it before the class, it suddenly had meaning. Since I didn't want to make a fool of myself in front of my peers, I memorized it and recited it correctly the next day, even though I had no idea what the sense of it was.

Brain scans have shown that when new learning is readily comprehensible (sense) and can be connected to past experiences (meaning), there is substantially more cerebral activity followed by dramatically improved retention (Maquire, Frith, & Morris, 1999).

Meaning Is More Significant. Of the two criteria, meaning has the greater impact on the probability that information will be stored. Think of all the television programs you have watched that are NOT stored, even though you spent one or two hours with the program. The show's content or story line made sense to you, but if meaning was absent, you just did not save it. It was *entertainment* and no learning resulted from it. You might have remembered a summary of the show, or whether it was enjoyable or boring, but not the details. On the other hand, if the story reminded you of a personal experience, then meaning was present and you were more likely to remember more details of the program.

Test Question No. 2: Learners who can perform a new learning task well are likely to retain it.

Answer: False. We cannot presume that because a learner performs a new learning task well, it will be permanently stored. Sense and/or meaning must be present in some degree for storage to occur.

Implications for Teaching. Now think of this process in the classroom. Every day, students listen to things that make sense but lack meaning. They may diligently follow the teacher's instructions to perform a task repeatedly, and may even get the correct answers, but if they have not found meaning after the learning episode, there is little likelihood of long-term storage. Mathematics teachers are often frustrated by this. They see students using a certain formula to solve problems correctly one day, but they cannot remember how to do it the next day. If the process was not stored, the information is treated as brand new again!

Sometimes, when students ask why they need to know something, the teacher's response is, "Because it's going to be on the test." This response adds little meaning to a learning. Students resort to writing the learning in a notebook so that it is preserved in writing, but not in memory. We wonder the next day why they forgot the lesson.

Teachers spend about 90 percent of their planning time devising lessons so that students will *understand* the learning objective (i.e., make sense of it). But to convince a learner's brain to persist with that objective, teachers need to be more mindful of helping students establish *meaning*. We should remember that what was meaningful for us as children may not be necessarily meaningful for children today.

Past experiences always influence new learning. What we already know acts as a filter, helping us attend to those things that have meaning (i.e., relevancy) and discard those that don't. If we expect students to find meaning, we need to be certain that today's curriculum contains connections to *their* past experiences, not just ours. Further, the enormous size and the strict separation of secondary curriculum areas do little to help students find the time to make relevant connections between and among subjects. Helping students to make connections between subject areas by integrating the curriculum increases meaning and retention, especially when students

> **Past experiences always influence new learning.**

recognize a future use for the new learning. Meaning is so powerful that most states prohibit trial lawyers from using what is dubbed the "golden rule" argument. It asks the jury, "If you were in this person's situation, what would you have done?"

Long-Term Storage

Storing occurs when the hippocampus encodes information and sends it to one or more long-term storage areas. The encoding process takes time and usually occurs during deep sleep. While learners may *seem* to have acquired the new information or skill in a lesson, there is no guarantee that storage will be permanent after the lesson. How do we know if retention has occurred? If the student can accurately recall the learning after a specific period of time has passed, we say that the learning has been retained. Because research on retention shows that the greatest loss of newly acquired information or a skill occurs within the first 18 to 24 hours, the 24-hour period is a reasonable guideline for determining if information was transferred into long-term storage. If a learner cannot recall new learning after 24 hours, there is a high probability that it was not permanently stored and, thus, can never be recalled. This point has implications for how we test students for retention of previously learned material. See the **Practitioner's Corner** at the end of this chapter on page 70 on how to test whether information is in long-term storage. Sometimes, we store only the gist of an experience, not the specifics. This may occur after watching a movie or television program. We store a generalization about the plot but few, if any, details.

Test Question No. 3: Reviewing material just before a test is a good practice to determine how much has been retained in long-term storage.

Answer: False. Reviewing material just before a test allows students to enter the material into working memory for immediate use. Thus, the test cannot verify that what the learner recalls actually came from long-term storage.

The long-term storage areas are represented in the model (Figure 2.1) as file cabinets— places where information is kept in some type of order. Although there are three file cabinets in the diagram for simplicity, we do not know how many long-term storage sites actually are in the brain. Memories are not stored as a whole in one place. Different parts of a memory are stored in various sites which reassemble when the memory is recalled. Long-term memory is a dynamic, interactive system that activates storage areas distributed across the brain to retrieve and reconstruct memories.

Long-Term Memory and Long-Term Storage

This is a good place to explain the difference between the terms *long-term memory* and *long-term storage,* as I use them in the model. Long-term memory refers to the process of storing and retrieving information, while long-term storage refers to the areas in the brain where the memories are kept.

The Cognitive Belief System

The total of all that is in our long-term storage areas forms the basis for our view of the world around us. This information helps us to make sense out of events, to understand the laws of nature, to recognize cause and effect, and to form decisions about goodness, truth, and beauty. This total construct of how we see the world is called the *cognitive belief system.* It is shown in the information processing model as a large triangle extending beyond the long-term storage areas (file cabinets). It is drawn this way to remind us that the thoughts and understandings that arise from the long-term storage data are greater than the sum of the individual items. In other words, one marvelous quality of the human brain is its ability to combine individual items in many different ways. As we accumulate more items, the number of possible combinations grows exponentially.

Because no two of us have the same data in our long-term storage (not even identical twins raised in the same environment have identical data sets), no two of us perceive the world in exactly the same way. People can put the same experiences together in many different ways. To be sure, there are areas of agreement: Gravity, for example (few rational people would dispute its effects), or inertia, since most people have experienced the lurch forward or backward when a moving vehicle rapidly changes speed. There can be strong disagreement, however, about what makes an object or person beautiful, or an act justified. The persistent debates over abortion and capital punishment are testimony to the wide range of perspectives that people have over any issue. These differences reflect the ways individuals use the experiences in their long-term storage areas to interpret the world around them.

> **The cognitive belief system is our view of the world around us and how it works.**

Here is a simple example of how people's experiences can cause them to interpret the same information differently. Close your eyes and form the mental image of an "old bat." Go ahead, try it! What picture comes to mind? For some baseball fans, it might be a marred wooden club that has been in too many games. A zoologist, however, might picture an aging fruit bat as it flies haltingly among the trees. Still others might recall an old hag whose complaining made their lives unpleasant. Here are at least three very different images generated by the same two words, each one formed by individuals whose experiences are different from the others.

Self-Concept

Deep within the cognitive belief system lies the *self-concept.* While the cognitive belief system portrays the way we see the world, the self-concept describes the way we view ourselves in that world. I might conceptualize myself as a good softball player, an above average student, or a poor mathematician. These and a long list of other descriptions form part of a person's self-concept.

The self-concept is represented in the information processing model (Figure 2.1) as a face and is placed at the apex of the triangle to emphasize its importance. *Self-concept* is used here as a neutral term that can run the gamut from very positive to very negative (Figure 2.5). The face on the diagram of the model has a smile, indicating a positive self-concept. But for some people, the face might have a frown because they may not see themselves as positive beings in their world. Emotions play an important role in forming a person's self-concept.

Self-Concept

Figure 2.5   Self-concept describes how we see ourselves in the world. It can range from very low to very high and vary with different learning situations.

Self-Concept and Past Experiences

Our self-concept is shaped by our past experiences. Some of our experiences, such as passing a difficult test or getting recognition for a job well done, raised our self-concept. Other experiences, such as receiving a reprimand or failing to accomplish a task, lowered our self-concept. These experiences produced strong emotional reactions that the brain's amygdala encoded and stored with the cognitive event. These emotional cues are so strong that we often reexperience the original emotion each time we recall the event. Over time, the addition of new positive and negative experiences moderate the self-concept and alter how we see ourselves in our world.

Accepting or Rejecting New Learning

Remember that the sensory register and temporary memory systems use past experiences as the guide for determining the importance of incoming stimuli to the individual. Thus, if an individual is in a new learning situation and past experience signals the sensory register that prior encounters with this information were successful, then the information is very likely to pass along to working memory. The learner now consciously recognizes that there were successes with this information and focuses on it for further processing. But if past experiences produced failure, then the sensory register is likely to block the incoming data, just as Venetian blinds are closed to block light. The learner resists being part of the unwanted learning experience and resorts to some other cerebral activity, internal or external, to avoid the situation. In effect, the learner's self-concept has closed off the receptivity to the new information. As mentioned earlier in discussing the hierarchy of data processing, when a curriculum concept struggles with an emotion, the emotion almost always wins. Of course, it is possible for the rational system (frontal lobe) to override the emotions, but that usually takes time and conscious effort.

> *People will participate in learning activities that have yielded success for them and avoid those that have produced failure.*

Let us use an example to explain this important phenomenon. Someone who was a very successful student in mathematics remembers how that success boosted self-concept. As a result, the individual now feels confident when faced with basic mathematical problems. On the other hand, for someone who was a poor mathematics student, lack of success would lower self-concept. Consequently, such an individual will avoid dealing with mathematical problems whenever possible. People will participate in learning activities that have yielded success for them and avoid those that have produced failure.

Implications for Teaching. Students who experience self-concept shutdown in the classroom often give signs of their withdrawal—folding their arms, losing themselves in other work, or causing distraction. Too often, teachers deal with this withdrawal by reteaching the material, usually slower and louder. But they are attacking the problem from the front end of the information processing system, and this is rarely successful. It is the equivalent of putting a brighter light outside the closed Venetian blinds, hoping the light will penetrate. If the blinds are fully closed and effective, no light will get through, regardless of how bright it may be.

The better intervention is to deal with the learner's emotions and convince the learner to allow the perceptual register to open the blinds and pass the information along. But since the self-concept controls the blinds, the learner must believe that participating in the learning situation will produce new successes rather than repeat past failures. When teachers provide these successes, they encourage students to open the sensory register and, ultimately, to participate and achieve in the once-avoided learning process. In short, the self-concept controls the feedback loop and determines how the individual will respond to almost any new learning situation. Recognizing this connection gives teachers new insight on how to deal with reluctant learners.

What's Coming Up?

This completes our trip through the information processing model. Remember that the brain is a parallel processor and deals with many items simultaneously. Even though it rejects much data, it always stores some. The next chapter will examine the nature of memory and the factors that determine and help in the retention of learning.

PRACTITIONER'S CORNER

Walking Through the Brain

Directions: In this activity, students/participants will assume the roles of the different parts of the information processing model.

1. Each participant gets one of the following assignments:

    3–4 persons for the **sensory register**

    1 person for the **immediate memory**

    1 person for the **working memory**

    3–4 persons for the **long-term storage**

    rest of the group represents **incoming information**

2. In an open area of the classroom, the participants should arrange themselves in a pattern that approximates the information processing model shown earlier in Figure 2.1.

3. All participants, except those representing **incoming information**, briefly explain their role and function in the model.

4. The participants representing incoming information then move through the model one at a time, explaining what is happening at each stage.

5. **Variations**: Replay the activity demonstrating how information can be accepted or rejected by the sensory register, immediate memory, and working memory. One of the participants representing **long-term storage** can also represent the feedback loop of past experiences.

6. After demonstrating several different possibilities, discuss how this activity may have enhanced your understanding of the model. Note the positive effect that kinesthetic activities can have on learning new material.

PRACTITIONER'S CORNER

Redesigning the Information Processing Model

This activity gives the students/participants the opportunity to redesign the information processing model explained in this chapter.

Directions: In the area below redesign the information processing model using a **different** metaphor (e.g., a sports game, taking a vacation, cooking recipe). Keep the same metaphor for each of the major parts of the model. Be prepared to explain the metaphor and why you chose it.

PRACTITIONER'S CORNER

Sensory Preferences and Learning Style

Although we use all five senses to collect information from our environment, they do not contribute equally to our knowledge base. Most people do not use sight, hearing, and touch equally during learning. Just as most people develop a left- or right-handed preference, they also develop preferences for certain senses as they gather information from their environment. Some people have a preference for learning by sight, for example. They are called *visual* learners. Others who use hearing as the preferred sense are known as *auditory* learners. Still others who prefer touch or whole-body involvement in their learning are called *kinesthetic* learners. Sensory (also called *modality*) preferences are an important component of an individual's learning style. Teachers need to

- **Understand** that students with different sensory preferences will behave differently during learning.

- **Recognize** that they tend to teach the way they learn. A teacher who is a strong auditory learner will prefer this modality when teaching. Students who also are strong auditory learners will feel comfortable with this teacher's methods, but visual learners can have difficulty in maintaining focus. They will doodle or look at other materials to satisfy their visual craving.

- **Note,** similarly, that students with auditory preferences want to talk about their learning and can become frustrated with teachers who use primarily visual strategies. Strong kinesthetic learners require movement while learning or they become restless—tapping their pencils, squirming in their seats, or walking around the room.

- **Avoid** misinterpreting these variations in learning style behavior as inattention or as intentional misbehavior. The variations may, in fact, represent the natural responses of learners with different and strong preferences.

- **Understand** that a teacher's own learning style and sensory preferences can affect learning and teaching. Teachers should design lessons that include activities to address all sensory preference and learning styles.

PRACTITIONER'S CORNER

Determining Your Sensory Preferences

This checklist indicates your sensory preference(s). It is designed for adults and is one of many that are available. You should not rely on just one checklist for self-assessment. Remember that sensory preferences are usually evident only during prolonged and complex learning tasks.

Directions: For each item, circle "**A**" if you **agree** that the statement describes you most of the time. Circle "**D**" if you **disagree** that the statement describes you most of the time. Move quickly through the questions. Your first response is usually the more accurate one.

1. I prefer reading a story rather than listening to someone tell it.   A   D

2. I would rather watch television than listen to the radio.   A   D

3. I remember names better than faces.   A   D

4. I like classrooms with lots of posters and pictures around the room.   A   D

5. The appearance of my handwriting is important to me.   A   D

6. I think more often in pictures.   A   D

7. I am distracted by visual disorder or movement.   A   D

8. I have difficulty remembering directions that were told to me.   A   D

9. I would rather watch athletic events than participate in them.   A   D

10. I tend to organize my thoughts by writing them down.   A   D

11. My facial expression is a good indicator of my emotions.   A   D

12. I tend to remember names better than faces.   A   D

13. I would enjoy taking part in dramatic events like plays.   A   D

14. I tend to subvocalize and think in sounds.   A   D

15. I am easily distracted by sounds.   A   D

16. I easily forget what I read unless I talk about it.   A   D

17. I would rather listen to the radio than watch television.   A   D

18. My handwriting is not very good.   A   D

19. When faced with a problem, I tend to talk it through.   A   D

20. I express my emotions verbally.   A   D

21. I would rather be in a group discussion than read about a topic.   A   D

22. I prefer talking on the phone rather than writing a letter to someone.   A   D

23. I would rather participate in athletic events than watch them.   A   D

24. I prefer going to museums where I can touch the exhibits.   A   D

25. My handwriting deteriorates when the space becomes smaller.   A   D

26. My mental pictures are usually accompanied by movement.   A   D

27. I like being outdoors and doing things like biking, camping,   A   D
    swimming, hiking, etc.

28. I remember best what was done rather than what was seen or talked about.   A   D

29. When faced with a problem, I often select the solution involving   A   D
    the greatest activity.

30. I like to make models or other hand-crafted items.   A   D

31. I would rather do experiments than read about them.   A   D

32. My body language is a good indicator of my emotions.   A   D

33. I have difficulty remembering verbal directions if I have not done the   A   D
activity before.

Interpreting Your Score

Total the number of "**A**" responses in items 1–11:   _____
This is your visual score.

Total the number of "**A**" responses in items 12–22:   _____
This is your auditory score.

Total the number of "**A**" responses in items 23–33:   _____
This is your tactile/kinesthetic score.

If you scored a lot higher in any one area: This sense is *very probably* your preference during a protracted and complex learning situation.

If you scored a lot lower in any one area: This sense is *not likely* to be your preference in a learning situation.

If you have similar scores in all three areas: You can learn things in almost any way they are presented.

Reflections

A. What was your preferred sense? Were you surprised?

B. How does this preference show up in your daily life?

C. How does this preference show up in your teaching?

PRACTITIONER'S CORNER

Developing a Classroom
Climate Conducive to Learning

Learning occurs more easily in environments free from threat or intimidation. Whenever a student detects a threat, thoughtful processing gives way to emotion or survival reactions. Experienced teachers have seen this in the classroom. Under pressure to give a quick response, the student begins to stumble, stabs at answers, gets frustrated or angry, and may even resort to violence.

There are ways to deal with questions and answers that reduce the fear of giving a wrong answer. The teacher could:

- Supply the question to which the wrong answer belongs:
  "You would be right if I had asked . . . "

- Give the student a prompt that leads to the correct answer.

- Ask another student to help.

Threats to students loom continuously in the classroom. The teacher's capacity to humiliate, embarrass, reject, and punish all constitute perceived threats. Many students even see grading more as a punitive than as a rewarding process. Students perceive threats in varying degrees, but the presence of a threat in *any* significant degree impedes learning. One's thinking and learning functions operate fully only when one feels secure.

Teachers can make their classrooms better learning environments by avoiding threats (even subtle intimidation) and by establishing democratic climates in which students are treated fairly and feel free to express their opinions during discussions. In these environments students:

- Develop trust in the teacher

- Exhibit more positive behaviors

- Are less likely to be disruptive

- Show greater support for school policy

- Sense that thinking is encouraged and nurtured

For Further Discussion

- What kinds of emotions in school could interfere with cognitive processing (i.e., have a negative effect on learning)?

_____

_____

- What strategies and structures can schools and teachers use to limit the threat and negative effects of these emotions?

_____

_____

- What factors in schools can foster emotions in students that promote learning (i.e., have a positive effect)?

_____

_____

- What strategies have you used to encourage the positive emotions that promote learning?

_____

_____

PRACTITIONER'S CORNER

Using Humor to Enhance
Climate and Promote Retention

Humor has many benefits when used frequently and appropriately in the classroom and other school settings.

Physiological Benefits

- **Provides More Oxygen**. Brain cells need oxygen and glucose for fuel. When we laugh, we get more oxygen into the bloodstream, so the brain is better fueled.

- **Causes an Endorphin Surge**. Laughter causes the release of *endorphins* in the blood. Endorphins are the body's natural painkillers, and they also give the person a feeling of euphoria. In other words, the person enjoys the moment in body as well as in mind. Endorphins also stimulate the brain's frontal lobes, thereby increasing the degree of focus and amount of attention time.

- **Moderates Body Functions.** Scientists have found that humor decreases stress, modulates pain, decreases blood pressure, relaxes muscle tension, and boosts immune defenses. These are all desirable outcomes.

Psychological, Sociological, and Educational Benefits

- **Gets Attention**. The first thing a teacher has to do when starting a lesson is to get the students' attention or focus. Because the normal human brain loves to laugh, starting with a humorous tale (such as a joke, pun, or story) gets the learner's attention. Self-deprecating humor ("You won't believe what happened to me this weekend.") is particularly effective with teens.

- **Creates a Positive Climate**. Students are going to be together in a classroom for about 180 days. We need to find ways to help this increasingly diverse student population get along. When people laugh together, they bond and a community spirit emerges—all positive forces for an climate conducive to learning.

- **Increases Retention and Recall**. We know that emotions enhance retention, so the positive feelings that result from laughter increase the probability that students will remember what they learned and be able to recall it later.

- **Improves Everyone's Mental Health**. Schools and all their occupants are under more stress than ever. Taking time to laugh can relieve that stress and give the staff and students better mental attitude with which to accomplish their tasks. Let's take our work seriously but ourselves lightly.

- **Provides an Effective Discipline Tool**. Good-natured humor (not teasing or sarcasm) can be an effective way of reminding students of the rules without raising tension in the classroom. Laughter also dampens hostility and aggression. Teachers who use appropriate humor are more likeable and students have a more positive feeling toward them. Discipline problems, therefore, are less likely to occur.

Using Humor as Part of Lessons. Humor should not be limited to an opening joke or story. Because of its value as an attention-getter and retention strategy, look for ways to use humor within the context of the learning objective. Droz and Ellis (1996) give many helpful suggestions on how to get students to use humor in lessons on writing, mathematics, science, and history.

Administrators and Humor. Administrators also need to remember the value of humor in their relationships with staff, students, and parents. As leaders, they set the example. In meetings and other settings, they can show that humor and laughter are acceptable in schools and classrooms.

Some Barriers to Humor in Classrooms

- **"I'm Not Funny."** Some teachers want to use humor in the classroom but don't perceive themselves as jokesters. They'll say: "I'm just not funny" or "I can't tell a joke." But the teacher doesn't have to be funny, just the material—and there's plenty of it. Books on humor are available in local stores, and don't forget that students themselves often provide humor by their responses in class and answers on tests. Be certain that you use this material appropriately, avoiding teasing or sarcasm.

- **"Students Won't Enjoy It."** Secondary teachers, particularly, believe that students won't find humor in corny jokes or that they are too sophisticated to laugh. But everyone likes to laugh (or groan) at humor. I suggest starting each class period with humor for three weeks, then stopping. I'm certain that students will say, "Hey, where's the joke?"—evidence that they *were* listening.

- **"It Takes Too Much Time."** This is a common concern. Secondary teachers often feel so pressured to cover curriculum material that they are reluctant to give time to what may seem like a frivolous activity. On the other hand, humor is an *efficient* as well as effective way to gain students' attention and improve retention of learning. It really is a useful investment of time.

Avoiding Sarcasm. All of the wonderful benefits mentioned above are the result of using wholesome humor that everyone can enjoy, and not sarcasm, which is inevitably destructive to someone. Even some well-intentioned teachers say, "Oh, I know my students very well, so they can take sarcasm." More than ever, today's students are coming to school looking for emotional support. Sarcasm is one of the factors that can undermine that support and turn students against their peers, the teacher, and the school. Besides, there are plenty of sources of good humor without sarcasm.

For a deeper look at the research on the effects of humor on the body and brain, see Cardoso (2000) and Schmidt (1995, 2002).

PRACTITIONER'S CORNER

Increasing Processing Time Through Motivation

Working memory is a temporary memory, so items have a limited time for processing. But the longer an item is processed (or rehearsed), the greater the probability that sense and meaning may be found, and therefore, that retention will occur. One way to increase processing time is through motivation, which is essentially an emotional response. Not surprisingly, recent research has validated long-standing beliefs that motivation is a key to the amount of attention devoted to a learning situation.

Motivation can come from within the individual, called *intrinsic motivation,* when an activity is related to a person's needs, values, interests, and attitudes. People spend hours on their hobbies because of intrinsic motivation. These internal attributes are so deeply rooted that they are difficult to change. But they can change over time.

Motivation that comes from the environment, such as rewards and punishment, is called *extrinsic motivation.* External motivators are used to control and reward behavior. Grades, stars, and praise are examples of external motivators used in schools. Although these incentives serve a purpose, they have little relationship to the internal process of learning. It's no secret that learning occurs best when the learner is intrinsically motivated (Wigfield & Eccles, 2002). External motivators can be of value by getting students started on a topic so that they can move toward intrinsic rewards.

Here are a few ideas about motivation for teachers to consider (Diamond & Hopson, 1998; Hunter, 2004; Moore, 2005):

- **Generate Interest.** If the learner is interested in the item, then the processing time can be extended significantly because the learner is dealing with the item in different ways and making new connections with past learnings that once were also of interest. The working memory is seeking ways to use this new learning to enhance the usefulness of the past learning. We all know students who won't give us five minutes of their undivided attention in class, but who spend hours working on a stamp collection, playing video games, or repairing a carburetor.

Teachers can identify these interests by having their students complete interest inventories at the beginning of the school year. The information gathered from these surveys can help teachers design lessons that include references to student interests as often as possible. Guidance counselors can provide information on the types and sources of interest inventories.

Today's novelty-seeking brain wants to get actively involved in the learning process. Active learning involves choices and actions that the learner finds pleasurable and effective for developing an understanding of the big picture as well as the relationship between and among the components of the learning objective. This approach stimulates intrinsic motivation and interest. Teachers, then, should:

- Make clear what the students should be able to do when the lesson objective is accomplished.

- Include provocative ideas and challenging activities.

- Involve the students in developing the criteria that will be used to assess their competency (e.g., assessment rubrics).

- Demonstrate how closely the content is connected to the real world.

- Give students choices in selecting activities and questions to pursue.

- **Establish Accountability.** When learners believe they will be held accountable for new learning, processing time increases. High school students have little difficulty staying on task in driver education classes. Not only do they have interest but they also know they will be legally accountable for their knowledge and skills long after they complete the license tests.

- **Provide Feedback.** When students get prompt, specific, and corrective feedback on the results of their thinking, they are more likely to continue processing, make corrections, and persist until successful completion. Frequent brief quizzes that are carefully corrected and returned promptly are much more valuable learning tools than the unit test, and are more likely to help students be successful. This success will improve self-concept and encourage them to try more difficult tasks. Computers are motivating because they provide immediate and objective feedback and allow students to evaluate their progress and understand their level of competence.

Another effective strategy suggested by Hunter (2004) for increasing processing time through motivation is called *level of concern*. This refers to how much the student cares about the learning. We used to think that if the students had anxiety about learning, then little or no learning occurred. But there is helpful anxiety (desire to do well) and there is harmful anxiety (feeling threatened). Having anxiety about your job performance will usually get you to put forth more effort to obtain positive results. When you are concerned about being more effective (helpful anxiety), you are likely to learn and try new strategies. This is an example of how emotions can increase learning.

Level of Concern vs. Degree of Learning

The graph shows that as the level of concern increases, so does the degree of learning. If the stress level gets too high, our focus shifts to the emotions and the consequences generated by the stress, and learning fades. Students need a certain level of concern to stimulate their efforts to learn. When there is no concern, there is little or no learning. But if there is too much concern, anxiety shuts down the learning process and adverse emotions take over. The teacher then has to seek the level of concern that produces the optimum processing time and learning. Hunter (2004) offers four ways to raise or lower the level of concern in a lesson.

- Consequences. Teachers raise the level of concern when they say "This is going to be on the test," and lower it with, "Knowing this will help you learn the next set of skills more easily."

- Visibility. Standing next to a student who is off-task will raise that student's concern; moving away from an anxious student will lower concern. Telling students their work will be displayed can also raise concern.

- Amount of Time. Giving students only a little time to complete a learning task will raise concern; extending the time will lower it.

- Amount of Help. If students have little or no help while completing a learning task, concern rises. On the other hand, if they have quick access to help, concern lowers. This can be a problem, however. If students can always get immediate help, they may become dependent and never learn to solve problems for themselves. There comes a time when the teacher needs to reduce the help and tell the students to use what they have learned to solve the problem on their own.

Reflections

A. What types of class activities increase the level of concern beyond the optimum level?

B. What strategies lower the level of concern raised by the activities in your answers to A above?

PRACTITIONER'S CORNER

Creating Meaning in New Learning

Meaning refers to the relevancy that students attach to new learning. Meaning isn't inherent in content, but rather is the result of how the students relate it to their past learnings and experiences. Questions like "Why do I need to know this?" reveal a learner who is having difficulty determining the relevancy of the new topic. Here are a few ways teachers can help students attach meaning to new learning.

- **Modeling**. Models are examples of the new learning that the learner can perceive in the classroom rather than relying on experience. Models can be concrete (an engine) or symbolic (a map). To be effective, a model should:

  - Accurately and unambiguously highlight the critical attribute(s) of new learning. A dog is a better example of a mammal than a whale.

  - Be given first by the teacher to ensure that it is correct during this period of prime time when retention is highest.

  - Avoid controversial issues that can evoke strong emotions and redirect the learner's attention.

- **Using Examples From Students' Experience.** These allow students to bring previous knowledge into working memory to accelerate making sense and attaching meaning to the new learning. Make sure that the example is clearly relevant to the new learning. This is not easy to do on the spot, so examples should be thought out in advance when planning the lesson.

- **Creating Artificial Meaning.** When it is not possible to identify exemplary elements from student experience to develop meaning, we can resort to other methods. Mnemonic devices help students associate material so they can remember it. Examples are HOMES to remember the Great Lakes and "Every good boy does fine" for the musical notes *e, g, b, d,* and *f* (See Chapter 3).

PRACTITIONER'S CORNER

Using Closure to Enhance Sense and Meaning

Closure describes the covert process whereby the learner's working memory summarizes for itself its perception of what has been learned. It is during closure that a student often completes the rehearsal process and attaches sense and meaning to the new learning, thereby increasing the probability that it will be retained in long-term storage.

- **Initiating Closure:** The teacher gives directions that focus the student on the new learning, such as "I'm going to give you about two minutes to think of the three causes of the Civil War that we learned today. Be prepared to discuss them briefly." In this statement, the teacher told the students how much quiet time they have for the cerebral summarizing to occur and identified the overt activity (discussion) that will be used for student accountability. During the discussion, the teacher can assess the quality and accuracy of what occurred during closure and make any necessary adjustments in teaching.

- **Closure Is Different From Review.** In review, the teacher does most of the work, repeating key concepts made during the lesson and rechecking student understanding. In closure, the student does most of the work by mentally rehearsing and summarizing those concepts and deciding whether they make sense and have meaning.

- **When to Use Closure.** Closure can occur at various times in a lesson.
  - It can start a lesson: "Think of the two causes of the Civil War we talked about yesterday and be prepared to discuss them."
  - It can occur during the lesson (called *procedural closure*) when the teacher moves from one sublearning to the next: "Review those two rules in your mind before we learn the third rule."
  - It should also take place at the end of the lesson (called *terminal closure*) to tie all the sublearnings together.

Closure is an investment that can pay off dramatically in increased retention of learning.

PRACTITIONER'S CORNER

Testing Whether Information
Is in Long-Term Storage

Information that the learner processes during a lesson remains in working memory where it eventually will be dropped out or saved for long-term storage. Just because students act as if they have learned the new information or skill doesn't mean it will be transferred to long-term storage. Extensive research on retention indicates that 70 to 90 percent of new learning is forgotten within 18 to 24 hours after the lesson. Consequently, if the new learning survives this time period intact, it is probably destined for long-term storage and will not deteriorate further.

This time requirement confirms that the processing and transfer between working memory and long-term storage needs adequate time for the encoding and consolidation of the new information into the storage networks. Thus, tomorrow is the earliest reliable time we can confirm that what was learned today has been indeed retained.

How to Test. If teachers want to test whether information actually has been transferred to long-term storage, the test needs to

- Be given no sooner than 24 hours after the learning

- Test precisely what should have been retained

- Come as a surprise to the learner, with no warning or preparation time

Rationale. If the learners have warning about the test, they are likely to review the material just before the test. In this case, the test may determine the amount of information the learners were able to cram and hold in working memory and not what they have recalled from long-term storage. While testing without warning may seem insensitive, it is the only way teachers can be sure that long-term storage was the source of the test information that the learners provided. Unannounced quizzes, then, should help students assess what they have remembered, rather than be a classroom management device to get students back on task.

Misuse of Tests. Some teachers use unannounced tests as punishment to get students back on task. This is a misuse of a valuable tool. Another approach is for teachers to

- **Establish** sense and meaning to increase the probability that retention will occur.

- **Explain** to students that unannounced tests help them see *what* as well as *how much* they have retained and learned over a given period of time.

- **Ensure** that the test or quiz matches the rehearsal when it was first taught. If the learning required essentially rote rehearsal, give a rote type of test. If it required elaborate rehearsal, use a test that allows the students more flexibility in their responses.

Using the Test Results. It is important that teachers

- **Analyze** immediately the results of the test to determine what areas need to be retaught or practiced. If some students forgot parts, consider forming cooperative learning groups that focus on reteaching the forgotten areas.

- **Record** the grades of only a small portion of these unannounced assessments. Rather, ask students to share their results and discuss in a think-pair-share format what strategies the students used to remember their correct responses. In this way, students talk about their memory processes and have a better understanding of how they learn and remember.

- **Decide** whether memory strategies such as concept maps, mnemonics, or chunking (see following chapters) can help in retention.

The analysis might also reveal areas of the curriculum to be reworked or updated for relevance, or it might show that the lesson should be retaught in a different way. A task analysis on a failed lesson is a good way to detect false assumptions about learning that the teacher may have made, and it recasts the lesson into a new presentation that can be more successful for both students and teacher.

Using tests as tools to help students to be right, rather than to catch them being wrong, will create a supportive learning climate that results in improved student performance.

PRACTITIONER'S CORNER

Using Synergy to Enhance Learning

Synergy describes how the joint actions of people working together increase each other's effectiveness. This strategy gets students moving and talking while learning. It is effective because it is novel, is multisensory, uses active participation, is emotionally stimulating, and encourages socialization. Each participant ends up having a better understanding as a result of this interaction (synergy). It can be used from the primary grades to graduate school. Here are the guidelines:

- **Provide Adequate Time for Reflection.** After teaching a concept, ask students to quietly review their notes and be prepared to explain what they have learned to someone else. Be sure to allow sufficient time for this mental rehearsal to occur (usually 1 to 3 minutes).

- **Model the Activity.** Working with a student, show the students how you want them to behave and interact during the activity.

- **Get Students to Stand, Move, and Deliver.** Ask students to walk across the room and pair up with someone they do not usually work with or know very well. They stand face-to-face and take turns explaining what they have learned. They add to their notes anything their partners have said that they do not have. When done, all students end up with more information and ideas than they would have had if they worked alone. If they cannot agree or don't understand something, they are to ask the teacher about it when the activity is over. (Note: Make sure students stand face-to-face—rather than just looking at each other's notes—so that they must talk to their partners. Allow pairs only—one trio, if you have an uneven number of students.)

- **Keep in Motion.** Move around the room using proximity to help students stay on task. Answer questions to get them back on track, but avoid reteaching the lesson. Otherwise, students will become dependent on your reteaching rather than on each other's explanations.

- **Provide Enough Time and Adjust As Needed.** Allow adequate time for this process to be effective. Start with a few minutes, adding more time if they are still on task and reducing the time when you sense they are done.

- **Ensure Accountability.** To help keep students on task, tell them that you will call on several students at random when the activity is over to explain what they discussed.

- **Clarify Any Misunderstandings.** Ask if there were any misunderstandings or items that need further explanation, and clarify them. An inviting statement would be "Is there anything I need to clarify?" rather than "Is there anything you didn't understand?"

- **Use Variety for the Pairing.** You can pair students by birth week or month, hair or eye color, height, musical cues, similar first names, etc. Aim for random pairing as much as practicable to enhance socialization (because students tend to work more with their friends) and to avoid monotony.

Some Potential Barriers to Using Synergy

- **"The Teacher Should Be Talking."** The long-standing practice of the teachers being the "deliverers" of information is tough to overcome. For that reason, some teachers are uncomfortable with this activity because they are not "working" (read "talking"). But one of the reasons this activity can be so effective is because it shifts the work to the students' brains, increasing the likelihood that they will find sense and meaning in the new learning.

- **"It Takes Too Much Time."** The question is: What would the teacher be doing otherwise? More talking? This is a useful investment of time because the students are talking about the lesson, thereby enhancing learning and retention.

- **"The Students Will Get Off Task."** This is a common and realistic concern. However, off-task behavior can be reduced significantly if the teacher continually moves around the room, listens in and asks questions of the student pairs, and holds them accountable for the learning at the end of the activity.

PRACTITIONER'S CORNER

NeuroBingo

Directions: In this activity the entire group gets up and moves around. Each person tries to find someone who can answer one of the questions in a box. The person who answers the question initials the box. The object is to get a bingo pattern (horizontally, vertically, or diagonally). No person may initial the same sheet twice. Time limit: 15 to 20 minutes, depending on the size and age of the group.

FIND A PERSON WHO IS ABLE TO

Explain the function of the sensory register	Explain the importance of sense and meaning to learning	Define "windows of opportunity"	Explain how the brain prioritizes incoming information	Explain the functions of the frontal lobes
State the two functions of the hippocampus	Tell you the function of immediate memory	Explain the function of the amygdala	Explain what is meant by the "novel" brain	Provide an example of how self-concept affects learning
Relate the cognitive belief system to learning	Tell you the functions of the cerebellum	Tell you the functions of the cerebrum	Describe the time limits of working memory	Explain synapses
Explain the meaning of sensory preferences	Describe the capacity limits of working memory	Explain what is meant by emotional control	Explain the function of neurotransmitters	Explain the function of longterm memory
Explain the value of humor in learning	Name the five senses	Describe the sources of brain research	Explain closure	Describe a neuron

Chapter 2—How the Brain Processes Information

Key Points to Ponder

Jot down on this page key points, ideas, strategies, and resources you want to consider later. This sheet is your personal journal summary and will help to jog your memory.

Chapter 3

Memory, Retention, and Learning

The memory should be specially taxed in youth, since it is then that it is strongest and most tenacious. But in choosing the things that should be committed to memory, the utmost care and forethought must be exercised; as lessons well learned in youth are never forgotten.

—Arthur Schopenhauer

Chapter Highlights: This chapter probes the nature of memory. It explains why our ability to retain information varies within a learning episode and with the teaching method used. It also discusses the value and pitfalls of practice, as well as techniques for increasing the capacity of working memory.

Memory gives us a past and a record of who we are and is essential to human individuality. Without memory, life would be a series of meaningless encounters that have no link to the past and no use for the future. Memory allows individuals to draw on experience and use the power of prediction to decide how they will respond to future events.

For all practical purposes, the capacity of the brain to store information is unlimited. That is, with about 100 billion neurons, each with thousands of dendrites, the number of potential neural

> **The brain goes through physical and chemical changes each time it learns.**

pathways is incomprehensible. The brain will hardly run out of space to store all that an individual learns in a lifetime. Learning is the process by which we *acquire* new knowledge and skills; memory is the process by which we *retain* the knowledge and skills for the future. Most of what makes up our cognitive belief system, we have learned. Investigations into the neural mechanisms required for different types of learning are revealing more about the interactions between learning new information, memory, and changes in brain structure. Just as muscles improve with exercise, the brain seems to improve with use. While learning does not increase the number of brain cells, it does increase their size, their branches, and their ability to form more complex networks.

The brain goes through physical and chemical changes when it stores new information as the result of learning. Storing gives rise to new neural pathways and strengthens existing pathways. Thus, every time we learn something, our long-term storage areas undergo anatomical changes that, together with our unique genetic makeup, constitute the expression of our individuality.

HOW MEMORY FORMS

What is a memory? Is it actually located in a piece of the brain at a specific spot? Are memories permanent? How does the brain manage to store a lifetime of memories in an organ the size of a melon? Is forgetting actually losing the memory or just access to it? The definitive explanation for memory is still elusive. Nevertheless, neuroscientists have discovered numerous mechanisms that occur in the brain that, taken together, define a workable hypothesis about memory formation, storage, and recall.

The Temporary Stimulus

You will recall from Chapter 1 that a stimulus (say, the color red, a whiff of perfume, or a musical note) causes nerve impulses to travel down the axon to the gap, or synapse, where neurotransmitter chemicals are released. These chemicals cross the synapse to the dendrite of the other neuron. As the chemical messages enter the neighboring neuron, they spark a series of electrochemical reactions that cause this second neuron to generate a signal, or "fire." The reaction continues and causes more receptor sites on other neurons to fire as well. This sequence forms a pattern of neuronal connections firing together.

The firing may last only for a brief time, after which the memory decays and is lost. If the second neuron is not stimulated again, it will stay in a state of readiness for hours, or days. What is created here is a perception, and even recognition, of an outside stimulus that quickly passes. We are bombarded with thousands of such events each day. The ability for these events to decay quickly means that our brain does not get cluttered with useless memories.

Forming the Memory

On the other hand, if the pattern is repeated during this standby period (through rehearsal and practice), the tendency for the associated group to fire together is increased. The faster a neuron fires, the greater the electrical charge it generates and the more likely it is to set off its neighbors. As the neighbors fire, the surfaces of their dendrites change to make them more sensitive to stimulation. This process of synaptic awareness and sensitivity is called *long-term potentiation* or *LTP*. Eventually, repeated firing of the pattern binds the neurons together so that if one fires, they all fire, ultimately forming a new memory trace, or *engram* (Figure 3.1). These individual traces associate and form networks so that whenever one is triggered, the whole network is strengthened, thereby consolidating the memory and making it more easily retrievable (Carter, 1998; Fields, 2005; Restak, 2003; Squire & Kandel, 1999).

Memories are not stored intact. Instead, they are stored in pieces and distributed in sites throughout the cerebrum. The shape, color, and smell of an orange, for example, are categorized and stored in different sets of neurons. Activating these sites simultaneously brings together a recollection of our thoughts and experiences involving an orange. There is also evidence that the brain stores an extended experience in more than one network. Which storage sites to select could be determined by the number of associations that the brain makes between new and past learnings. The more connections that are made, the more understanding and meaning the learner can attach to the new learning, and the more likely it is that it will be stored in different networks. This process now gives the learner multiple opportunities to retrieve the new learning.

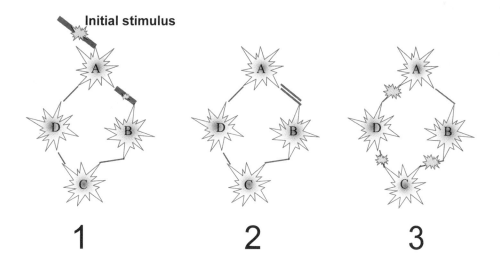

Figure 3.1   Memories are formed when a group of neurons fires together when activated. (1) Neuron A receives a stimulus, which causes it to set off neuron B. (2) If neuron A fires again soon, a link is established. Later, neuron A can just fire weakly to set off neuron B. (3) The firing of neurons A and B may set off neighboring neurons C and D. If this happens repeatedly, the four cells become a network and will fire together in the future—forming a memory.

> *The more understanding and meaning the learner can attach to the new learning, the more likely it is that it will be stored in different networks. This process now gives the learner multiple opportunities to retrieve the new learning.*

Smart Drugs to Enhance Memory

Drugs will soon be available that enhance the ability of the neurons to form and recall engrams. Pharmaceutical companies are working on "smart drugs," several of which are already being tested on humans (Lynch, 2002). One approach is to use substances called ampakines that affect long-term potentiation to increase synaptic transmission. Another is to enhance the effectiveness of certain neurotransmitters during memory formation. Although researchers are aiming to develop drugs that will help patients with memory disorders, these same drugs will help normal people perform memory tasks, such as test taking, with greater success. This prospect will pose some interesting ethical questions for classroom teachers. How do we deal with a student who takes a legal smart drug just before we give a test?

STAGES AND TYPES OF MEMORY

Scientists have been debating for decades how best to classify forms of memory. Numerous case studies of people experiencing memory loss, the results of experiments designed to test memory, and analysis of brain scans all suggest that memories exist in different forms. The problem is getting neuroscientists to agree on a set taxonomy that defines the stages and types of human memory. Furthermore, as new research results emerge, the taxonomy and nomenclature change accordingly. I have attempted here to present what most active researchers seem to accept as a workable model for describing memory systems at the time of publication.

Stages of Memory

The stages of memory are the following: sensory/immediate, working, and long-term. In Chapter 2, we looked at the nature of sensory/immediate and working memories, which you will recall are temporary memories. Some stimuli that are processed in these temporary memories are eventually transferred to long-term memory sites where they actually change the structure of the neurons so they can last a lifetime.

Types of Memory

Although neuroscientists are not in total agreement with psychologists as to all of the characteristics of long-term memory, there is considerable agreement on some of their types, and their description is important to understand before setting out to design learning activities accordingly. Long-term memory can be divided into two major types, *declarative memory* and *nondeclarative memory*. Figure 3.2 shows the stages of memory and the various types of long-term memory.

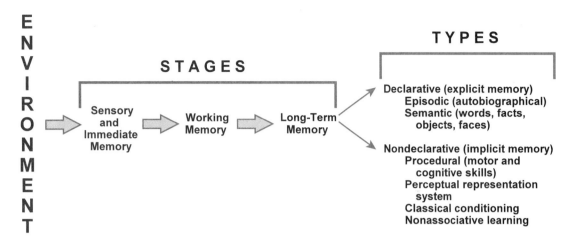

Figure 3.2   The hypothesized structure of human memory showing the relationship among different forms of memory.

Declarative Memory

Declarative memory (also called *conscious* or *explicit* memory) describes the remembering of names, facts, music, and objects (e.g., where you live and the kind of car you own), and is processed by the hippocampus and cerebrum. Think for a moment about a person who is now important in your life. Try to recall that person's image, voice, and mannerisms. Then think of an important event you both attended, one with an emotional connection, such as a concert, wedding, or funeral. Once you have the context in mind, note how easily other components of the memory come together. This is declarative memory in its most common form—a conscious and almost effortless recall. Declarative memory can be further divided into *episodic memory* and *semantic memory*.

Episodic Memory. Episodic memory refers to the conscious memory of events in our own life history, such as our sixteenth birthday party, falling off a new bicycle, or what we had for breakfast this morning. It helps us identify the time and place when an event happened and gives us a sense of self. Episodic memory is the memory of *remembering*.

Semantic Memory. Semantic memory is knowledge of facts and data that may not be related to any event. It is knowing that the Eiffel Tower is in Paris, how to tell time, how to multiply two numbers, and who the fortieth president was. Semantic memory is the memory of *knowing*. A veteran knowing that there was a Vietnam War in the 1970s is using semantic memory; remembering his experiences in that war is episodic memory.

Nondeclarative Memory

Nondeclarative memory (sometimes called *implicit* memory) describes all memories that are *not* declarative memories, that is, memories that can be used for things that cannot be declared or explained in any straightforward manner. Because nondeclarative memories do not require the intentional recall of experiences, they have been of particular interest to researchers. As a result, the descriptions and names of the categories of nondeclarative memories have changed over the last decade in light of new research. To date, the generally accepted categories of nondeclarative memory include *procedural memory, perceptual representation system, classical conditioning,* and *nonassociative learning.*

Procedural Memory. Procedural memory refers to the learning of motor and cognitive skills, and remembering *how* to do something, like riding a bicycle, driving a car, swinging a tennis racket, and tying a shoelace. As practice of the skills continues, these memories become more efficient and can be performed with little conscious thought or recall. The brain process shifts from *reflective* to *reflexive.* For example, you may remember the first time you drove an automobile by yourself. No doubt you gave a lot of conscious attention to your speed, maneuvering the vehicle, putting your foot

> *Procedural memory helps us to learn things that don't require conscious attention and to habituate ourselves to the environment.*

on the correct pedal, and observing surrounding traffic (reflective thought). However, as you continued to practice this routine, the skills were stored in procedural memory and became more automatic (reflexive activity). Now, aren't you sometimes amazed at how you can drive from home to work and not even recall what happened on the road? "Did I really stop at that stop sign back there?" "What was that thump I heard a while ago?" Procedural memory was driving the car while working memory was planning your day.

Much of what we do during the course of a day involves the performance of skills. We go through the morning grooming and breakfast rituals, read the newspaper, get to work, and shake the hand of a new acquaintance. We do all of these tasks without realizing that we have learned them and without being aware that we are using our memory. Although learning a new skill involves conscious attention, skill performance later becomes unconscious and relies essentially on nondeclarative memory.

We also learn *cognitive skills,* such as reading, discriminating colors, identifying tones in music, and figuring out a *procedure* for solving a problem. Cognitive skills are different from cognitive concept building in that cognitive skills are performed automatically and rely on procedural memory rather than declarative memory. Perceptual and cognitive skill acquisition involve some different brain processes and memory sites from cognitive concept learning. If they are learned differently, should they be taught differently?

Perceptual Representation System (PRS). The perceptual representation system (PRS) refers to the structure and form of words and objects in memory that can be prompted by prior experience, without explicit recall. The PRS used to be included as part of procedural memory. But recent studies have identified unique characteristics of this recall system that merit it a separate category. Essentially, the PRS describes our ability to complete fragments of words or tell whether objects in drawings could exist in the real world. Not surprisingly, our success at completing these tasks is much improved if we have seen the entire words and pictures on a previous occasion, even if we only glimpsed at the words and pictures and did not have time to study them intently. This is a form of implicit (nondeclarative) memory because no explicit processing of the words or pictures was involved.

Classical Conditioning. Classical conditioning (also called Pavlovian conditioning) occurs when a conditioned stimulus to an organism prompts an unconditioned response from that organism. Remember Pavlov ringing a bell as he fed his dogs? Because the response gets associated with the stimulus, this form of learning is called *associative learning.* Experienced teachers know exactly how to respond in school when the fire alarm bell sounds. They have learned to associate the sound of the alarm with the procedures needed to safely evacuate the building.

Nonassociative learning. Nonassociative learning occurs in two forms. *Habituation* helps us to learn not to respond to things that don't require conscious attention, and to accustom ourselves to the environment. Thus, we can become accustomed to the clothes we wear, the daily noisy traffic outside the school, a ticking clock in the den, or the sounds of construction. This adjustment to the environment allows the brain to screen out unimportant stimuli so it can focus on those that matter.

In *sensitization,* we increase our response to a particularly noxious or threatening stimulus. For example, Californians who have been through an earthquake respond quickly and vigorously to any weak noise or vibration thereafter, even though it may be unrelated to an earthquake.

It seems that procedural and declarative memories are stored differently. Studies of brain-damaged and Alzheimer's victims show that they may still be perfectly capable of riding a bicycle (procedural) without remembering the word, *bicycle* or when they learned to ride (declarative). Procedural and declarative memory seem to be stored in different regions of the brain, and declarative memory can be lost while procedural is spared (Rose, 2005).

Emotional Memory

Earlier taxonomies of memory systems usually listed *emotional memory* as a form of nondeclarative memory. But in refining their memory categories, scientists have identified situations requiring explicit (i.e., declarative) learning and memory. So emotional memories can be both implicit and explicit. In either case, the amygdala is heavily involved in processing emotional learning and memory. For example, sometimes, an experience is stored merely as an emotional *gist* or summary of the event, that is, we remember whether we liked it or not. A year after seeing a movie, for example, we might be able to recall only bits of the storyline (declarative memory) and perhaps its mood and our reaction (nondeclarative memory). Students often can remember whether they liked a particular topic, but cannot recall many details about it.

Emotional Memory and Learning

In Chapter 2, we learned how emotions can positively or negatively affect the acquisition of new learning. Emotions impact on learning in two distinct ways. One is the emotional climate in which the learning occurs. The other is the degree to which emotions are associated with the learning content. Figure 3.3 illustrates two ways that emotions impact directly on learning.

The Learning Climate. Emotions that students associate with a learning experience (but not the content) become part of the nondeclarative memory system. Emotional climate is directly

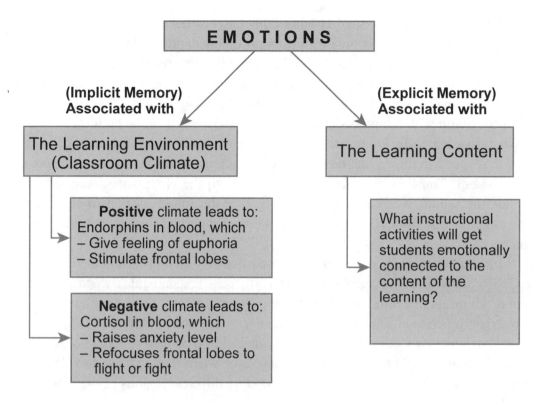

Figure 3.3   The chart shows the two ways that emotions impact on learning. One way is the emotional climate of the environment in which the learning takes place. The other deals with the emotions that the learner experiences while processing the content of the learning.

related to classroom climate, which is regulated by the teacher. Students ask: Do I have a good rapport with the teacher? Is my opinion respected? Does the teacher make me feel dumb when I ask for help? Am I the butt of sarcastic remarks? Does the teacher care whether I succeed? The answers to these questions generate emotions that determine how a student *feels* about the learning situation. These unconscious responses can turn them toward or away from their teachers and future learning experiences.

When students feel positive about their learning environment, endorphins are released in the brain. Endorphins produce a feeling of euphoria and stimulate the frontal lobes, thereby making the learning experience more pleasurable and successful. Conversely, if students are stressed and have a negative feeling about the learning environment, cortisol is released. Cortisol is a hormone that travels throughout the brain and body and activates defense behaviors, such as fight or flight. Frontal lobe activity is reduced to focusing on the cause of the stress and how to deal with it. Little attention is given to the learning task. Cortisol appears to interfere especially with the recall of emotional memories (Kuhlmann, Kirschbaum, & Wolf, 2005).

Connect Content to Emotions. Students are much more likely to remember curriculum content in which they have made an emotional investment. For this to happen, teachers often need to use strategies that get students emotionally involved with the learning content. For example, I once sat in a high school classroom where students had been asked to create some original material that showed how their study of the Civil War had affected them emotionally. Taking turns, the students sang songs, recited poems, displayed sketches and watercolors depicting battle scenes, and acted out skits of major Civil War events. I suspect that more students will remember the causes and results of that war for many years to come. Simulations, role-playing, journal writing, and real world experiences are all examples of strategies that teachers can use to help students connect emotions to content.

Flashbulb Memories

A powerful emotional experience can cause an instantaneous and long-lasting memory of an event, called a *flashbulb memory*. An example is remembering where you were and what you were doing when the *Challenger* space shuttle exploded or when the World Trade Center was attacked. Although these memories are not always accurate, they do attest to the brain's ability to record and recall emotionally significant experiences. This ability most likely results from the stimulation of the amygdala and the release throughout the body of emotion-arousing substances, such as adrenalin (Cahill & McGaugh, 1998). This process puts vivid memory tags on emotionally charged events. As a result, confidence in the recollection is high, although flashbulb memories seem to be no more accurate than the recall of memories of everyday experiences (Gazzaniga et al., 2002).

Implications for Teaching

How the learner processes new information presented in school has a great impact on the quality of what is learned and is a major factor in determining whether and how it will be retained. Memories, of course, are more than just information. They represent fluctuating patterns of associations and connections across the brain from which the individual extracts order and meaning. Teachers with a greater understanding of the types of memory and how they form can select strategies that are more likely to improve the retention and retrieval of learning.

LEARNING AND RETENTION

Learning and retention are different. Learning involves the brain, the nervous system, and the environment, and the process by which their interplay acquires information and skills. Sometimes, we need information for just a short period of time, like the telephone number for a pizza delivery, and then the information decays in just a few seconds. Thus, learning does not always involve long-term retention.

A good portion of the teaching done in schools centers on delivering facts and information to build concepts that explain a body of

> *Learning and retention are different. We can learn something for just a few minutes and then lose it forever.*

knowledge. We teach numbers, arithmetic operations, ratios, and theorems to explain mathematics. We teach about atoms, momentum, gravity, and cells to explain science. We talk about countries, famous leaders, and their trials and battles to explain history, and so on. Students may hold on to this information in working memory just long enough to take a test, after which it readily decays and is lost. (See the **Practitioner's Corner** in Chapter 2 on testing whether information is in long-term storage, p. 70.) Retention, however, requires that the learner not only give conscious attention but also build conceptual frameworks that have sense and meaning for eventual consolidation into the long-term storage networks.

FACTORS AFFECTING RETENTION OF LEARNING

Retention refers to the process whereby long-term memory preserves a learning in such a way that it can locate, identify, and retrieve it accurately in the future. As explained earlier, this is an inexact process influenced by many factors including the degree of student focus, the length and type of rehearsal that occurred, the critical attributes that may have been identified, the student's learning style, and, of course, the inescapable influence of prior learnings.

The information processing model in Chapter 2 identifies some of these factors and sets the stage for finding ways to transfer what we know into daily classroom practice. Let us look more specifically at the way the brain processes and retains information during a learning episode, how the nature of that processing affects the degree of retention, and how the degree of retention varies with the length of the episode.

Rehearsal

> *Rehearsal deals with the repetition and processing of information whereas practice generally refers to the repetition of motor skills.*

The assignment of sense and meaning to new learning can occur only if the learner has adequate time to process and reprocess it. This continuing reprocessing of information is called *rehearsal,* and it is a critical component in the transference of information from working memory to long-term storage. Rehearsal is different from practice in that rehearsal deals with the repetition and processing of information whereas practice, for our purposes, refers to the repetition of motor skills.

The concept of rehearsal is not new. Even the Greek scholars of 400 BC knew its value. They wrote:

> *Repeat again what you hear; for by often hearing and saying the same things, what you have learned comes complete into your memory.*

—from the *Dialexeis*

Two major factors should be considered in evaluating rehearsal: The amount of time devoted to it, which determines whether there is both initial and secondary rehearsal, and the type of rehearsal carried out, which can be *rote* or *elaborative.*

Time for Initial and Secondary Rehearsal

Time is a critical component of rehearsal. Initial rehearsal occurs when the information first enters working memory. If the learner cannot attach sense or meaning, and if there is no time for further processing, then the new information is likely to be lost. Providing sufficient time to go beyond the initial processing to secondary rehearsal allows the learner to review the information, to make sense of it, to elaborate on the details, and to assign value and relevance, thus increasing significantly the chance of long-term storage. When done at the end of a learning episode, this rehearsal is called closure (see Chapter 2).

Scanning studies indicate that the frontal lobe is very much involved during the rehearsal process and, ultimately, in long-term memory formation. This makes sense because working memory is also located in the frontal lobe. Several studies using fMRI scans of humans showed that during longer rehearsals the amount of activity in the frontal lobe determined whether items were stored or forgotten (Buckner, Kelley, & Petersen, 1999; Wagner et al., 1998). Students carry out initial and secondary rehearsal at different rates of speed and in different ways, depending on the type of information in the new learning and their learning styles. As the learning task changes, learners automatically shift to different patterns of rehearsal.

Rote and Elaborative Rehearsal

Rote Rehearsal. This type of rehearsal is used when the learner needs to remember and store information exactly as it is entered into working memory. This is not a complex strategy, but it is necessary to learn information or a cognitive skill in a specific form or sequence. We use rote rehearsal to remember a poem, the lyrics and melody of a song, multiplication tables, telephone numbers, and steps in a procedure.

Elaborative Rehearsal. This type of rehearsal is used when it is not necessary to store information exactly as learned, but when it is more important to associate the new learnings with prior learnings to detect relationships. This is a more complex thinking process in that the learner reprocesses the information several times to make connections to previous learnings and assign meaning. Students use rote rehearsal to memorize a poem, but elaborative rehearsal to interpret its message.

When students get very little time for, or training in, elaborative rehearsal, they resort more frequently to rote rehearsal for nearly all processing. Consequently, they fail to make the associations or discover the relationships that only elaborative rehearsal can provide. Also, they continue to believe that learning is merely the recalling of information as learned rather than its value for generating new ideas, concepts, and solutions.

Rote rehearsal is valuable for certain limited learning objectives. Nearly all of us learned the alphabet and the multiplication tables through rote rehearsal. But rote rehearsal simply allows us to acquire information in a certain sequence. It doesn't mean we understand the information or can apply it to new situations. Too often, students use rote rehearsal to memorize important terms and facts in a lesson, but are unable to use the information to solve problems. They will probably do fine on a true-false or fill-in-the-blank test. But they will find difficulty answering higher-order questions that require them to apply their knowledge to new situations.

The goal of learning is not just to acquire knowledge, but to be able to use that knowledge in a variety of different settings. To do this, students need a deeper understanding of the concepts involved in the learning. For example, we could teach students the various types of government, such as monarchy, parliamentary, republic, totalitarian state, dictatorship, and theocracy. On a test, we could ask them to write and define the types of government and even to name a country as an example of each type.

> **There is almost no long-term retention of cognitive concepts without rehearsal.**

All this could be accomplished through rote rehearsal. But if we want students to understand why people are willing to die to change their type of government, or to make predictions about how different governments will react to a crisis, then they must have a much deeper grasp of the concepts of government and governing. That requires elaborative rehearsal. Perhaps one reason students are bored in school is that they spend too much time memorizing but not understanding.

When deciding on how to use rehearsal in a lesson, teachers need to consider the time available as well as the type of rehearsal appropriate for the specific learning objective. Keep in mind that rehearsal only contributes to, but does not guarantee that information will transfer into, long-term storage. However, there is almost no long-term retention *without* rehearsal.

Test Question No. 4: Increased time on task increases retention of new learning.

Answer: False. Simply increasing a student's time on a learning task does not guarantee retention if the student is not allowed the time and help to personally interact with the content through rehearsal.

Retention During a Learning Episode

When an individual is processing new information, the amount of information retained depends, among other things, on *when* it is presented during the learning episode. At certain time intervals during the learning, we will remember more than at other intervals. Let's try a simple activity to illustrate this point. You will need a pencil and a timer. Set the timer to go off in 12 seconds. When you start the timer, look at the list of 10 words. When the timer sounds, cover the list and write as many of the 10 words as you remember on the lines to the right of the list. Write each word on the line that represents its position on the list (i.e., the first word on line one, etc.). Thus, if you cannot remember the eighth word, but you remember the ninth, write it on line number nine.

Ready? Start the timer and stare at the word list for 12 seconds. Now cover the list and write the words you remember on the lines to the right. Don't worry if you did not remember all the words.

KEF	1.	——————
LAK	2.	——————
MIL	3.	——————
NIR	4.	——————
VEK	5.	——————
LUN	6.	——————
NEM	7.	——————
BEB	8.	——————
SAR	9.	——————
FIF	10.	——————

Turn to your list again and circle the words that were correct. To be correct, they must be spelled correctly and be in the proper position on the list. Look at the circled words. Chances are you remembered the first 3 to 5 words (lines 1 through 5) and the last 1 to 2 words (lines 9 and 10), but had difficulty with the middle words (lines 6-8). Read on to find out why.

Primacy-Recency Effect

Your pattern in remembering the word list is a common phenomenon that is referred to as the *primacy-recency effect* (also known as the *serial position effect*). In a learning episode, we tend to remember best that which comes first, and remember second best that which comes last. We tend to remember least that which comes just past the middle of the episode. This is not a new discovery. Ebbinghaus published the first studies on this effect in the 1880s.

More recent studies help to explain why this is so. The first items of new information are within the working memory's functional capacity so they command our attention, and are likely to be retained in semantic memory. The later

> *During a learning episode, we remember best that which comes first, second best that which comes last, and least that which comes just past the middle.*

information, however, exceeds the capacity and is lost. As the learning episode concludes, items in working memory are sorted or chunked to allow for additional processing of the arriving final items, which are likely held in working memory and will decay unless further rehearsed (Gazzanniga et al., 2002; Terry, 2005).

Figure 3.4 shows how the primacy-recency effect influences retention during a 40-minute learning episode (Buzan, 1989; Thomas, 1972). The times are approximate and averages. Note that it is a bimodal curve, each mode representing the degree of greatest retention during that time period. For future reference, I will label the first or primacy mode *prime-time-1,* and the second or recency mode *prime-time-2.* Between these two modes is the time period in which retention during the lesson is least. I will refer to that area as the *down-time.* This is not a time when no retention takes place, but a time when it is most difficult for retention to occur.

Figure 3.4 The degree of retention varies during a learning episode. We remember best that which comes first (prime-time-1) and last (prime-time-2). We remember least that which comes just past the middle.

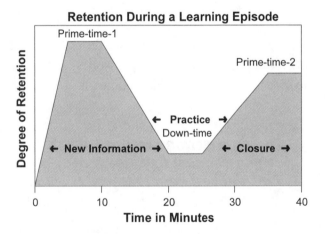

Figure 3.5 New information should be presented in prime-time-1, and closure in prime-time-2. Practice is appropriate for the down-time segment.

Implications for Teaching

Teach New Material First

There are important implications of the primacy-recency effect for teaching a lesson. The learning episode begins when the learner focuses on the teacher with intent to learn (indicated by "0" in the Figure 3.4 graph). New information or a new skill should be taught first, during prime-time-1, because it is most likely to be remembered. Keep in mind that the students will remember almost any information coming forth at this time. It is important, then, that only *correct* information be presented. This is not the time to be searching for what students may know about something. I remember watching a teacher of English start a class with, "Today, we are going to learn about a new literary form called *onomatopoeia*. Does anyone have any idea what that is?" After several wrong guesses, the teacher finally defined it. Regrettably, those same wrong guesses appeared in the follow-up test. And why not? They were mentioned during the most powerful retention position, prime-time-1.

The new material being taught should be followed by practice or review during the down-time. At this point, the information is no longer new, and the practice helps the learner organize it for further processing. Closure should take place during prime-time-2, since this is the second most powerful learning position and an important opportunity for the learner to determine sense and meaning. Adding these activities to the graph in Figure 3.5 shows how we can take advantage of research on retention to design a more effective lesson.

Misuse of Prime-Time

Even with the best of intentions, teachers with little knowledge of the primacy-recency effect can do the following: After getting focus by telling the class the day's lesson objective, the teacher takes attendance, distributes the previous day's homework, collects that day's homework, requests notes from students who were absent, and reads an announcement about a club meeting after school. By the time the teacher gets to the new learning, the students are already at the down-time. As a finale, the teacher tells the

> *When you have the students' focus, teach the new information. Don't let prime-time get contaminated with wrong information.*

students that they were so well-behaved during the lesson that they can do anything they want during the last five minutes of class (i.e., during prime-time-2) as long as they are quiet. I have observed this scenario, and I can attest that the next day those students remembered who was absent and why, which club met after school, and what they did at the end of the period. The new learning, however, was difficult to remember because it was presented at the time of least retention. See the **Practitioner's Corner** on p. 121 on using the primacy-recency effect in the classroom.

Retention Varies With Length of Teaching Episode

Another fascinating characteristic of the primacy-recency effect is that the proportion of prime-times to down-time changes with the length of the teaching episode. Look at Figure 3.6. Note that during a 40-minute lesson, the two prime-times total about 30 minutes, or 75 percent of the teaching time. The down-time is about 10 minutes, or 25 percent of the lesson time. If we double the length of the learning episode to 80 minutes, the down-time increases to 30 minutes, or 38 percent of the total time period.

As the lesson time lengthens, the percentage of down-time increases faster than for the prime-times. The information is entering working memory faster than it can be sorted or checked, and it accumulates. This cluttering interferes with the sorting and chunking processes and reduces the learner's ability to attach sense and meaning, thereby decreasing retention. Think back to some of those college classes that lasted for two hours or more. After about the first 20 minutes, didn't you find yourself concentrating more on taking notes rather than on processing and learning what was being presented?

Figure 3.6 also shows what happens when we shorten the learning time to 20 minutes. The down-time is about 2 minutes, or 10 percent of the total lesson time. As we shorten the learning episode, the down-time decreases faster than the prime-times. This finding indicates that there is a higher probability of effective learning taking place if we can keep the learning episodes short and, of course, meaningful. Thus, teaching two 20-minute lessons provides 20 percent more prime-time (approximately 36 minutes) than one 40-minute lesson (approximately 30 minutes). Note, however, that a time period shorter than 20 minutes may not give the learner sufficient time to determine the pattern and organization of the new learning, and is thus of little benefit.

Table 3.1 summarizes the approximate number of minutes in the prime-times and down-times of the learning cycle for episodes of 20, 40, and 80 minutes. Remember that the times are averages over many episodes. Nonetheless, these data confirm what we may have long suspected: More retention occurs when lessons are shorter and meaningful.

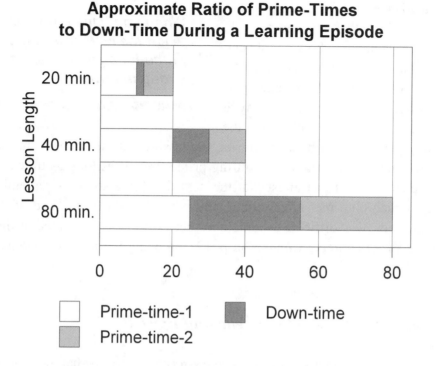

Figure 3.6   The proportion of down-time to prime-times for 20-, 40-, and 80-minute learning episodes, when taught as one lesson.

Shorter Is Better: Impact on Block Scheduling

Because today's students are accustomed to quick change and novelty in their environment, many find it difficult to concentrate on the same topic for long periods of time. They fidget, drift, send text messages to each other, and get into off-task conversations. This is particularly true if the teacher is doing most of the work, such as lecturing. The primacy-recency effect has a particularly important impact on block scheduling, in which a learning episode of 80 or more minutes can be a blessing or a disaster, depending on how the time is used. Figure 3.7 shows that a block containing four 20-minute segments will often be much more productive than one continuous lesson. Further, only one or two of the four block segments should be teacher directed. (See the **Practitioner's Corner** on p. 123 on block scheduling.)

Rest Between Block Lesson Segments

Most teachers believe that staying on-task throughout the learning period is best. During 1994-1997, while an adjunct professor at Seton Hall University, I asked secondary teachers to conduct action research projects in their block schedule classrooms to determine if going off-task between lesson segments (for example, telling a joke or story, playing music, taking a quiet rest break, or getting students up and moving around) resulted in more, less, or the same amount of attending

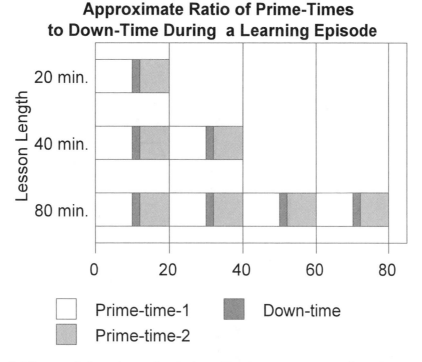

Figure 3.7 By dividing each learning episode into 20-minute segments, there is proportionately more prime-time to down time

	Prime-Times		Down-Time	
Episode Time	**Total Number of Minutes**	**Percentage of Total Time**	**Number of Minutes**	**Percentage of Total Time**
20 minutes	18	90	2	10
40 minutes	30	75	10	25
80 minutes	50	62	30	38

Table 3.1 Average Prime- and Down-times in Learning Episodes

(measured by the speed with which the students returned to task) than if they had stayed continuously on-task.

Figure 3.8 is the compilation of their results, which are similar to Tony Buzan's (1989) findings in the 1980s. The graph suggests that teachers are more likely to keep students focused *during*

Comparison of Degree of Attending Using On-Task or Off-Task Activities Between Segments

Figure 3.8   Compilation of 18 action research studies in secondary school classrooms comparing the degree of attending (focus) to on-task and off-task behavior between lesson segments of a block period.

the lesson segments if they go off-task *between* the segments. Granted, this is not a scientifically controlled study, but the results are not surprising given the higher novelty-seeking behavior of today's students. Teachers in nonblock classes (i.e., 40 to 45 minutes in length) who take an off-task break about half-way through the period have reported similar results.

Retention Varies With Teaching Method

The learner's ability to retain information is also dependent on the type of teaching method used. Some methods result in more retention of learning than others. The learning pyramid shown in Figure 3.9, devised in the 1960s by the National Training Laboratories of Bethel, Maine (now the NTL Institute of Alexandria, Virginia), comes from studies on retention of learning after students were exposed to different teaching methods. The pyramid shows the percentage of new learning that students can recall after 24 hours as a result of being taught *primarily* by the teaching method indicated. (Note: As discussed earlier, information recalled after 24 hours is presumed to be in long-term storage.) Although this study was conducted four decades ago, more recent studies on the factors affecting retention of learning generally support the original results. It is possible that the percentages may have changed somewhat over the years. For example, Moore (2005) reports studies showing that retention after three days is 10 percent from lecturing and 20 percent from demonstration.

The percentages (from the original study) are rounded to the nearest 5 percent and are not additive. At the top of the pyramid is lecture—the teaching method that results in an average retention of only 5 percent of learning after 24 hours. This is not surprising because lecture involves verbal processing with little student active participation or mental rehearsal. In this

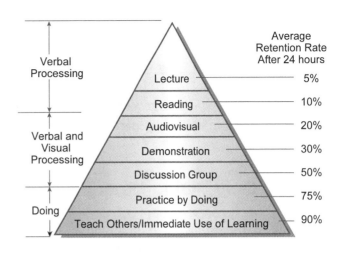

Figure 3.9 The diagram shows the average percentage of retention of material after 24 hours for each of the instructional methods.

format, the teacher is telling and the students are listening just enough to convert the teacher's auditory output into written notes. Rote rehearsal predominates as auditory information moves onto the notebook paper. Elaborative rehearsal is minimal or nonexistent. Despite the impressive amount of evidence about how little students retain from lecture, it continues to be the most prevalent method of teaching, especially in secondary and higher education. No one doubts that the lecture method allows a lot of information to be presented in a short period of time. But the question is not what is presented, but what is learned.

Moving down the pyramid, input changes to verbal and visual processing as students become more involved in the learning process, and retention increases. The methods at the bottom of the pyramid involve having the students doing something through practice, and teaching others or using the new learning immediately. This results in from 75 to 90 percent retention after 24 hours. We have known for a long time that the best way to learn something is to prepare to teach it. In other words, whoever explains, learns. This is one of the major components of cooperative learning groups and helps to explain the effectiveness of this instructional technique.

Lecture continues to be the most prevalent teaching method in secondary and higher education, despite evidence that it produces the lowest degree of retention for most learners.

No One Teaching Method Is Best. No one teaching method exists that is best for all students all the time. Sometimes, lecture is the appropriate method when a lot of information needs to be given in a short period of time. But neither lecture, nor any other method for that matter, should be used almost all the time. Successful teachers use a variety of methods, keeping in mind that students are more likely to retain and achieve whenever they are actively engaged in the learning.

LEARNING MOTOR SKILLS

Scanning studies show that a person uses the frontal lobe, motor cortex, and cerebellum while learning a new physical skill. Learning a motor skill involves following a set of procedures and can be eventually carried out largely without conscious attention. In fact, too much conscious attention directed to a motor skill while performing it can diminish the quality of its execution.

Brain Activity During Motor Skill Acquisition

When first learning the skill, attention and awareness are obviously required. The frontal lobe is engaged because working memory is needed, and the motor cortex of the cerebrum (located across the top of the brain) interacts with the cerebellum to control muscle movement. As practice continues, the activated areas of the motor cortex become larger as nearby neurons are recruited into the new skill network. However, the memory of the skill is not established (i.e., stored) until after practice stops. It takes about 4 to 12 hours for this consolidation to take place in the cerebellum, and most of it occurs during deep sleep. Once the skill is mastered, brain activity shifts to the cerebellum, which organizes and coordinates the movements and the timing to perform the task. Procedural memory is the mechanism, and the brain no longer needs to use its higher-order processes as the performance of the skill becomes automatic (Penhume & Doyon, 2005; Press, Casement, Pascual-Leone, & Robertson, 2005; Shadmehr & Holcomb, 1997; Walker, Stickgold, Alsop, Gaab, & Schlaug, 2005).

Continued practice of the skill changes the brain structurally, and the younger the learner is, the easier it is for these changes to occur. Most music and sports prodigies began practicing their skills very early in life. Because their brains were most sensitive to the structural changes needed to acquire the skills, they can perform them masterfully. These skills become so much a part of the individual that they are difficult to change later in life. In the 1990s, Michael Jordan tried to become a major league baseball player at the age of 31 after a stellar career as a lead basketball scorer for the Chicago Bulls. Despite much effort, his attempt at baseball failed. Jordan had started playing basketball at the age of 8 and had developed a finely tuned set of motor skills in procedural memory that allowed him to be an expert basketball player. Trying to learn a new set of motor and perceptual skills to be a successful baseball player in a short period of time was just not possible.

The Problem of Learning Two Similar Skills

A surprising finding from these studies was that if the person practiced a very similar skill during the 4- to 12-hour down-time, the second skill interfered with the consolidation and mastery of the first skill—and vice versa. Consequently, the person was not able to perform either skill well (Oberauer & Kliegl, 2004; Witney, 2004). This appears to be evidence that negative transfer (see Chapter 4) can occur during the learning of motor

> *Learning two skills that are too similar at the same time causes memory interference so that the student learns neither skill well.*

skills as well as during the learning of cognitive concepts. Think of the implications that this has for teaching, wherein similarity is one of the major criteria we use to decide the sequence for presenting information and skills. See the **Practitioner's Corner** on p. 117 on how similarity can interfere with new motor skill learning.

Test Question No. 5: Two very similar concepts or motor skills should be taught at the same time.

Answer: False. Teaching two very similar concepts or skills at the same time can cause interference so that the student learns neither.

Does Practice Make Perfect?

Practice refers to learners repeating a skill over time. It begins with the rehearsal of the new skill in working memory, the motor cortex, and the cerebellum. Later, the skill memory is recalled and additional practice follows. The quality of the practice and the learner's knowledge base will largely determine the outcome of each practice session.

Over the long term, repeated practice causes the brain to assign extra neurons to the task, much as a computer assigns more memory for a complex program. The assignment of these additional neurons is more or less on a permanent basis. Professional keyboard and string musicians, for example, have larger portions of the motor cortex devoted to controlling finger and hand movements. Furthermore, the earlier their training started, the bigger the motor cortex (Schlaug, Jancke, Huang, & Steinmetz, 1995). If practice is stopped altogether, the neurons that are no longer being used are eventually assigned to other tasks and skill mastery will decline (Amunts et al., 1997). In other words, use it or lose it!

The old adage that "practice makes perfect" is rarely true. It is very possible to practice the same skill repeatedly with no increase in achievement or accuracy of application. Think of the people you know who have been driving, cooking, or even teaching for many years with no improvement in their skills. I am a self-taught bowler, and although I have been bowling for 25 years, I do not improve. My bowling scores are embarrassingly low and remain there despite years of repeated bowling. Why is this?

> *Practice does not make perfect.*
> *Practice makes permanent.*

How is it possible for one to continuously practice a skill with no resulting improvement in performance?

Conditions for Successful Practice

For practice to *improve* performance, four conditions must be met (Hunter, 2004):

1. The learner must be sufficiently motivated to *want* to improve performance.
2. The learner must have all the knowledge necessary to understand the different ways that the new knowledge or skill can be applied.
3. The learner must understand how to apply the knowledge to deal with a particular situation.
4. The learner must be able to analyze the results of that application and know what needs to be changed to improve performance in the future.

Teachers help learners meet these conditions when they do the following:

*   Start by selecting the smallest amount of material that will have maximum meaning for the learner.
*   Model the application process step-by-step. Studies show that the brain also uses observation as a means for determining the spatial learning needed to master a motor skill (Petrosini et al., 2003).
*   Insist that the practice occur in their presence over a short period of time while the student is focused on the learning.
*   Watch the practice and provide the students with prompt and specific feedback on what variable needs to be altered to correct and enhance the performance. Feedback seems to be particularly important during the learning of complex motor skills (Wulf, Shea, & Matschiner, 1998).

Guided Practice, Independent Practice, and Feedback

Practice does make permanent, thereby aiding in the retention of learning. Consequently, we want to ensure that students practice the new learning correctly from the beginning. This early practice (referred to as *guided practice),* then, is done in the presence of the teacher, who can now offer corrective feedback to help students analyze and improve their practice. When the practice is correct, the teacher can then assign *independent practice,* in which the students can rehearse the skill on their own to enhance retention.

> **Avoid giving students independent practice before guided practice.**

This strategy leads to perfect practice, and, as Vince Lombardi said, "Perfect practice makes perfect." In my case, I go bowling every few months to be with the same close friends, who are very busy professionals. Bowling is simply the means that allows us to catch up on our lives, and our scores are of little importance. Thus, I have no *motivation* to improve—and, believe me, I don't.

Teachers should avoid giving students independent practice before guided practice. Because practice makes permanent, allowing students to rehearse something for the first time while away from the teacher is very risky. If they unknowingly practice the skill incorrectly, then they will learn the incorrect method well! This will present serious problems for both the teacher and learner later on because it is very difficult to change a skill that has been practiced and remembered, even if it is not correct.

Unlearning and Relearning a Skill. If a learner practices a skill incorrectly but well, unlearning and relearning that skill correctly is very difficult. The degree to which the unlearning and relearning processes are successful will depend on the

- Age of the learner (i.e., the younger, the easier to relearn)
- Length of time the skill has been practiced incorrectly (i.e., the longer, the more difficult to change)
- Degree of motivation to relearn (i.e., the greater the desire for change, the more effort that will be used to bring about change).

Sometimes, students who are young, and who have practiced the skill wrong for only a brief time, are so annoyed at having wasted their time with the incorrect practice that they lose motivation to learn the skill correctly.

Practice and Rehearsal Over Time Increases Retention

Hunter (2004) suggested that teachers use two different types of practice over time, massed and distributed. (Here, Hunter uses practice to include rehearsal.) Practicing a new learning during time periods that are very close together is called massed practice. This produces fast learning, as when you may mentally rehearse a new telephone number if you are unable to write it down. Immediate memory is involved here and the information can fade in seconds if it is not rehearsed quickly.

Teachers provide massed practice when they allow students to try different examples of applying new learning in a short period of time. Cramming for an exam is an example of massed practice. Material can be quickly chunked into working memory but can also be quickly dropped or forgotten if more sustained practice does not follow soon. This happens because the material has no further meaning, and thus the need for long-term retention disappears. Sustained practice over time, called distributed practice, is the key to retention. If you want to remember that new telephone number later on, you will need to use it repeatedly over time. Thus, practice that is distributed over longer periods of time sustains meaning and consolidates the learnings into long-term storage in a form that will ensure accurate recall and applications in the future. The graph in Figure 3.10 shows that recall after periodic review improves over time. This is the rationale behind the idea of the spiral

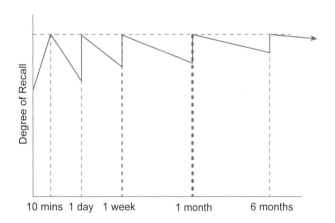

Figure 3.10 Practicing learnings over time (distributed practice) increases their degree of recall.

curriculum, whereby critical information and skills are reviewed at regular intervals within and over several grade levels.

Effective practice, then, starts with massed practice for fast learning and proceeds to distributed practice later for retention. As a result, the student is continually practicing previously learned skills throughout the year(s). Each test should not only test new material but also allow students to practice important older learnings. This method not only helps in retention but reminds students that the learnings will be useful for the future, not just for the time when they were first learned and tested.

DAILY BIOLOGICAL RHYTHMS AFFECT TEACHING AND LEARNING

Circadian Rhythms

Many of our body functions and their components, such as temperature, breathing, digestion, hormone concentrations, etc., go through daily cycles of peaks and valleys. These daily cycles are called circadian (from the Latin, "about a day") rhythms. The timing of these cycles is determined by the brain's exposure to daylight. Thus, some of the rhythms are related to the sleep-wake cycle and are controlled by a pair of small clusters of just 10,000 neurons in a tiny region of the brain located in the front part of the limbic area. These clusters are called the *suprachiasmatic nuclei* because they sit immediately above (supra) the optic chiasm—the area where the optic nerves from the left and right eye meet on their way to the brain.

One of these circadian rhythms regulates our ability to focus on incoming information with intent to learn. It can be referred to as the *psychological-cognitive cycle*. This cycle has drawn the attention of several research studies on the awake-and-asleep cycles of students (Carskadon, Acebo, Wolfson, Tzischinsky, & Darley, 1997; Millman, 2005). The findings show that the cognitive rhythm is about the same for a preadolescent and an adult, but starts later in an adolescent. This is because the onset of puberty shifts this particular cycle roughly an hour later than in the preadolescent. It returns to its previous level when the adolescent enters adulthood around the age of 22 to 24 years.

Figure 3.11 shows a comparison of the pre-/postadolescent, and adolescent cycles. Note the trough that occurs for both groups just past the middle of the day. This is a low point of focus.

Learning can still occur during this 20- to 60-minute period, but it will require more *effort*. I refer to the trough as the "dark hole of learning." Some cultures refer to it as the "siesta," having recognized long ago how difficult it is to accomplish much learning during this time.

Note that the adolescent cycle has shifted and that these students don't reach their peak until about an hour later. Note, too, that the second peak is flatter than for the other groups. This graph explains why adolescents are sleepier in the morning and tend to stay up later at night.

CIRCADIAN RHYTHMS
The Psychological/Cognitive Cycle

Figure 3.11 A comparison of the typical pre/postadolescent and adolescent cognitive cycles during the day. Note the trough that develops just past the middle of the day. This is a time when teaching and learning require more effort.

What Are the Implications? The different rhythms among preadolescents, adolescents, and their teachers have several implications. For example,

- How do the start times at elementary and secondary schools compare to the times when the students they serve are at their cognitive peak?
- Can the performance of students on standardized tests be affected when we test the whole K–12 population of students at the same time—usually in the morning?
- Can classroom climate in high schools be affected in the early afternoon when the teacher is in the trough and the students still at their peak?
- Can starting high schools later in the morning when students are more apt to be attentive result in lowering the drop-out rate?
- Would alternative high schools be more successful if they started in the afternoon?

See the **Practitioner's Corner** on p. 127 on the impact of circadian rhythms on schools and classrooms at the end of this chapter.

Importance of Sleep in Learning and Memory

The encoding of information into the long-term memory sites occurs during sleep, more specifically, during the rapid-eye movement (REM) stage. This is a slow process that can flow more easily when the brain is not preoccupied with external stimuli. When we sleep, the brain reviews the events and tasks of the day, storing them more securely than at the time we originally processed them. What we think and talk about while awake very likely influences the nature and shape of the memory consolidation that occurs during sleep (Tuma, 2005). This may explain why people who review important information before going to sleep are likely to remember that information the next day during a test. Why not share this information with students?

> *Teenagers are not getting enough sleep. This sleep deprivation affects their ability to store information, increases irritability, and leads to fatigue which can cause accidents.*

Adequate sleep is vital to the memory storage process, especially for young learners. Most teenagers need about nine hours of sleep each night. Many teenagers are not getting enough sleep. Several factors are responsible for eroding sleep time. In the morning, high schools start earlier, teens spend more time grooming, and some travel long distances to school. At the end of the day, there are athletic and social events, part-time jobs, homework, television, and video games. Add to this the shift in teens' body clocks that tends to keep them up later, and the average sleep time is more like five to six hours.

Delayed Sleep Phase Disorder

This problem is becoming so prevalent in middle and high schools that some neuroscientists and psychiatrists are convinced that it is a chronic disorder of the adolescent population. Called Delayed Sleep Phase Disorder (DSPD), it is characterized by a persistent pattern that includes difficulty falling asleep at night and getting up in the morning, fatigue during the day, and alertness at night. Caused mainly by the shift in the adolescent's circadian rhythm (Figure 3.11), DSPD is aggravated by other conditions.

Figure 3.12 shows the stages and cycles of sleep for teenagers and adults. Most of the encoding of information and skills into long-term storage is believed to occur during the rapid-eye movement (REM) phases. During the normal sleep time of eight to nine hours, five REM cycles occur. Adolescents getting just five to six hours of sleep lose out on the last two REM cycles, thereby reducing the amount of time the brain has to consolidate information and skills into long-term storage. This sleep deprivation not only disturbs the memory storage process but can lead to other problems as well. Students may nod off in class or become irritable. Worse, their decreased alertness due to fatigue can lead to accidents in school and in their cars (Acebo, Wolfson, & Carskadon,1997; Millman, 2005; Schacter, 1996).

Some studies show that students who get less sleep are more likely to get poorer grades in school than students who sleep longer. Sleep-deprived students also had more daytime sleepiness and depressed moods (Wolfson & Carskadon, 1998). It is important to remind students of the

Normal Sleep Cycles

Figure 3.12   The chart shows the cycles of sleep from Waking through Stage 1 (Transitional), Stage 2 (Light Sleep), and Stages 3 to 4 (Deep Sleep). Long-term storage occurs during the rapid-eye movement (REM) phase.

significance of sleep to their mental and physical health and to encourage them to reexamine their daily activities to provide for adequate sleep. It should be noted that REM sleep is not required for *all* memory consolidation. Subsequent memory consolidation can occur when awake, especially the encoding of declarative memories, which seem to be less dependent on REM sleep.

INTELLIGENCE AND RETRIEVAL

Intelligence

Our modern notion of what constitutes human intelligence is growing increasingly complex. At the very least, it represents a combination of varied abilities and skills. For many years psychologists referred to a general mental ability, called the *g* factor. People who scored high on tests of general mental ability (i.e., I.Q. tests) were smarter than those who scored lower. The study of human intelligence took a major leap in the 1980s when psychologists Howard Gardner and Robert Sternberg proposed separate models of different types and patterns of intelligence. Their work changed our concept of intelligence from a singular entity to a multifaceted aptitude that varies even within the same person. Many educators have been using the ideas of Gardner and Sternberg in their curriculum, teaching, and school organization.

Different Views of Intelligence

Howard Gardner. In 1983, Howard Gardner defined intelligence as an individual's ability to use a learned skill, create products, or solve problems in a way that is valued by the society of that individual. This approach expands our understanding of intelligence to include divergent thinking and interpersonal expertise. Gardner differentiates between the terms *intelligence* and *creativity,* and suggested that in everyday life people can display intelligent originality in any of seven (now eight) intelligences. They are: musical, logical-mathematical, spatial, bodily-kinesthetic, linguistic, interpersonal, intrapersonal, and naturalist (Gardner, 1993).

Gardner made clear that intelligence is not just how a person thinks, but it also includes the materials and the values of the situation where and when the thinking occurs. The availability of appropriate materials and the values of any particular context or culture will thus have a significant impact on the degree to which specific intelligences will be activated, developed, or discouraged. A person's combined intellectual capability, then, is the result of innate tendencies (the genetic contribution) and the society in which that individual develops (the environmental contribution).

This theory suggests that at the core of each intelligence is an information-processing system (similar perhaps to that in Chapter 2) unique to that intelligence. The intelligence of an athlete is different from that of a musician or physicist. He also suggests that each intelligence is semi-autonomous. A person who has abilities in athletics but who does poorly in music has enhanced athletic intelligence. The presence or absence of music capabilities exists separately from the individual's athletic prowess.

Richard Sternberg. Two years after Gardner's work appeared, Robert Sternberg (1985) at Yale proposed a theory that distinguishes three patterns of intelligence: analytical, creative, and practical. People with analytical intelligence (the analyzers) have abilities in analyzing, critiquing, and evaluating. Those who are creatively intelligent (the creators) are particularly good at discovering, inventing, and creating. By contrast, the practically intelligent (the practitioners) excel at applying, utilizing, and implementing.

In this model, intelligence is defined by these three patterns of behavior, and intelligence refers to the ability to perform the skills in one or more of these areas with accuracy and efficiency. According to Sternberg, various combinations of these three areas produce different patterns of intelligence. This concept was tested in several studies conducted by Sternberg and his colleagues. Students were assessed for their memory as well as their analytical, creative, and practical achievement. The results showed that those students who were taught in ways that best matched their achievement patterns outperformed those whose method of instruction was not a good fit for their pattern of abilities (Sternberg, Ferrari, Clinkenbeard, & Grigorenko, 1996; Sternberg, et al., 2000).

Jeff Hawkins. In 2004, Jeff Hawkins, the inventor of the PalmPilot and a major researcher in artificial intelligence, described human intelligence as being measured by the capacity to remember and predict patterns in the world, including mathematics, language, social situations, and the properties of objects. The brain receives patterns from the outside world through experience, stores them as memories, and makes predictions by combining what it has seen before to what is happening now. In other words, to Hawkins, prediction, not behavior, is the proof of intelligence (Hawkins & Blakeslee, 2004).

It is clear that no agreement exists about what intelligence is, and major efforts to define intelligence are not likely to be advanced significantly by brain imaging anytime in the near future. PET scans and fMRIs do show some localization of brain activity for certain tasks. However, there is no scientific basis for equating the task with a particular type or pattern of

Figure 3.13 This composite MRI shows the key areas in the frontal lobes and left hemisphere where people with higher IQ scores had more gray matter than those with lower scores (Adapted from Haier et al., 2004).

intelligence. For example, visual stimuli are processed first in the visual cortex at the rear of the brain, and then in other parts of the brain for spatial perception and recognition. If anything, recent brain scans and case studies are revealing how remarkably integrated brain activity is when performing even the simplest task. Although most neuroscientists agree that there are areas that are specialized for certain tasks, areas rarely, if ever, work in isolation in the normal brain (See more about brain specialization in Chapter 5). Some researchers suggest that it is better to think of the brain as having a number of cerebral systems that are primarily responsible for processing the specific contents associated with each intelligence. For example, the motor cortex and cerebellum would take the lead in processing new skills associated with the bodily-kinesthetic area.

One interesting discovery is that general intelligence (that *g* factor) is closely linked to the amount of gray matter in key areas of the frontal lobes (Figure 3.13). People with more gray matter in their frontal lobes tend to score higher on tests of intelligence (Haier, Jung, Yeo, Head, & Alkire, 2004). The unanswered chicken-and-egg question is: Does the early development of more gray matter make a person more intelligent, or do challenging learning experiences result in the production of more gray matter? No one knows.

PET scans and EEGs also depict that people who score high on tests of reasoning and intelligence show less cerebral activity than people who score lower. These results imply that intelligence may be primarily a matter of *neural efficiency*, whereby the brain eventually learns to use fewer neurons or networks to accomplish a repetitive task (Neubauer, Grabner, Freudenthaler, Beckmann, & Guthke, 2004; Restak, 2003). If so, think of the implications this concept has for altering the way we allocate learning time as well as design and deliver lessons. It suggests, at the very least, that we should vary learning time to accommodate the task at hand and move learners to intensive practice as soon as comprehension is established. This approach is one of the basic components of differentiated instruction.

> *It is clear that no agreement exists about what intelligence is, and major efforts to define intelligence are not likely to be advanced significantly by brain imaging anytime in the near future.*

Figure 3.14   These PET images show the level of brain activity while playing a computer game. With the light colored areas indicating high levels of activity, the scans indicate that the expert player (right) uses significantly less energy than the novice player (left), an example of increased neural efficiency.

Further evidence of neural efficiency exists in PET scans taken of the brain while playing a computer game. When first learning the game there is a large amount of neural activity. As the player masters the game, the amount of brain activity diminishes significantly (Figure 3.14). Further, the higher the I.Q. of the player, the more quickly the neural activity drops while learning the game. Future research may describe these systems in greater detail and provide a neurological framework for better interpreting how data from the neurosciences support the notion of multiple intelligences.

For now, these current notions continue to move us away from the traditional model of intelligence as a singular entity, fixed at birth, and best measured by vocabulary and reading. They help us understand that the environment can have significant impact on intelligence, and that human beings can be smart in different ways.

Perhaps the next step is to realize that each of the intelligences described by Gardner, Sternberg, and others has many skills contained within it, and thus, there are *innumerable* ways that each brain can manipulate information and skills during the learning process. Expanding our view beyond separate intelligences to an integrated wealth of intelligences is supported by neuroscience, and it also reduces the chances that we will label kids as "word smart" or "music dumb." Rather, we can accept that the best teaching and learning occurs when we use the greatest variety of techniques, thereby making it more likely that all learners will succeed (Shearer, 2004).

Retrieval

It takes less than 50 milliseconds (a millisecond is 1/1,000th of a second) to retrieve an item from working memory. Retrieving a memory from long-term storage, however, can be complicated and comparatively time-consuming. One curious finding in recent years is that encoding information into memory involves the left hemisphere more than the right, and retrieval involves the right hemisphere more than the left. Although both processes involve the frontal lobes, it appears that encoding and retrieval activate separate neural systems.

The brain uses two methods to retrieve information from the long-term storage sites, *recognition* and *recall*. Recognition matches an outside stimulus with stored information. For example, the questions on a multiple-choice test involve recognizing the correct answer (assuming the learner stored it originally) among the choices. This method helps explain why even poor students almost always do better than expected on multiple-choice tests. Recall is quite different and more difficult. It describes the process whereby cues or hints are sent to long-term memory, which must search and retrieve information from the long-term storage sites, then consolidate and decode it back into working memory.

Both methods require the firing of neurons along the neural pathways to the storage site(s) and back again to working memory. The more frequently we access a pathway, the less likely it is to be obscured by other pathways. Information we use frequently, such as our name and telephone number, are quickly retrieved because the neural impulses to and from those storage sites keep the pathways clear. When the information is moved into working memory, we reprocess it to determine its validity and, in effect, relearn it.

> *Whenever we retrieve something from long-term storage into working memory, we relearn it.*

Factors Affecting Retrieval

The rate at which the retrieval occurs depends on a number of factors.

- **Adequacy of the Cues.** The cue used to stimulate the retrieval of a memory may prompt a fully accurate recall or an ambiguous one. Since memory is not a videocassette recorder, the rememberer must reconstruct the memory based on the information retrieved by that cue. Having a strong memory does not seem to be as important as the retrieval cues (Schacter, 1996).
- **Mood of the Retriever.** Studies show that people in a sad mood more easily remember negative experiences, while those in a happy mood tend to recall pleasant experiences.
- **Context of the Retrieval.** Accurate recall is more likely to occur if the context during retrieval is very similar to the context of the period during which it was learned. Thus, testing for information in the same location in which it was learned is likely to result in better retrieval.
- **System of Storage.** Declarative memories get stored across brain structures, most likely in the areas that perceive and process incoming stimuli. Thus, the interests and past experiences of the learner will influence the type of cerebral networks that are constructed to contain the memory.

Students store the same item of information in different networks, depending on how they link the information to their past learnings. These storage decisions affect the amount of time it will take to retrieve the information later. This explains why some students need more time than others to retrieve the same information. When teachers call on the first hands that go up, they inadvertently signal to the slower retrievers to stop the retrieval process. This is an unfortunate strategy for two reasons: First, the slower retrieving students feel that they are not getting teacher recognition, thereby lowering their self-concept. Second, by not retrieving the information into working memory, they miss an opportunity to relearn it.

> *Calling on the first hands that go up signals the slower retrievers to stop the retrieval process.*

Rates of Learning and Retrieval

It is no secret that some people learn a particular item faster or slower than others. The amount of time it takes someone to learn cognitive information with sufficient confidence that it will be consolidated into long-term memory is called the *rate of learning.* The rate of learning can vary within the same individual because it can be affected by motivation, emotional mood, degree of focus, and the context in which the learning occurs.

In the information processing model in Chapter 2, the rate of learning is represented by the data arrows flowing from left to right, from the senses through the sensory register to immediate memory and into working memory. The *rate of retrieval* is represented by the recall arrow moving information from right to left, from long-term storage to working memory. *These two rates are independent of each other.* This notion is quite different from classic doctrine which holds that the retrieval rate is strongly related to the rate of learning and, thus, anchored in genetic inheritance. The doctrine is further fueled in our society by timed tests and quiz programs that use the speed of retrieving answers as the main criterion for judging success and intelligence. The disclosure that the rate of retrieval is linked to the nature of the learner's storage method—a learned skill—rather than to the rate of learning is indeed significant. Because it is a *learned* skill, it can be taught. There is now great promise that techniques can be developed for helping us refine our long-term storage methods for faster and more accurate retrieval. (See the **Practitioner's Corners** on retention on pp. 118 and 130–132 at the end of this chapter.)

> **The rate of learning and the rate of retrieval are independent of each other.**

Because the rate of learning and the rate of retrieval are independent, individuals can be fast or slow learners, fast or slow retrievers, and every combination in between. Although most people tend to fall midrange, some are at the extremes. Actually, not only have we had experience with learners possessing the extreme combinations of these two rates, but we have also (perhaps unwittingly) made up labels to describe them. An individual who is a fast learner and a fast retriever we call *gifted* or a *genius.* Such students retrieve answers quickly. Their hands go up first. Their responses are almost always correct, and they get reputations as "brains." Teachers call on them when they want to keep the lesson moving.

A student who is a fast learner but slow retriever we call an *underachiever.* Teachers say to these students, "Come on, John, I know you know this . . . keep trying." We often run out of patience and admonish them for not studying enough. A slow learner and fast retriever, we call an *overachiever.* These students respond quickly, but their answers may be incorrect. Teachers sometimes mistakenly view them as trying too hard to learn something that may be beyond them.

Test Question No. 6: The rate at which a learner retrieves information from memory is closely related to intelligence.

Answer: False. The rate of retrieval is independent of intelligence. It is more closely tied to how and where the information was stored originally.

For the student who is a slow learner and slow retriever, we have a whole list of uncomplimentary labels. More regrettable is that too often we interpret "slow learner" to mean "unable to learn." What being a slow learner really means is that the student

Too often we interpret "slow learner" to mean "unable to learn".

is unable to learn something in the amount of time we have arbitrarily assigned for that learning. All these labels are unfortunate because they perpetuate the mistaken notion that the major factors promoting successful learning are beyond the control of the learner and teacher.

Teachers can help students improve their rate of retrieval by using instructional strategies that assist the learners' brain in deciding how and where to consolidate the new learning in long-term memory. One strategy deals with chunking, and is the next topic of discussion. The other involves identifying the critical attributes and is discussed in Chapter 4.

Chunking

There are three limits to our power of reasoning and thinking: our limited attention span, working memory, and long-term memory. Is it possible to consciously increase the number of items that working memory can handle at one time? The answer is yes, through a process called *chunking*. Chunking occurs when working memory perceives a set of data as a single item, much as we perceive *information* as one word (and, therefore, one item) even though it is composed of 11 separate letters. Going back to the number exercise in Chapter 2, some people may have indeed remembered all 10 digits in the right sequence. These may be people who spend a lot of time on the telephone. When they see a 10-digit number, their experience helps them to group it by area code, prefix, and extension. Thus, they see the second number, 4915082637, as (491) 508-2637, which is now three chunks, not 10. Since three are within the working memory's functional capacity, the digits can be remembered accurately.

Some researchers suggest that chunking occurs in two ways (Gobet et al., 2001). In one situation, chunking is a deliberate, goal-oriented process initiated and controlled by the learner. For example, in learning a poem, we are likely to rehearse the first line, then the first two lines, then three lines, and so on, gradually increasing the size of the chunk until we know the whole poem. The other mechanism is more subtle, automatic, continuous, and linked to perceptual processes. This occurs, for instance, when we learn to read. The brain gradually expands the number of words it processes at one time from a single word to two words, to a phrase, and so on. During this process, fMRIs show increased activity in the frontal lobes as working memory encodes the learning content into higher capacity chunks (Bor, Duncan, Wiseman, & Owen, 2003).

Chunking allows us to deal with a few large blocks of information rather than many small fragments. Problem solving involves the ability to access large amounts of relevant knowledge from long-term memory for use in working memory. The key to that skill is chunking. The more a person is able to chunk in a particular area, the more expert the person becomes. These experts have the ability to use their experiences to group or chunk all kinds of information into discernable patterns. Chunking is also a valuable strategy when learning a complicated procedure, especially if the learners are reading aloud the procedures while carrying them out (Duggan & Payne, 2001). Chunking is also a valuable strategy for learning a new language, especially when the chunking is combined with imagery (Carter, Hardy, & Hardy, 2001).

This ability to chunk is much more a reflection of how the expert's knowledge base is organized rather than a superior perceptual ability. Experience has changed the experts' brains so that they can encode relevant information in greater detail and more fully than the nonexperts. As they gain experience, more patterns are chunked and linked and the expertise becomes less conscious and more intuitive. Here are some examples:

- An experienced physician takes much less time to diagnose a medical condition than an intern.
- Expert waiters remember meal combinations rather than single menu items.
- Expert musicians recall long passages, not single notes.
- Chess masters recall board layouts as functional clusters rather than separate pieces.
- Expert readers take in phrases, not individual words.

Test Question No. 7: The amount of information a learner can deal with at one time is genetically linked.

Answer: False. The amount of information a learner can deal with at one time is linked to the learner's ability to add more items to the chunks in working memory—a learned skill.

Effect of Past Experiences on Chunking

Let's show how past experiences affect chunking. First, look at the following sentence:

Grandma is buying an apple.

This sentence has 22 letters, but only five chunks (or words) of information. Because the sentence is one complete thought, most people treat it as just one item in working memory. In this example, 22 bits of data (letters) become one chunk (complete thought). In addition, visual learners probably formed a mental image of a grandmother buying that apple.

Now let's add more information to working memory. Stare at the next sentence below for about 10 seconds. Now close your eyes and try recalling the two sentences.

Hte plpae si edr.

Having trouble with the second? That's because the words make no sense, and working memory is treating each of the 13 letters and three spaces as 16 individual items (plus the first sentence as 1 item, for a total of 17). The 5- to 9-item functional capacity range of working memory is quickly exceeded.

Let's rearrange the letters in each word of the second sentence to read as follows:

The apple is red.

Stare at this sentence for 10 seconds. Now close your eyes again and try to remember the first sentence and this sentence. Most people will remember both sentences because they are now just 2 items instead of 17 and their meanings are related. Experience, once again, helps the working memory decide how to chunk items.

Here's a frequently used example of how experience can help in chunking information and improving achievement. Get the pencil and paper again. Now stare at the letters below for 10 seconds. Then look away from the page and write them down in the correct sequence and groupings. Ready? Go.

LSDN BCT VF BIU SA

Check your results. Did you get all the letters in the correct sequence and groupings? Probably not, but that's OK. Most people would not get 100 percent by staring at the letters in such a short period of time.

Let's try it again. Same rules: Stare at the letters below for 10 seconds and write the letters down. Ready? Go.

LSD NBC TV FBI USA

How did you do this time? Most people do much better on this example. Now compare the two examples. Note that the letters in both examples are *identical and in the same sequence*! The only difference is that the letters in the second example are grouped—or chunked—in a way that allows past experience to help working memory process and hold the items. Working memory usually sees the first example as 14 letters plus 4 spaces (i.e., the grouping is important) or 18 items—much more than its functional capacity. But the sec-

> *Chunking is an effective way of enlarging working memory's capacity and for helping the learner make associations that establish meaning.*

ond example is quickly seen as only 5 understandable items (the spaces no longer matter) and, thus, within the limits of working memory's capacity. Some people may even pair NBC with TV, and FBI with USA, so that they actually deal with just 3 chunks. These examples show the power of past experience in remembering—a principle of learning called *transfer,* which we will discuss in the next chapter.

Chunking is a very effective way of enlarging working memory's capacity. It can be used to memorize a long string of numbers or words. Most of us learned the alphabet in chunks—for some it may have been *abcd, efg, hijk, lmnop, qrs, tuv, wxyz.* Chunking reduced the 26 letters to a smaller number of items that working memory could handle. Even people can be chunked, such as couples (for example, Romeo and Juliet, Gilbert and Sullivan, Bonnie and Clyde), in which recalling the name of one immediately suggests the name of the other. Although working memory has a functional capacity limit as to the number of chunks it can process at one time, there appears to be no limit to the number of items that can be combined into a chunk. Teaching students (and yourself) how to chunk can greatly increase learning and remembering.

Test Question No. 8: It is usually not possible to increase the amount of information that the working memory can deal with at one time.

Answer: False. By increasing the number of items in a chunk, we can increase the amount of information that our working memory can process simultaneously.

Cramming Is Chunking

Cramming for a test or interview is another example of chunking. The learner loads into working memory as many items as can be identified as needed. Varying degrees of temporary associations are made among the items. With sufficient effort and meaning, the items can be carried in working memory, even for days, until needed. If the source of the crammed items was outside the learner, that is, from texts or class notes, then it is possible for none of the crammed items to be transferred to long-term storage. This practice (which many of us have experienced) explains how a learner can be conversant and outwardly competent in the items tested on one day (while the items were in working memory) and have little or no understanding of them several days later after they drop out of working memory into oblivion. We cannot recall later what we have not stored. Is there anything teachers can do about this? See the **Practitioner's Corner** on p. 70 of Chapter 2 on "Testing Whether Information Is in Long-Term Storage."

Forgetting

Ask teachers how long they want their students to remember what they were taught, and the answer is a resounding, "forever." Yet, that is not usually the case. Much of what is taught in school is forgotten over time, sometimes within a few days. Forgetting is often viewed as the enemy of learning. But, on the contrary, forgetting plays an important role in promoting learning and facilitating recall.

The human brain processes an enormous amount of incoming information every day. Much of that information remains in temporary memory sites and soon fades. For example, the name of a person that one has just met may remain in memory for just a few minutes. Yet the name of one's best friend is turned into a long-term memory and lasts a lifetime. Why do we forget so much and preserve so little? Forgetting manifests itself in two major ways: the process of discarding newly acquired information, and the decay that occurs with memories already in long-term storage.

Forgetting New Information

The first major studies on forgetting were conducted by Hermann Ebbinghaus (1850 - 1909), a German psychologist, whose work led to the development of a forgetting curve. The curve was a mathematical representation of how quickly new experiences were forgotten. Subsequent studies have somewhat modified his findings. When the brain is exposed to new information, the greatest amount of forgetting occurs shortly after the learning task is completed, and continues rapidly throughout the first day. Items that do not make sense to the learner are usually forgotten first. Conversely, traumatic and vivid experiences are rarely forgotten, although what we recall of them may change over time. But for most information, forgetting slows down after two weeks when there is not much left to forget.

Forgetting new material can occur as a result of interference from earlier learning. This is a component of a process called transfer, which will be discussed in greater detail in Chapter 4. Even *how* one acquires new learning can affect forgetting. For most people, it is easier to forget what is heard than what is read. When listening to new information, extraneous sounds can divert the brain's attention. But reading is a much more focused activity, thereby reducing the effect of distractions (see Figure 3.9). Stress and lack of sleep also contribute to forgetting.

Forgetting has some definite advantages. When the brain is presented with a large amount of information, forgetting prevents irrelevant information from interfering with the acquisition, remembering, and recall of relevant information. By screening out the unimportant, the essential data and experiences have a chance to be fully consolidated into long-term memories. Forgetting may be frustrating, but it is most likely a survival adaptation of memory. There is little value in remembering everything that has happened to us. Forgetting the trivial leaves room for the more important and meaningful experiences that shape who we are and establish our individuality.

> *By forgetting the trivial, we leave room for the more important and meaningful experiences that shape who we are and establish our individuality.*

Teachers, of course, believe that the material they present in class is relevant. Why doesn't the student's brain perceive it that way, too? We already answered that question in Chapter 2. You will recall that sense and meaning (relevancy) are key factors that affect whether new information will be remembered or forgotten.

Forgetting Past Memories

Imagine if the brain remembered everything for a lifetime. Just trying to recall the name of a childhood friend would be a significant challenge. The brain would have to search though thousands of names scattered among the long-term memory sites. At best, the name would take a long time to find; at worst, the result could be confusion, resulting in the recall of the wrong name. By gradually forgetting the names that are not important, the recall process becomes more efficient.

Forgetting also helps to update obsolete information. As one changes jobs and relocates, for example, new data, such as addresses and telephone numbers, overwrite the old data. The old data may still reside in long-term memory, but if it is not recalled and rehearsed, it will eventually become less accessible.

Exactly what happens in the brain to old memories over time is still an open question. Some researchers suggest that memory loss of a specific experience can occur if the memory has not been recalled for a long time. They believe that this leads to the slow but steady disassociation of the network of brain cells that form the memory, making retrieval increasingly difficult. Eventually, the integrity of the network fails and the memory is lost, perhaps forever. Such a process, the researchers say, frees up memory resources so that they become available for new information (Wixted, 2004).

Other researchers contend that old memories remain intact, though other factors somehow block access to them. These factors can include medications, drugs, vivid new experiences, stroke, and Alzheimer's disease. Recent studies have also found that some people can voluntarily block an unwanted past experience with such persistence that it results in forgetting (Fleck, Berch, Shear, & Strakowski, 2001). Does it make any difference whether forgetting is the deterioration of the memory sites or losing the pathways? Is not the result the same, the inability to recall the memory? Sure, the result is the same, but since our understanding of the storage process has changed, so has the method for trying to recall it. We can use a therapy that helps us to find the original pathway, or an alternate pathway, to the memory sites.

Here is an example. Suppose you try to recall the name of the teacher you had when you were in second grade. Unless you have thought recently about that teacher, the pathway to that name has not been used for a long time. It is blocked by newer pathways, and you will have difficulty finding it. The name is still there, but it may take you as long as several days to find it. It will probably come to you when you least expect it.

Another example: Suppose you start thinking about finding an old sweater that you have not seen in several years. If you believe you gave it away, you will not even begin to look for it. That is the same as if you believe that your forgotten memory has been destroyed over time; you will not even try to recall it. On the other hand, if you are convinced that the sweater is somewhere in that big attic, then it is just a matter of time before your hunt pays off and you find it. You'll probably start by thinking of the last time you wore it. This is the same process of memory therapy that is used with brain-damaged individuals. The therapy helps the patient seek other neural connections to find the original or an alternate pathway to the memory sites (Rose, 2005; Schacter, 2001).

Implications for Teaching. More research is needed before scientists can draw any conclusions about the mechanisms that result in the forgetting of old memories. Meanwhile, teachers can take advantage of what *is* known. Namely, that important information that students have already learned is more likely to be accurately and firmly consolidated in long-term memory if it is recalled and rehearsed periodically as the students progress through grade levels. Too often, information deemed important is taught just once, and the students are expected to remember it for a lifetime. They may even be tested on it years after they initially learned it. Something worth remembering is worth repeating. If important information is purposefully revisited throughout a student's entire school experience, then firmly consolidated and robust memories will be available for a long time to come.

Confabulation

Have you ever been discussing an experience with someone who had shared it with you and started arguing over some of the details? As described earlier, long-term memory is the process of searching, locating, retrieving, and transferring information to working memory. Rote recall, especially of frequently used information, such as your name and address, is actually simple. These pathways are clear and retrieval time is very short. Retrieving more complex and less frequently used concepts is much more complicated. It requires signaling multiple storage sites through elaborate, cluttered pathways for intermediate consolidation and ultimate decoding into working memory. It is less accurate. First, most of us do not retain 100 percent of elaborate experiences, such as an extensive vacation. Second, we store parts of the experience in many storage areas.

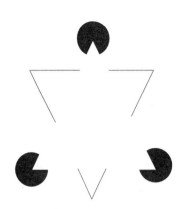

Figure 3.14 The white triangle you may see does not exist. It is a result of confabulation.

When retrieving such an experience, the long-term memory may not be able to locate all the events being requested, either because of insufficient time or because they were never retained. Moreover, older memories can be modified or distorted by the acquisition of newer information. During the retrieval process, memory can unconsciously fabricate the missing or incomplete information by selecting the next closest item it can recall. This process is called *confabulation* and occurs because the brain is always active and creative, and seems to abhor incompleteness. Confabulation is not unlike the way the brain completes visual patterns that do not exist, as in optical illusions. Take a look at Figure 3.14. Although you may see a white triangle in the diagram, it does not exist. It is the result of confabulation as the brain seeks to make sense of the pattern.

Confabulation is *not* lying, because it is an unconscious rather than a deliberate process, and the individual believes the fabricated information to be true. This explains why two people who participated in the same experience will later recall slightly—or even significantly—different versions of the same event. Neither individual stored 100 percent of the experience. If each stored 90 percent, it would not be the *same* 90 percent for both. Their missing and different 10 percent will be fabricated and will cause each to question the accuracy of the other's memory. The less of the experience remembered, the more the brain must fabricate. Over time, the fabricated parts are consolidated into the memory network. As we systematically recall this memory, minor alterations may continue to be made through confabulation. Gradually the original memory is transformed and encoded into a considerably different one that we believe to be true and accurate. Although we all fall victim to confabulation at one time or another, damage to certain brain areas can cause chronic and extreme confabulation where the recalled memories deviate significantly from

Our brain fabricates information and experiences that we believe to be true.

reality (Shallice, 1999). The left hemisphere seems to be the driving force behind confabulation. Experiments show that the left hemisphere is so intent on looking for order that it will find it even when there is none (Gazzaniga, 1998a). See more about this in Chapter 5.

Implications for Teaching. Confabulation also happens in the classroom. When recalling a complex learning, the learner is unaware of which parts are missing and, thus, fabricated. The younger the learner, the more inconsistent the fabricated parts can be. The teacher may react by thinking the student is inventing answers intentionally and may discipline accordingly. In another situation, a list of similar words or concepts may induce the confabulation of words or concepts *not* on the list. Studies show that this is a common phenomenon (Roediger & McDermott, 1995). In these cases, the teacher should be aware of confabulation as a possibility, identify the fabricated parts, and provide the feedback needed to help the student correct the inaccurate material. Through practice, the learner will incorporate the corrected material and transfer it to long-term memory.

Confabulation has implications for the justice system. This tendency for the brain to fabricate information rather than admit its absence can have serious consequences in court trials where eyewitnesses, under the pressure of testifying, feel compelled to provide complete information. Confabulation also raises questions about the accuracy of witnesses recalling very old memories of unpleasant events, such as a childhood accident or abuse. Experiments have shown how easy it is to distort a person's recollection of even recent events, or to "implant" memories. In the absence of independent verification, it is impossible to decide what events in the recalled "repressed memory" actually occurred and which are the result of confabulation (Loftus, 1997).

What's Coming Up?

One of the most important goals of education is to teach students how to apply what they learned to future situations they will encounter—what is known as the transfer of learning. Transfer affects old learning, new learning, memory, and recall. The nature and power of transfer as well as how it can help or hinder teaching and learning are unveiled in the next chapter.

PRACTITIONER'S CORNER

Avoid Teaching Two Very Similar Motor Skills

When a learner practices a new skill (in this example, swinging a baseball bat), the motor cortex (across the top of the cerebrum) coordinates with the cerebellum to establish the pathways that will consolidate the movements to perform the skill. After the learner stops the practice, it takes about 4 to 12 hours (down-time) for this consolidation to occur. Further memory pathways are established as the learner sleeps. Practicing the skill the next day will be much easier and more accurate.

If, during the 4- to 12-hour down-time, the learner practices a second skill (in this example, swinging a golf club) that is very similar to the first skill, the pathways for the two skills get confounded. As a result, the learner is able to perform *neither* skill well.

Implications for Practice:

- Avoid teaching two motor skills that are very similar to each other in the same day. When in doubt, make a list of their similarities and differences. If the similarities far outweigh the differences, it is best not to teach them together.

- When the time comes to teach the second skill, teach the *differences* first. This ensures that the differences are recognized during prime-time-1, which is the most powerful position for remembering.

PRACTITIONER'S CORNER

Using Rehearsal to Enhance Retention

Rehearsal refers to the learner's reprocessing of new information in an attempt to determine sense and meaning. It occurs in two forms. Some information items have value only if they are remembered *exactly* as presented, such as the letters and sequence of the alphabet, spelling, poetry, telephone numbers, notes and lyrics of a song, and the multiplication tables. This is called *rote rehearsal.* Sense and meaning are established quickly, and the likelihood of long-term retention is high. Most of us can recall poems and telephone numbers that we learned years ago.

More complex concepts require the learner to make connections and to form associations and other relationships in order to establish sense and meaning. Thus, the information may need to be reprocessed several times as new links are found. This is called *elaborative rehearsal.* The more senses that are used in this elaborative rehearsal, the more reliable the associations. Thus, when visual, auditory, and kinesthetic activities assist the learner during this rehearsal, the probability of long-term storage rises dramatically. That is why it is important for students to talk about what they are learning *while* they are learning it, and to have visual models as well.

Rehearsal is teacher initiated and teacher directed. Recognizing that rehearsal is a necessary ingredient for retention of learning, teachers should consider the following when designing and presenting their lessons:

Rote Rehearsal Strategies

- **Simple Repetition.** For remembering short items (telephone numbers, names, and dates), simply repeat aloud a set of items over and over until it can be recalled in correct sequence.

- **Cumulative Repetition.** For longer sets of items (song, poem, list of battles) the learner rehearses the first few items. Then the next set of items in the sequence is added to the first set and rehearsed, and so on. For example, to remember a poem of four stanzas, the learner starts by rehearsing the first stanza, then rehearsing the second stanza alone, followed by the first two stanzas together. With those in place, the learner rehearses the third stanza and then the three stanzas together. The process is repeated by rehearsing the fourth stanza alone, and finally, all four stanzas together.

Elaborative Rehearsal Strategies

- **Paraphrasing.** Students orally restate ideas in their own words, which then become familiar cues for later storage. Using auditory modality helps the learner attach sense, making retention more likely.

- **Selecting and Note Taking.** Students review texts, illustrations, and lectures, deciding which portions are critical and important. They make these decisions on the basis of criteria from the teacher, authors, or other students. Students then paraphrase the idea and write it into their notes. Adding the kinesthetic exercise of writing furthers retention.

- **Predicting.** After studying a section of content, the students predict the material to follow or what questions the teacher might ask about that content. Prediction keeps students focused on the new content, adds interest, and helps them apply prior learnings to new situations, thus aiding retention.

- **Questioning.** After studying content, students generate questions about the content. To be effective, the questions should range from lower-level thinking of recall, comprehension, and application to higher-level thinking of analysis, evaluation, and synthesis (see Bloom's Taxonomy in Chapter 7). When designing questions of varying complexity, students engage in deeper cognitive processing, clarify concepts, and predict meaning and associations—all contributors to retention.

- **Summarizing.** Students reflect on and summarize in their heads the important material or skills learned in the lesson. This is often the last and critical stage where students can attach sense and meaning to the new learning. Summarizing rehearsal is also called *closure* (see the **Practitioner's Corner** on closure on p. 69 in Chapter 2 for further explanation).

General Guidelines

If the retention of new information or skills beyond the immediate lesson is an important expectation, then rehearsal must be a crucial part of the learner's processing. The following considerations should be incorporated into decisions about using rehearsal.

- **Teach** students rehearsal activities and strategies. As soon as they recognize the differences between rote and elaborative rehearsal, they can understand the importance of selecting the appropriate type for each learning objective. With practice, they should quickly realize that fact and data acquisition require rote rehearsal, whereas analysis and evaluation of concepts require elaborative rehearsal.

- **Remind** students to continuously practice rehearsal strategies until they become regular parts of their study and learning habits.

- **Keep** rehearsal relevant. Effective elaborative rehearsal relies more on making personally meaningful associations to prior learning than on time-consuming efforts that lack these student-centered connections. Any associations that focus on the teacher's experiences may not be relevant to students.

- **Remember** that time alone is not a trustworthy indicator of the effectiveness of rehearsal. The degree of meaning associated with the new learning is much more significant than the time allotted.

- **Have** learners verbalize their rehearsal to peers or teachers while they are learning new material, as this increases the likelihood of retention.

- **Provide** more visual and contextual clues to make rehearsal meaningful and successful. Students with limited verbal competence will focus on visual and concrete lesson components to assist in their rehearsal. This will be particularly true of students whose first language is not English.

- **Vary** the rehearsal strategies that you initiate to ensure that there is plenty of novelty in the process. Students will bore quickly if the same method of rehearsal (e.g., sharing with the same partner) is used all the time.

PRACTITIONER'S CORNER

Using the Primacy-Recency Effect in the Classroom

The primacy-recency effect describes the phenomenon whereby, during a learning episode, we tend to remember best that which comes first (prime-time-1), second best that which comes last (prime-time-2), and least that which comes just past the middle (down-time). Proper use of this effect can lead to lessons that are more likely to be remembered.

Below is a sketch of two lessons. One is taught by Mr. Blue and the other by Mr. Green. Study their lesson sequences and look for any application of the primacy-recency effect.

Mr. Blue	Lesson Sequence	Mr. Green
"Get ready to tell me the two causes of the Civil War we discussed yesterday." After getting this he then says, "Today we will learn the third and most important cause as we are still living with its aftereffects 140 years later." "Before I tell you, let me give back some homework, collect today's homework, collect the notes from Bill and Mary who were absent yesterday, take attendance, and read a brief announcement."	Prime-time-1	"Get ready to tell me the two causes of World War I we discussed yesterday." After getting this he then says, "Today we will learn the third and most important cause as it set the stage for another world war just 30 years later." "And here is the third cause!" (He presents third cause, gives examples, and relates it to yesterday's two causes.)
"Here is the third cause." (He presents third cause, gives examples, and relates it to yesterday's two causes.)	Down-time	"Go into your discussion groups and discuss this third cause. Not only tie it to the two causes we learned yesterday but also to other wars we have learned so far. What are the similarities and differences?"
"OK, we've got only 5 minutes to the end of the period. You've listened attentively so you can do anything you want as long as you are quiet."	Prime-time-2	"Take 2 minutes to review quietly to yourself what you learned about this third cause. Be prepared to share your thoughts with the class."

If these sequences are representative of what happens most of the time in these two teachers' classes, whose students are more likely to remember what they have learned over time? Why? What are some other implications of using the primacy-recency effect in the classroom?

Here are some other considerations for using this effect in the classroom.

- **Teach the new material first** (after getting the students' focus) during prime-time-1. This is the time of greatest retention. Alternatively, this would also be a good time to **reteach** any concept that students may be having difficulty understanding.

- **Avoid asking students** at the beginning of the lesson if they know anything about a *new* topic being introduced. If it is a new topic, the assumption is that most students do not know it. However, there are always some students ready to take a guess—no matter how unrelated. Because this is the time of greatest retention, almost anything that is said, including incorrect information, is likely to be remembered. Give the information and examples yourself to ensure that they are correct.

- **Avoid using precious prime-time** periods for classroom management tasks, such as collecting absence notes or taking attendance. Do these before you get focus, or during the down-time.

- **Use the down-time** portion to have students practice the new learning or to discuss it by relating it to past learnings. Remember that retention of learning does occur during the down-time, but it just takes more effort and concentration.

- **Do closure during prime-time-2.** This is the learner's last opportunity to attach sense and meaning to the new learning, to make decisions about it, and to determine where and how it will be transferred to long-term storage. It is important, then, that the student's brain do the work at this time. If you wish to do a review, then do it *before* closure to increase the chances that the closure experience is accurate. Doing review *instead* of closure is of little value to retention.

- **Try to package lesson objectives** (or sublearnings) in teaching episodes of about 20 minutes. Link the sublearnings according to the total time period available (for example, two 20-minute lessons for a 40-minute teaching period, three for an hour period, and so on).

PRACTITIONER'S CORNER

Strategies for Block Scheduling

More high schools (and some middle schools, too) are converting from the standard 40- to 45-minute daily period to a block schedule consisting of longer teaching periods, usually 80 to 90 minutes. Although there are various formats for the blocks, the main goal of this change is to allow more time for student participation in the learning process.

The benefits of this approach are many: There is less fragmentation to the school day, more time to dig into concepts and allow for transfer to occur, and more time to develop hands-on activities, such as projects. It also allows for more performance-based assessments of student learning, reducing the reliance on paper-and-pencil tests.

The block experience is likely to be more successful if the teacher recognizes the value and need for novelty, and resists the temptation to be the focus of the block during the entire time period. Here are some suggestions for a brain-compatible block lesson.

- **Remember the primacy-recency effect.** Teaching a 90-minute episode as one continuous lesson will mean a down-time of about 35 minutes. Plan for four 20-minute learning segments and your down-time is reduced substantially to about 10 minutes. This down-time can also be productive if the students are engaged in discussions about the new learning.

- **Be in direct control of just one segment.** You may wish to do some direct instruction during one of the lesson segments. If so, use the first segment for this, and then shift the work burden to the students for the other segments. Remember that the brain that does the work is the brain that learns.

- **Go off-task between segments.** Figure 3.8 (p. 94) shows how going off-task between the lesson segments can increase the degree of focus when the students return to task. This is because of the novelty effect. If you prefer to stay on-task, however, then use a joke, story, or cartoon that is related to the learning. You still get the novelty effect without losing focus.

- **Eliminate the unnecessary.** Block scheduling is designed to give students a chance to dig deeper into concepts. To get the time to do this, scrap less important topics that sneak into the curriculum over time. We all know that everything in the curriculum is not of equal importance. Perform this selective abandonment on a regular basis.

- **Work with your colleagues.** Block activities offer an excellent opportunity for teachers to work together in planning the longer lessons. This collegial process can be very productive and interesting, especially when teachers deliver lessons together. Such planning can be within or across subject areas.

- **Vary the blocks.** Novelty means finding ways to make each of the segments different and multisensory. Here are just a few examples of block activities that you can use for the lesson segments:

Teacher talk	Guest speakers
Research	Videos, movies, slides
Cooperative learning groups	Audiotapes
Reading	Reflection time
Student peer coaching	Jigsaw combinations
Laboratory experiences	Discussion groups
Computer work	Role-playing and simulations
Journal writing	Instructional games and puzzles

- **Vary the assessment techniques.** Block scheduling offers students opportunities to explore content in many different ways. Thus, assessment techniques should also be varied to allow students different methods of showing what they have learned. Here are a few examples of assessment techniques to consider:

Written tests	Interviews
Questionnaires	Journals
Portfolios	Presentations
Exhibitions	Video production
Demonstrations	Dioramas
Modeling	Music and dance

PRACTITIONER'S CORNER

Using Practice Effectively

Practice does not make perfect, it makes *permanent*. Practice allows the learner to use the newly learned skill in a new situation with sufficient accuracy so that it will be correctly remembered. Before students begin practice, the teacher should model the thinking process involved and guide the class through each step of the new learning's application.

Since practice makes permanent, the teacher should monitor the students' early practice to ensure that it is accurate and to provide timely feedback and correction if it is not. This guided practice helps eliminate initial errors and alerts students to the critical steps in applying new skills. Here are some suggestions by Hunter (2004) for guiding initial practice:

- **Amount of Material to Practice.** Practice should be limited to the smallest amount of material or skill that has the most relevancy for the students. This allows for sense and meaning to be consolidated as the learner uses the new learning.

- **Amount of Time to Practice.** Practice should take place in short, intense periods of time when the student's working memory is running on prime- time. When the practice period is short, students are more likely to be intent on learning what they are practicing.

- **Frequency of Practice.** New learning should be practiced frequently at first so that it is quickly organized. This is called *massed practice.* If we expect students to retain the information in active storage and to remember how to use it accurately, it should continue to be practiced over increasingly longer time intervals. This is called *distributed practice*, and it is the real key to accurate retention and application of information and mastery of skills over time.

- **Accuracy of Practice.** As students perform guided practice, the teacher should give prompt and specific feedback on whether the practice is correct or incorrect and why. This process gives the teacher valuable information about the degree of student understanding and whether it makes sense to move on or reteach portions that may be difficult for some students.

PRACTITIONER'S CORNER

Relearning Through Recall

Every time we recall information from long-term storage into working memory, we relearn it. Therefore, teachers should use classroom strategies that encourage students to recall previously learned information regularly so they will relearn it. One strategy for doing this is to maintain learner participation throughout the lesson. Called *active participation*, this principle of learning attempts to keep the mind of the student consistently focused on what is being learned or recalled through covert and overt activities.

The covert activity involves the teacher asking the students to recall previously learned information and to process it in some way. It could be, "Think of the conditions that existed in America just after the Civil War that we learned yesterday, and be prepared to discuss them in a few minutes." This statement informs the students that they will be held accountable for their recall. This accountability increases the likelihood that the students will recall the desired item and, thus, relearn it. It also alleviates the need for the teacher to call on every student to determine if the recall has occurred. After sufficient wait time (see the **Practitioner's Corner** on wait-time, p. 129), overt activities are used to determine the quality of the covert recall.

Some suggestions follow on how to use active participation strategies effectively:

- **State the question** and allow thinking time *before* calling on a student for response. This holds all students accountable for recalling the answer until you pick your first respondent.

- **Give clear and specific directions** as to what the students should recall. Focus on the lesson objectives and not on the activities unless they were a crucial part of the learning. Repeat the question using different words and phraseology. This increases the number of cues that the learners have during their retrieval search.

- **Avoid predictable patterns** when calling on students, such as alphabetical order, up and down rows, or raised hands. These patterns signal the students *when* they will be held accountable, thereby allowing them to go off-task before and after their turns.

PRACTITIONER'S CORNER

Impact of Circadian Rhythms on Schools and Classrooms

This chapter explained the differences in circadian rhythms of adolescents compared to pre/postadolescents (Figure 3.11, p. 101). The adolescent rhythm is about an hour later, and these differences have implications for elementary and secondary schools. For example:

- **Planning Elementary School Lessons.** Remember that both the teacher and elementary school students are in the trough together. The tendency here would be for all to just take a nap! That's probably not an option, so we have to decide how to deal with the trough. Here are two things to consider:

  (1) Many elementary teachers can decide what time of day to teach certain subjects. Avoid teaching the same subject every day during the trough time. Because of low focus levels, it is boring for the students and tedious for the teacher. Varying the subject taught in the trough provides novelty and interest.

  (2) Keep assignments short, and frequently hold the students accountable for what they are learning. For example, instead of assigning 30 minutes of silent reading (a common practice during the trough time), assign just five minutes for the class to read two pages and give a specific assignment related to the reading. You might say: "After five minutes to read pages 12 and 13, decide what other choices the main character could have made, and why. I will call on some of you for your answers." Repeating this process results in four or five mini-lessons that will be more productive than trying to attempt a single 30-minute lesson.

- **School Start Times.** Because of this shift in rhythm, teenagers are sleepier in the morning and tend to stay up later at night. They come to school sleep deprived (i.e., many suffer from Delayed Sleep Phase Disorder), and often with an inadequate breakfast (i.e., lacking glucose, the brain's fuel). Meanwhile, students often face a long bus ride to get to high schools that are starting earlier. District leaders should consider realigning opening times and course schedules more closely with the students' biological rhythms to increase the chances of successful learning. School districts that have adopted later starting times for their high schools are reporting positive results. These same positive results apply to elementary schools that start earlier than the traditional time of 9:00 a.m.

- **Classroom Lighting.** Adolescents with Delayed Sleep Phase Disorder have a high amount of melatonin (the hormone that induces sleep) in their bodies. One of the best ways to reduce melatonin levels is with bright light. Keep classroom lights on, open blinds, lift shades, and look for ways to get the students into outdoor light, especially in the morning (Kripke, Youngstedt, & Elliot, 1997).

- **Testing.** School districts usually give standardized tests to all students in the morning. However, high school students tend to perform better in problem-solving and memory tasks later in the day rather than earlier. It is probable that a number of high school students do not do as well on these tests as they could because of the testing times. Some school districts have reported that testing high school students later in the morning and early afternoon improved their performance and scores.

- **Classroom Climate.** Classroom climate problems can arise in high schools if the teacher is in the postnoon trough while the students are still at their pretrough peak. The teacher is likely to be irritable, and minor discipline annoyances can easily escalate into major confrontations. High school administrators in charge of discipline often report a marked rise in student referrals in the early afternoon. One way to deal with this is for high school teachers to plan student-directed activities during this time, such as computer work, simulations, cooperative learning groups, and research projects. These strategies redirect student energy to productive tasks. Meanwhile, the teacher needs to walk around the room, not only to monitor student work, but also to overcome the lower energy levels experienced during the trough.

PRACTITIONER'S CORNER

Using Wait-Time to Increase Student Participation

Wait-time is the period of teacher silence that follows the posing of a question before the first student is called on for a response. Studies first conducted by Mary Budd Rowe (1974) and others indicate that high school teachers had an average wait-time of just over one second. Elementary teachers waited an average of three seconds. Although no major studies have been done in recent years, one can speculate that these wait-times have not increased, given the large amount of curriculum content that needs to be covered and the increased emphasis that many schools have placed on preparing for high-stakes tests. If anything, the times now may be even shorter.

One to three seconds is hardly enough time for slower retrievers, many of whom may know the correct answer, to locate that answer in long-term storage and retrieve it into working memory. And as soon as the teacher calls on the first student, the remaining students **stop the retrieval process** and lose the opportunity to relearn the information. Rowe found that the following happened when teachers extended the wait-time to at least **five** seconds or more:

- The length and quality of student responses increased.
- There was greater participation by slower learners.
- Students used more evidence to support inferences.
- There were more higher-order responses.

These results occurred at all grade levels and in all subjects.

Rowe also noted positive changes in the behavior of teachers who consistently used longer wait-times. Specifically, she observed that these teachers

- Used more higher-order questioning
- Demonstrated greater flexibility in evaluating responses
- Improved their expectations for the performance of slower learners

One effective method for using wait-time is Think-Pair-Share. In this strategy, the teacher asks the students to think about a question. After adequate wait-time, the students form pairs and exchange the results of their thinking. Some students then share their ideas with the entire class.

PRACTITIONER'S CORNER

Using Chunking to Enhance Retention

Chunking is the process whereby the brain perceives several items of information as a single item. Words are common examples of chunks. *Elephant* is composed of eight letters, but the brain perceives them as one item of information. The more items we can put into a chunk, the more information we can process in working memory and remember at one time. Chunking is a learned skill and, thus, can also be taught. There are different types of chunking.

Pattern Chunking: This is most easily accomplished whenever we can find patterns in the material to be retained.

- Say we wanted to remember the number 3421941621776. Without a pattern, these 13 digits are treated as separate items and exceed working memory's functional capacity of about seven items. But we could arrange the numbers in groups that have meaning. For example, 342 (my house number), 1941 (when the U.S. entered World War II), 62 (my father's age), and 1776 (the Declaration of Independence). Now the number is only four chunks with meaning: 342 1941 62 1776.

- The following example, admittedly contrived, shows how chunking can work at different levels. The task is to memorize the following string of words:

COW   GRASS   FIELD   TENNIS   NET   SODA   DOG   LAKE   FISH

We need a method to remember the sequence, because nine is more than the typical functional capacity of seven. We can chunk the sequence of items by using a simple story. First, we see a **cow** eating **grass** in a **field.** Also in the field are two people playing **tennis.** One player hits the ball way over the **net.** They are drinking **soda** while their **dog** runs after the ball that went into the **lake.** The dog's splashing frightens the **fish.**

- Learning a step-by-step procedure for tying a shoelace or copying a computer file from a CD-ROM to a hard disk are examples of pattern chunking. We group the items in a sequence and rehearse it mentally until it becomes one or a few chunks. Practicing the procedure further enhances the formation of chunks, and subsequent performance requires little conscious attention.

Categorical Chunking: This is a more sophisticated chunking process in that the learner establishes various types of categories to help classify large amounts of information. The learner reviews the information looking for criteria that will group complex material into simpler categories or arrays. The different types of categories can include the following:

- **Advantages and Disadvantages.** The information is categorized according to the pros and cons of the concept. Examples include energy use, global warming, genetically altered crops, abortion, and capital punishment.

- **Similarities and Differences.** The learner compares two or more concepts using attributes that make them similar and different. Examples are comparing the Articles of Confederation to the Bill of Rights, mass to weight, mitosis to meiosis, and the U.S. Civil War to the Vietnam War.

- **Structure and Function.** These categories are helpful with concepts that have parts with different functions, such as identifying the parts of an animal cell, a short story, or the human digestive system.

- **Taxonomies.** This system sorts information into hierarchical levels according to certain common characteristics. Examples are biological taxonomies (kingdom, phylum, class, etc.), taxonomies of learning (cognitive, affective, and psychomotor), and governmental bureaucracies.

- **Arrays.** These are less ordered than taxonomies in that the criteria for establishing the array are not always logical, but are more likely based on observable features. Human beings are classified, for example, by learning style and personality type. Dogs can be grouped by size, shape, or fur length. Clothing can be divided by material, season, and gender.

PRACTITIONER'S CORNER

Using Mnemonics to Help Retention

Mnemonics (from the Greek "to remember") are very useful devices for remembering unrelated information, patterns, or rules. They were developed by the ancient Greeks to help them remember dialogue in plays and for passing information to others when writing was impractical. There are many types of mnemonic schemes. The good news is that ordinary people can greatly improve their memory performance with appropriate strategies and practice (Ericsson, 2003). Here are two strategies that can be easily used in the classroom. Work with students to develop schemes appropriate for the content.

- **Rhyming Mnemonics.** Rhymes are simple yet effective ways to remember rules and patterns. They work because if you forget part of the rhyme or get part of it wrong, the words lose their rhyme or rhythm and signal the error. To retrieve the missing or incorrect part, you start the rhyme over again, and this helps you to relearn it. Have you ever tried to remember the fifth line of a song or poem without starting at the beginning? It is very difficult to do because each line serves as the auditory cue for the next line.

Common examples of rhymes we have learned are "*I* before *e*, except after *c* . . .," "Thirty days hath September . . . ," and "Columbus sailed the ocean blue . . . ". Here are some rhymes that can help students learn information in other areas:

The Spanish Armada met its fate
In fifteen hundred and eighty-eight.

Divorced, beheaded, died;
Divorced, beheaded, survived.
(the fate of Henry VIII's six wives, in chronological order)

The number you are dividing by,
Turn upside down and multiply.
(rule for dividing by fractions)

This may seem like a clumsy system, but it works. Make up your own rhyme, alone or with the class, to help you and your students remember more information faster.

- **Reduction Mnemonics:** In this scheme, you reduce a large body of information to a shorter form and use a letter to represent each shortened piece. The letters are either combined to form a real or artificial word or are used to construct a simple sentence. For example, the real word **HOMES** can help us remember the names of the great lakes (Huron, Ontario, Michigan, Erie, and Superior). **BOY FANS** gives us the coordinating conjunctions in English (but, or, yet, for, and, nor, and so). The name **ROY G BIV** aids in remembering the seven colors of the spectrum (red, orange, yellow, green, blue, indigo, and violet). The artificial word **NATO** recalls North Atlantic Treaty Organization. The sentence **My Very Earnest Mother Just Served Us Nine Pizzas** can help us remember the nine planets of the solar system in order from the sun (Mercury, Venus, Earth, Mars, Jupiter, Saturn, Uranus, Neptune, and Pluto). Here are other examples:

Please Excuse My Dear Aunt Sally.

(the order for solving algebraic equations: Parenthesis, Exponents, Multiplication, Division, Addition, Subtraction)

Frederick Charles Goes Down And Ends Battle.

(F, C, G, D, A, E, B: the order that sharps are entered in key signatures; reverse the order for flats)

In Poland, Men Are Tall.

(the stages of cell division in mitosis: Interphase, Prophase, Metaphase, Anaphase, and Telophase)

King Phillip Came Over From Greece Sailing Vessels.

(the descending order of zoological classifications: Kingdom, Phylum, Class, Order, Family, Genus, Species, Variety)

King Henry Doesn't Mind Drinking Cold Milk.

(the descending order of metric prefixes: Kilo, Hecto, Deca, (measure), Deci, Centi, and Milli)

Sober Physicists Don't Find Giraffes In Kitchens.

(the order of names for orbital electrons: s, p, d, f, g, i, and k)

Chapter 3—Memory, Retention, and Learning

Key Points to Ponder

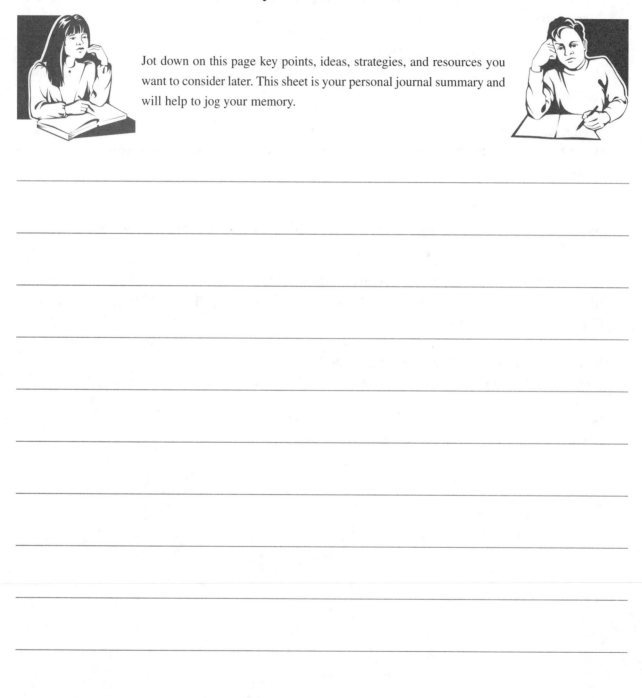

Jot down on this page key points, ideas, strategies, and resources you want to consider later. This sheet is your personal journal summary and will help to jog your memory.

_____

_____

_____

_____

_____

_____

_____

_____

_____

Chapter 4

The Power of Transfer

*Transfer is the basis of all creativity, problem solving
and the making of satisfying decisions.*
                                        —Madeline Hunter,
                                             Mastery Teaching

---

Chapter Highlights: This chapter explains the components of the
most powerful principle of learning, transfer. It examines the factors
that affect transfer and how teachers can use past learnings effectively to enhance present and future learning.

The brain is a dynamic creation that is constantly organizing and reorganizing itself when it receives new stimuli. More networks are formed as raw items merge into new patterns. Just as musicians in an orchestra join the individual sounds of their instruments in new and melodious ways, so does the brain unite disconnected ideas with wonderful harmony. We can add beauty and clarity, and forge isolated ideas into spectacular visions.

Transfer is one process that allows this amazing inventiveness to unfold. It encompasses the ability to learn in one situation and then use that learning, possibly in a modified or generalized form, in other situations. Transfer is the core of problem solving, creative thinking, and all other higher mental processes, inventions, and artistic products. It is also one of the ultimate goals of teaching and learning.

WHAT IS TRANSFER?

The principle of learning, called *transfer*, describes a two-part process:

(1) **Transfer *during* learning.** This refers to the effect that past learning has on the processing and acquisition of new learning.

(2) **Transfer *of* learning.** This refers to the degree to which the new learning is applied by the learner in future situations. Some researchers further separate this type of transfer into near and far transfer. Near transfer describes using the new learning in very similar and closely related settings. Far transfer includes the ability to use the new learning in a similar setting as well as the ability to solve novel problems that are not very similar but do share common elements with the learning that was initially acquired (Mestre, 2002).

Transfer During Learning

The process goes something like this: Whenever new learning moves into working memory, long-term memory (most likely stimulated by a signal from the hippocampus) simultaneously searches the long-term storage sites for any past learnings that are similar to, or associated with, the new learning. If the experiences exist, the memory networks are activated and the associated memories are reconsolidated in working memory (Hunter, 2004; Perkins & Salomon, 1988).

How much past learning affects the learner's ability to acquire new knowledge or skills in another context describes one phase of the powerful phenomenon called transfer. In other words, the information processing system depends on past learnings to associate with, make sense of, and treat new information. This recycling of past information into the flow not only reinforces and provides additional rehearsal for already-stored information but also aids in assigning meaning to new information. The degree of meaning attributed to new learning will determine the connections that are made between it and other information in long-term storage. Consider the following pieces of information:

1. There are seven days in the week.

2. Force = mass **X** acceleration.

3. North Korea is an evil country.

4. . . . They also serve who only stand and wait.

5. Jesus is the son of God.

6. There's a sucker born every minute.

In each instance, the meaning of the information depends on the experience, education, and state of mind of the reader. The third and last statements can arouse passionate agreement or disavowal. The second and fourth statements would be meaningless to a second grader, but not the first statement. The fifth could provoke an endless debate among adherents of different religions.

Meaning often depends on context. The transfer process not only provides interpretation of words, but often includes nuances and shadings that can result in very different meanings. "He is a piece of work!" can be either a compliment or a sarcastic comment, depending on tone and context.

These connections and associations give the learner more options to cope with new situations in the future (Figure 4.1).

Types of Transfer

Positive Transfer. When past learning *helps* the learner deal with new learning, it is called *positive transfer.* Suppose a violin player and a trombone player both want to learn to play the viola, an instrument similar to the violin. Who will learn the new instrument more easily? The violin player already possesses the skills and knowledge that will help in learning the viola. The trombone player, on the other hand, may be a very accomplished trombonist but possesses few skills that will help to play the viola. Similarly, Michelangelo, DaVinci, and Edison were able to transfer a great deal of their knowledge and skills to create magnificent works of art and invention. Their prior learnings made greater achievement possible.

Negative Transfer. Sometimes past learning *interferes* with the learner's understanding of new learning, resulting in confusion or errors. This process is called *negative transfer.* If, for example, you have been driving cars with only automatic shift, you will have quite a surprise the first time you drive a standard-shift car. You were accustomed to keeping your left foot idle or using it to brake (not recommended). In either case, the left foot has a very different function in a standard-shift car. If it keeps doing its automatic-shift functions (or does nothing), you will have great difficulty driving the standard-shift car. In other words, the skills that the driver's brain assigned to the left foot for the automatic-shift car are not the skills it needs to cope with the standard-shift car. The skill it used before is now interfering with the skill needed in the new situation, an example of negative transfer.

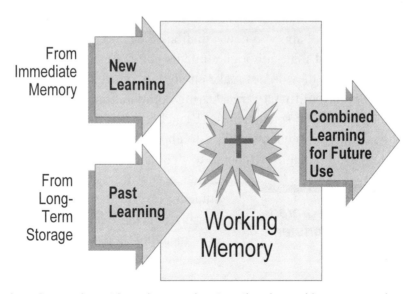

Figure 4.1 New learning and past learning coming together in working memory is one part of transfer. The learner's understanding of how the combined learning can be used in the future is the other part of transfer.

During a lesson, students are dealing continually with transfer as they process and practice new information and skills. Because students' experiences vary, the extent of what transfers also varies. Whether that transfer aids or impedes the acquisition of new learning is a major factor in determining the degree of success each student has in accomplishing the lesson objective.

Never underestimate the power of transfer. Past learning always influences the acquisition of new learning.

For example, teachers who teach Romance languages to native English speakers are frequently helped by positive transfer and plagued by negative transfer. Words like *rouge* in French and *mucho* in Spanish help to teach *red* and *much,* respectively, but when students see the French *librairie* and are told it is a place where books are found, experience prompts them to think that it means "library." It really means "bookstore." Never underestimate the power of transfer. Past learning *always* influences the acquisition of new learning.

Transfer of Learning

A review of any curriculum reveals that transfer is an integral component and expectation of the learning process. Every day, teachers deliberately or intuitively refer to past learning to make new learning more understandable and meaningful. For the long term, students are expected to transfer the knowledge and skills they learn in school to their daily routines, jobs, and ventures outside the school. Writing and speaking skills should help them communicate with others, scientific knowledge should inform their decisions on environmental and health issues, and their understanding of history should guide their responses to contemporary problems at personal, social, and cultural levels. Obviously, the more information students can transfer from their schooling to the context of everyday life, the greater the probability that they will be good communicators, informed citizens, critical thinkers, and successful problem solvers.

Yet studies continue to show that students are not successful in recognizing how the skills and knowledge they learned in school apply to new situations they encounter in other classes or outside school. One recent study found that, although students can spontaneously make inferences from one curriculum area to another, they do not make enough inferences to support fully fledged transfer and, thus, for example, have difficulty transferring computational skills they learned in mathematics class to solving problems in science class (Blanchette & Dunbar, 2002).

These studies suggest that the students' ability to apply knowledge to new situations is limited. Apparently, we are not doing enough in schools to deliberately make the transfer connections to enhance new learning. The more connections that students can make between past learning and new learning, the more likely they are to determine sense and meaning and thus retain the new learning. Moreover, when these connections can be extended across curriculum areas, they establish a framework of associative networks that will be recalled for future problem solving.

Thematic units and an integrated curriculum enhance the transfer process.

Successful transfer can be enhanced by educators who advocate thematic units and an integrated curriculum. This approach provides more stimulating experiences for students, and helps them see the commonalities among diverse topics, while reinforcing understanding and meaning for future applications. Thematic units, for instance, could focus on the environment (global warming, recycling, air quality), history (the Civil War, exploring the West, Black history month), science (sources of electrical power, space exploration, ecosystems), or language arts (tall tales, realistic fiction, poetry) (Roberts & Kellough, 2003). Integrated thematic units cut across curriculum areas. The Internet is an excellent source of ideas for integrated units (see Internet sites in the **Resources** section). Figure 4.2 is an example of an integrated thematic unit that could be adapted for elementary and secondary grade levels. Beyond restructuring curriculum, the question now becomes: How can we select teaching that will ensure transfer?

TEACHING FOR TRANSFER

Transfer is more frequently provoked by the environment than consciously by the learner. Have you ever heard a song that brings back a flood of memories? You could not really control that recall unless something else in the present environment now demanded your immediate attention, such as your crying baby or a ringing fire alarm. So who represents a large portion of the environment for students in school? Yes, the teachers! Teachers are the instruments of transfer for students. If teachers

> *Teachers are frequently the provokers of transfer for their students.*

are not aware of that, they can inadvertently provoke negative transfer during learning situations just as easily as they can provoke positive transfer.

Figure 4.2   Here is an example of an integrated thematic unit on water. Students have opportunities to gain a deeper understanding of how water directly affects their daily lives. This approach increases the chances of transfer of learning to future situations.

Test Question No. 9: Most of the time, the transfer of information from long-term storage is under the conscious control of the learner.

Answer: False. The transfer process is more often provoked by the learner's present environment.

Example of Transfer in a Literature Class. The following anecdote illustrates how transfer can impede or promote a lesson objective. I once observed a senior class in British literature in a large urban high school. It was late April, and as the students entered the class, they were discussing the upcoming final examinations, the prom, and preparations for graduation. After the opening bell rang, the teacher admonished the students to pay attention and said, "Today, we are going to start another play by William Shakespeare." The moans and groans were deafening and abated only after the teacher used every threat short of ripping up their forthcoming diplomas. Judging from their reactions and unsolicited comments, the students' perceptions of past experiences with Shakespeare were hardly positive. Without realizing it, the teacher's brief introduction had provoked negative transfer; getting the students to focus constructively on the new play now would not be easy.

Later that afternoon, I found myself in a different teacher's British literature class. A large television monitor and a videocassette recorder in the front of the classroom got the students' attention as they entered. The teacher asked the students to "watch a videotape and be prepared to discuss what they saw." What unfolded over the next 15 minutes was a cleverly edited collection of scenes from the movie *West Side Story*. There was enough story to get the plot and enough music to maintain interest. The students were captivated; some even sang along. As the showdown between Tony and Maria's brother came on the screen, the teacher stopped the tape. The students complained, wanting to see who won the fight. The teacher noted that this was really an old story set in modern times, and that she had the script of the original play. The characters' names and the location were different, but the plot was the same. While the students were discussing what they had seen, she distributed Shakespeare's *Romeo and Juliet*. Many students eagerly flipped through the pages trying to find the outcome of the fight scene! The teacher's understanding of positive transfer was evident, and she had used it magnificently.

To use transfer effectively, teachers need to purposefully identify factors that facilitate learning (positive transfer) while minimizing or eliminating factors that can cause interference (negative transfer).

Factors Affecting Transfer

How quickly transfer occurs during a learning situation depends on the rate of retrieval. As noted earlier, the rate of retrieval is largely dependent on the storage system that the learner has created and how the learning was originally stored. Designing the filing system in long-term storage is a *learned* skill and can run the gamut from very loose connections to a highly organized series of networks. Working memory uses a sensory cue that it encodes with the material and files it in a network containing similar items.

The cue helps long-term memory locate, identify, and select the material for later retrieval, similar to the way the label on a file folder helps to locate and identify what is in the file. If the learner is recalling a complex concept, information has to come from various storage areas to the frontal lobes for assembly, verification, and decoding into working memory. Many factors in a learning system affect the nature of this transfer process. Researchers have identified four of these: the context and degree of original learning, similarity, critical attributes, and association. No factor is more important than the others, and they often work together (Hunter, 2004).

Context and Degree of Original Learning

The quality of transfer that occurs during new learning is largely dependent on the quality of the original learning. Most of us can recall easily our Social Security number or even a poem we learned in our early school years. If the original learning was well learned and accurate, its influence on new learning will be more constructive and help the student toward greater achievement. Students who did not learn the scientific method well, for example, will not be very effective in laboratory analysis, and they will not be able to transfer this learning to future success.

If something is worth teaching, it is worth teaching well. Rote learning does not tend to facilitate transfer, but learning with understanding does. Thus, trying to learn too many concepts too quickly may hinder transfer because the learner is simply memorizing isolated facts with little opportunity to organize the material in a meaningful fashion and link it to prior related knowledge.

> *Rote learning does not tend to facilitate transfer.*

If we teach students to be conscious of both the new learning and the context into which it fits, we are helping them forge strong associations for future recall. If the new learning is too tightly bound to the context, then learners may fail to transfer that knowledge or skill to different contexts. When students perceive, for example, that grammatical correctness matters only in English class, then their writing in other classes gets careless.

In another example, a major study found that students who learned to solve arithmetic progression problems in algebra class were able to transfer the method they learned to solve similar physics problems involving velocity and distance in their science classes. On the other hand, students who learned to solve the physics problems first were unable to transfer the method to solve similar arithmetic progression problems in their algebra class (Bassok & Holyoak, 1989). The transfer of learning from physics to arithmetic was apparently blocked because the physics equations were embedded within the specific subject area context, thereby preventing the students from seeing their application to another context—algebra.

Not surprisingly, one study revealed that when students were required to process information more thoroughly for meaning, there was a high degree of transfer to new situations. The researchers found that students who did more thorough processing used the underlying conceptual information when they were asked to generate analogies, but they used superficial information when asked to do simple rote recall of similar information (Blanchette & Dunbar, 2000).

We discussed in the previous chapter that information is more likely to be remembered if the learner has multiple opportunities to rehearse and use it. But too often, we have time enough only to study a topic until the students reach some low level of mastery and then move on to the next topic. But research on transfer suggests that transfer is improved when students visit important topics often rather than just one intense exposure.

> *Today's learning is tomorrow's transfer. Therefore, if something is worth teaching, it is worth teaching well.*

When using transfer, we ask students to bring learnings from their past forward to today. If the past learning was taught well, it should help the students acquire today's learning. What is taught today becomes past learning tomorrow. If it is taught well today, the positive transfer will enhance tomorrow's learning, and so forth. In other words, today's learning is tomorrow's transfer.

Similarity

Transfer can be generated by the similarity of the situation in which something is being learned and the situation to which that learning may transfer. Thus, skills learned in one environment tend to transfer to other environments that are similar. For example, commercial jet pilots are first trained in flight simulators before they sit in the cockpit of the actual plane. All the training and learnings they acquired in the simulator, an exact replica of the actual plane, will transfer to the real flying situation. This positive transfer helps the pilot get accustomed quickly to the actual plane, and it reduces errors. If you have ever rented a car, you realize that it does not take you very long to get accustomed to it and drive away. The environment is similar to your own car, and most of the important components are in familiar places. You may need a few moments, however, to locate the windshield wiper and light switches.

Teachers often use similarity when introducing new material. They may have students learn words with similar spelling patterns, such as *beat, heat, meat,* and *neat.* Students may use their skills at finding locations on a road map to help place ordered numbers on a graph grid. However, as we shall discuss shortly, presenting two items of information at the same time that are *too* similar can cause problems during retention. Other examples of using similarity are fire and tornado drills. Even giving students major tests in the room where they learned the material being tested uses similarity of the environment for positive transfer.

Similarity of sensory modalities is another form of transfer. Using the color red to represent danger can alert us to traffic lights, the location of fire alarm boxes, or hazardous areas. Sensory similarity can also cause error. Students may confuse *there, their,* and *they're* because they sound alike, or they may not be able to pronounce *read* until they know the word's context.

The more specific the cue that working memory attaches to a new learning, the easier it is for long-term memory to identify the item being sought. This process leads to an interesting phenomenon regarding long-term storage and retrieval: We store by similarity, but we retrieve by difference. That is, long-term memory most often stores new learnings into a network that contains learnings with similar characteristics or associations, as perceived by the learner. This network identification is one

Figure 4.3 We tend to store information in networks by similarity, but retrieve it back into working memory by difference.

of the connections made in working memory during rehearsal and closure. To retrieve an item, long-term memory identifies how it is *different* from all the other items in that network (Figure 4.3).

For example: How would you recognize your best friend in a crowd? It is not because he has two arms, two legs, a head, and a torso. These characteristics make him *similar* to all the others. Rather, it is his more subtle *differences,* such as facial features, walk, and voice, that allow you to distinguish him from everyone else. His unique characteristics are called his *critical attributes.* If your friend is an identical twin, however, you might have difficulty picking him out from his brother if both are in the crowd. Similarly, the high degree of similarity between two concepts, coupled with few differences, makes it difficult for the learner to tell them apart.

Take, for example, the concepts of latitude and longitude. The similarities between these two ideas far outweigh their differences. Both use identical units of measure, deal with all four compass points, are imaginary lines, locate points on the Earth's surface, and are similar in sound and spelling. Their only real difference is their orientation in space. Teaching them together can be very difficult because their many similarities obscure their singular difference. The problem of similarity can be pervasive because curriculums are often written with the most alike concepts taught together. In fact, a useful task for a committee rewriting a curriculum is to list those concepts that students find the most difficult. Then determine if the difficulty is that two very similar concepts or motor skills are taught together, resulting in confusion. See the **Practitioner's Corner** at the end of this chapter, p. 151, for precisely when this can be a problem and how to deal with it.

> *Two concepts that are very similar to each other ordinarily should not be taught at the same time.*

Critical Attributes

Transfer is sometimes generated when a special property, called a *critical attribute,* is recalled. Critical attributes, characteristics that make one idea unique from all others, are the cues of *difference* that learners can use as part of their storage process. Statements like *Amphibians live both on land and in water, Homonyms are words that sound alike but have different spellings and meanings*, and *To produce sound, something must vibrate* are examples of identifying a concept's critical attributes.

Identifying the critical attributes of a concept is a powerful memory tool, but it is not an easy task. We live in a culture driven by a quest for equality for all. This culture places a higher value on similarities than on differences. Thus, our cerebral networks are organized around similarity from an early age, and teachers frequently use similarity in the classroom to introduce new ideas. Successful retrieval from mental storage areas is accomplished by identifying differences among concepts. Consequently, teachers can help learners process new learnings accurately by having them identify the unique characteristics that make one concept different from all others. For example, what are the critical attributes of an explorer? Will these attributes help to separate Vasco da Gama from Napoleon Bonaparte? Students can use critical attributes to sort concepts so that they are stored in logical networks with appropriate cues. This will facilitate long-term memory's searches and increase the probability that it will accurately identify and retrieve the concept being sought.

Another useful task for a committee that is updating curriculum is to identify the critical attributes of all the major concepts that will be taught. If the committee members have difficulty agreeing on the critical attributes of a particular topic, imagine the challenge this will pose for the learner. See the **Practitioner's Corner** at the end of this chapter, p. 153, on how to identify critical attributes.

Association

Whenever two events, actions, or feelings are learned together, they are said to be *associated,* or bonded, so that the recall of one prompts the spontaneous recall of the other. The word *Romeo* elicits *Juliet,* and *Batman* gets *Robin.* A song you hear being played at a mall may elicit memories of some event that are associated with that song. The odor of a cologne once worn by a close friend from the past triggers the emotions of that relationship. Trademarks and product symbols, such as McDonald's golden arches, are designed to recall the product. Although there is no similarity between the two items, they were learned together and are, therefore, recalled together.

Here is a simple example of transfer. Look at the words listed below. On the lines to the right, write one or two words that come to mind as you read each word in the list.

Monday _____ _____

dentist _____ _____

Mom _____ _____

vacation _____ _____

babies _____ _____

emergency _____ _____

money　　　　_____　　　　_____

Sunday　　　　_____　　　　_____

What you wrote down represents thoughts that you have associated with each word in the list. Here are some responses that others have written for Monday: *work, blues, quarterback, beginning.* For Mom, others have written: *love, apple pie, caring, important, security, dad.* Were your words anything like these? Maybe they were, or maybe not. Show the list to your family and friends and note their responses. Each of us makes different connections with concepts based on our unique experiences; this activity points out the variety of associations that different people can make with the same thought.

> **The more we learn and retain, the more we can learn.**

Making associations expands the brain's ability to retain information. New connections are formed between neurons and new insights are encoded. Much like a tree growing new branches, everything we remember becomes another set of branches to which memories can be attached. The more we learn and retain, the more we *can* learn and retain.

Emotions Associated With Learning. Association is particularly powerful when feelings or emotions are associated with a learning. We mentioned earlier that the brain's amygdala encodes emotional messages when they are strong and bonds them to learnings for long-term storage. We also noted that emotions usually have a higher priority than cognitive processing for commanding our attention. Words like *abortion, Holocaust,* and *capital punishment* often evoke strong feelings. Math anxiety is an example of a strong feeling (probably failure) associated with mathematics. Some students will avoid new situations involving learning mathematics to avoid the negative feelings that are recalled with the content. On the other hand, people devote hours to their hobbies because they associate feelings of pleasure and success with these activities. Thus, teachers should strive to bond positive feelings to new learnings so that students feel competent and can enjoy the process. Positive emotions can be associated with learning whenever teachers do the following:

- Use humor (not sarcasm) as an integral part of the lesson.
- Design and tell stories that enhance understanding of the concepts. Studies show that stories engage all parts of the brain because they touch on the learner's experiences, feelings, and actions (Schank, 1990; Scott-Simmons, Barker, & Cherry, 2003).
- Incorporate real-world examples and activities that have meaning for the learners.
- Demonstrate that they really *care* about their students' success. This means spending less time on the class rules and test schedule, and more time on asking "How do *you* learn? What teaching strategies work best for you?" A 2004 Gallup poll of students indicated that they respond best to teachers who have plenty of latitude to be highly creative, to build strong relationships, and to tailor the learning process to the needs of each individual student (Gallup, 2004b).
- Learning new concepts is rarely a smooth-flowing linear progression. Rather, it is a dynamic with fits and starts, successes generating positive emotions and failures leading to negative feelings. When learning stalls, the teacher helps the student overcome negative emotions associated with failure by providing the support that leads the student to success—no matter how small that success is.

Teaching Methods

Teachers should not assume that transfer will automatically occur after students acquire a sufficient base of information. Significant and efficient transfer occurs only if we teach to achieve it. Hunter (2004), Mestre (2002), Perkins and Salomon (1988), and others have suggested that when teachers understand the factors that affect transfer, they can plan lessons that use the power of positive transfer to help students learn faster, solve problems, and generate creative and artistic products that enrich the learning experience.

To teach for transfer, we need to consider two major factors: The time sequence and the complexity of the transfer link between the learnings. The time sequence refers to the way the teacher will use time and transfer in the learning situation. Transfer can occur from past to present or from present to future.

Transfer From Past to Present

> **Past Learning** ⟶ **Helps in** ⟶ **Present Learning**

In this, the teacher links something from the learner's past that helps add sense and meaning to the new learning. It is important to select an experience that is clear, unambiguous, and closely relevant (not just related) to the new learning. Some examples are as follows:

- An English teacher uses *West Side Story* to introduce *Romeo and Juliet* so that students transfer their knowledge about street gangs and feuds to help them understand Shakespeare's plot.
- A science teacher asks students to recall what they have learned about plant cells to study the similarities and differences in animal cells.
- A social studies teacher asks students to think of the causes of the U.S. Civil War to see if they can also explain the causes of the Vietnam War.

Transfer From Present to Future

> **Present Learning** ⟶ **Helps in** ⟶ **Future Learning**

The teacher makes the present learning situation as similar as possible to a future situation to which the new learning should transfer. For the transfer to be successful, students must attain a high degree of original (current) learning and be able to recognize the critical attributes and concepts that make the situations similar and different. For example,

- Students learn the critical attributes of fact and opinion so they can transfer that learning in the future when evaluating advertising, news reports, election campaigns, and the like.

- Students learn how to read graphs, pie charts, and tables so that in the future they can evaluate data presented to them for analysis and action.
- Students learn safe personal and interpersonal hygiene practices to protect their health throughout their lives.

Teaching techniques, such as *bridging* and *hugging*, are designed to help students make transfer links from past to present, and present to future. They can be used in all subject areas and for learning both cognitive concepts and psychomotor skills. Examples of these techniques are found in the **Practitioner's Corners** at the end of this chapter on pp. 157 and 159.

Complexity of the Link Between Learnings

The way that transfer occurs during a learning situation can range from a very superficial similarity to a sophisticated, abstract association. For example, when renting a car, it takes just a few minutes to get accustomed to the model, find the windshield wiper and light controls, and drive off. Interpreting a pie chart in the school budget requires the recall of graph analysis skills from a prior mathematics course. The new learning environments are perceived as being *similar* to others that the learner has practiced, and that similarity automatically triggers the same learned behaviors.

> *Metaphors can convey meaning of abstract material as well and as rapidly as literal language.*

Metaphor, Analogy, and Simile. The transfer connection can also be much more complex, requiring the learner to make an abstract application of knowledge and skills to the new situation. Metaphors, analogies, and similes are useful devices for promoting abstract transfer. The *metaphor* is the application of a word or phrase to an object or concept that it does not literally denote to suggest a comparison with another object or concept. A person may say "It's raining cats and dogs outside. I'm drowned!" Obviously, it is not raining animals and the person did not drown. He is speaking figuratively and the metaphor compares things that are essentially dissimilar. An *analogy* compares partial similarity between two things, such as comparing a heart to a pump. The *simile* compares two unlike things: *She is like a rose.*

Metaphors can often convey meaning of abstract material as well and as rapidly as literal language. Metaphors help to explain complex concepts or processes. A geologist explains the movement of glaciers as flowing like batter on a griddle, and that the glacier was like an enormous plow upon the land. Comparing life to taking a long trip also is a metaphor. We ask the learner to reflect on how the situations encountered on the road compare to those encountered in life. How can the meaning of bumps, detours, road signs and billboards, places we have visited, passed through, or stayed in for a while all compare to life situations? Complex transfer patterns can reach back to the past: *How does the thinking strategy I used when I encountered a major detour help me to decide what course to choose in life now?* They can also transfer to the future: *The planning I used in preparing for the trip should help me prepare for other major decisions I need to make in my life that require extensive planning.*

These strategies are rich in imagery and enhance the thinking process by encouraging students to seek out associations and connections that they would not ordinarily make. They gain insights into relationships among ideas that help to forge a more thorough understanding of new learning. See more on imagery in Chapter 5; see also the **Practitioner's Corner** on p. 161 on using metaphors to enhance transfer.

Journal Writing for Transfer

Transfer is more likely to occur when students have an opportunity to reflect on their new learning. This reflection time can occur during closure, and is more likely to take place if the student is given a specific task. Journal writing is a very useful technique for closure because the specific steps help students to make connections to previous knowledge and organize concepts into networks for eventual storage. The strategy takes but a few minutes, but it can have enormous payback in terms of increased understanding and retention of learning. See the **Practitioner's Corner** on p. 163 for the specific steps that are likely to make this a successful effort.

> *Journal writing is a highly effective strategy for closure and transfer.*

Transfer and Constructivism

The proper and frequent use of transfer greatly enhances the constructivist approach to learning. Constructivist teachers (Brooks & Brooks, 1999) are those who:

- Use student responses to alter their instructional strategies and content
- Foster student dialogue
- Question student understanding before sharing their own
- Encourage students to elaborate on their initial responses
- Allow students time to construct relationships and create metaphors

All these strategies have been discussed here and in previous chapters and are characteristic of teachers who are proficient in using transfer deliberately throughout their lessons.

Additional Thoughts About Transfer

Transfer can be referred to as the "so what?" phase of learning. The context in which students learn information and skills is often different from the context where they will apply that learning. If students do not perceive how the information or skill can be used for the future, they will tend to pay little attention and exert even less effort. The cognitive research supports the notion that transfer occurs easier if students have processed the initial learning in ways that promote deep, abstract understanding of the material, rather than emphasizing the rote application of superficial similarities. Teachers help students achieve deep, abstract understandings when they involve students in multiple examples that illustrate the critical attributes in as wide a variety as possible.

Of course, there are times when some rote memorization is needed to facilitate transfer. In fact, research in areas such as reading and early mathematical development suggests that both conceptual learning and rote activities (e.g., decoding skills for reading, number facts for early mathematics) are important (Mestre, 2002).

Teaching strategies mentioned elsewhere in this book can enhance transfer. For example, using music and songs, or performing some physical movements when learning a particular concept allows students to associate these activities with the concept and assist in recall at some future time.

Transfer and High Stakes Testing. The recent attention to accountability and high stakes testing may actually work against efforts to increase the transfer of learnings. Teaching to the high stakes test might emphasize rote activities in place of strategies that foster the deep understandings needed for transfer. We need to devise tests that assess transfer of knowledge. Computer programs, for instance, can aid in devising assessments that look at deep conceptual processing. Assessments that focus on preparedness for future learning (e.g., solving a relatively complex novel problem) may be more revealing of transfer than those focused strictly on solving superficial problems in an isolated subject area.

What's Coming Up?

One of the most interesting discoveries about the brain in the last 40 years is the research evidence showing that each hemisphere specializes in performing certain functions. Subsequent studies have given researchers fascinating insights into how the brain is organized and clues about a broad range of cognitive processes. Brain specialization has also spawned some myths and stories that endure to this day. What are the facts and fallacies about the left and right sides of the brain? Why is this information so important for teachers and parents? The answers to these and other intriguing questions about brain specialization are found in the next chapter.

PRACTITIONER'S CORNER

Strategies for Connecting to Past Learnings

Transfer helps students make connections between what they already know and the new learning. It is important to remember that the connections are of value only if they are relevant to the *students'* past, not necessarily the teacher's. This process also helps the teacher find out what the students already know about the new material. If students already have knowledge of what is planned for the new lesson, then teachers should make some adjustments and move on. (The curriculum is notably cluttered with too much repetition at every grade level and in every subject area.) This method also alerts the teacher to any prior knowledge that may interfere with new learning (negative transfer). Here are a few suggestions to discover what students already know so that prior learnings can help facilitate new learning (positive transfer). Note that the activities use novelty and shift the task burden to the student. Choose those that are grade-level appropriate.

- **Short Story.** Students write short stories to describe what they already know about a given topic. This can be used in any subject area because writing is a skill that should be continually practiced. (Note: This activity is not journal writing, which serves a different purpose.)

- **Interviews.** In a think-pair-share format, students interview their partners to determine their knowledge levels.

- **Graphic Organizers.** Students select an appropriate graphic organizer to explain and relate their past learning.

- **Mural or Collage.** Students make a mural or collage to communicate their current knowledge.

- **Music Activity.** Students write a song that tells of their prior knowledge.

- **Models.** Students build or draw models to express what they know.

- **Student Ideas.** Students may suggest other ways of showing what they know, such as writing a poem, painting a picture, creating a quiz show, etc.

PRACTITIONER'S CORNER

Avoid Teaching Concepts That Are Very Similar

Teachers often use similarity to introduce new topics. They say, "You already learned something about this topic when we . . . " This helps students to use positive transfer by recalling similar items from long-term storage that can assist in learning new information. But as we saw in the Chapter 3 discussion on learning motor skills, similarity can also be a problem.

Whenever two concepts have many more similarities than differences, such as latitude and longitude, mitosis and meiosis, or simile and metaphor, there is a high risk that the learner cannot tell them apart. In effect, the similarities overwhelm the differences, resulting in the learner attaching the same retrieval cues to both concepts. Thus, when the learner uses that cue later to retrieve information, it could produce either or both concepts and the learner may not recognize which is correct.

How to Deal With This Problem. When planning a lesson with two very similar concepts, list their similarities and differences. If the number of similarities and differences is about the same, there is less chance the students will be confused, but if the number of similarities is far greater than the differences, confusion is likely. In that case, try the following:

- **Teach the Two Concepts at Different Times.** Teach the first concept. Make sure that the students thoroughly understand it and can practice it correctly. Then teach a related concept to give the first concept time to be consolidated accurately and fully into long-term storage. Teach the second concept a few weeks later. Now information from the first concept acts for positive transfer in learning the second concept.

- **Teach the Difference(s) First.** Another option is to start by teaching the difference(s) between the two concepts. This works better with older students because they have enough prior learnings to recognize subtle differences. For example, teach that the only real difference between latitude and longitude is their orientation in space, and that this can cause confusion when labeling a location. Focusing on and practicing the difference gives learners the warnings and the cues they need to separate the two similar concepts and identify them correctly in the future.

It seems so logical that two concepts that have many similarities should be taught at the same time. And so, for years, teachers have struggled with introducing concepts like the following in the same lesson: latitude and longitude; mitosis and meiosis; simile, analogy, and metaphor; complementary and supplementary angles; monarchy, oligarchy, plutocracy; writing lower-case b, d, p, and q, and many others. But the very fact that they are *so* similar can lead to retrieval problems.

To see how similarity may affect your work, try this activity:

A. Think about and list two or more concepts that are so similar they could cause confusion.

_____

_____

_____

_____

_____

_____

B. How could these concepts be presented to minimize confusion?

_____

_____

_____

_____

_____

_____

PRACTITIONER'S CORNER

Identifying Critical Attributes for Accurate Transfer

Critical attributes are characteristics that make one concept *unique* among all others. Teachers need to help students identify these attributes so students can use them for eventual and accurate retrieval. Hunter (2004) suggested a five-step process:

1. **Identify the Critical Attributes.** Suppose the learning objective is for the students to understand how mammals are different from all other animals. The two critical attributes of mammals are that (a) they nurse their young through mammary glands, and (b) they have hair.

2. **Teacher Gives Simple Examples.** The teacher offers some simple examples, such as the human being, cat, dog, and gerbil, to establish the concept. The teacher gives the examples at this point, not the students. Because this new learning is occurring in prime-time-1 when retention is highest, the examples must be correct. Be sure to match the example to the two critical attributes.

3. **Teacher Gives Complex Examples.** Now the teacher gives more complex examples, such as the porpoise and whale, which, unlike most mammals, live in water. It is important here to show again how the critical attributes apply.

4. **Students Give Examples.** Here the teacher checks for student understanding to ensure that the critical attributes are used correctly and that the concept is firmly in place. The students must also prove that the attributes apply to their examples.

5. **Teach the Limits of the Critical Attributes.** The learner must recognize that critical attributes may have limits and not apply in every instance. In this lesson, these attributes will accurately identify all mammals, but may incorrectly identify some nonmammals. There is a small group of animals called *platypuses*, that exhibit not only mammalian characteristics but also those of amphibians and birds. They are in a separate classification.

Take each major concept you teach and use the five-step process above to identify its critical attributes. These attributes help students clearly recognize what makes this concept *different* from all others. These attributes become valuable cues for accuracy and later retrieval.

By identifying the critical attributes, the student learns how one concept is different from all other similar concepts. This leads to clearer understanding, concept attainment, the ability to relate the new concept properly to others, and the likelihood that it will be stored, remembered, and recalled accurately. All subject areas have major concepts whose critical attributes should be clearly identified. Here are a few simple examples:

Social Studies

Law	Rule made by a government entity that is used for the control of behavior, is policed, and carries a penalty if broken.
Culture	The common behavior of a large group of people who can be identified by specific foods, clothing, art, religion, and music.
Democracy	A system of government in which the citizens have power through their elected representatives.

Science

Atom	The smallest part of an element that still retains the properties of that element.
Mammal	An animal that has hair and mammary glands.
Planet	A natural heavenly body that revolves around a star, rotates on its axis, and does not produce its own light.

Mathematics

Triangle	A two-dimensional figure that is closed and three-sided.
Prime	An integer with a value greater than 1 whose only positive factors are itself and 1.
Histogram	A bar graph that shows how many data values fall into a certain interval.

Language Arts

Sonnet	A poem of 14 lines, written in iambic pentameter with a specific rhyming pattern.
Simile	A figure of speech that compares two unlike things.
Hyperbole	An intentional exaggeration not intended to be taken literally.

Try the activity on the next page to help identify the critical attributes of important concepts from your own teaching or learning experiences.

A. Work with a partner to complete the worksheet on the next page, *Identifying Unique and Unvarying Elements*. Begin by using the Analogy Map below to help you decide on the differences between two similar concepts.

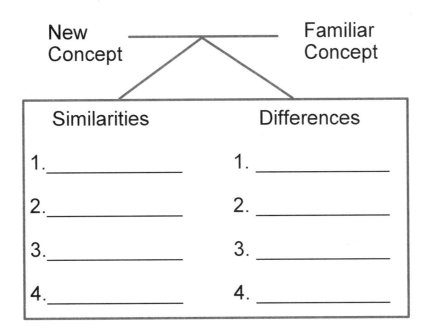

B. After completing the worksheet, decide what benefits are provided to the learner by identifying the unique and unvarying elements/critical attributes.

C. List here some concepts in your curriculum that would be good candidates for this strategy.

Worksheet on Identifying Unique and Unvarying Elements (Critical Attributes)

Identify a major concept and decide on its unique and unvarying elements (critical attributes).

Concept:_____

1. Its unique and unvarying elements (critical attributes) are

_____

_____

2. Simple examples are

_____

_____

3. Complex example(s) are

_____

_____

4. Student examples could be

_____

_____

5. Limits of the unique and unvarying elements (if any) are

_____

_____

PRACTITIONER'S CORNER

Teaching for Transfer: Bridging

Perkins and Salomon (1988), among others, have suggested various techniques for teachers to use to achieve positive transfer. In the technique called *bridging,* the teacher invokes transfer by helping students see the connection and abstraction from what the learner knows to other new learnings and contexts. There are many ways this can be accomplished. Here are a few:

- **Brainstorming.** When introducing a new topic, ask students to brainstorm ways this new learning can be applied in other situations. For example, can students use the skills they have just learned in analyzing charts, tables, and graphs? How else can they use their understandings about the law of supply and demand? What future value is there in knowing about nuclear power generation and alternative energy sources?

- **Analogies.** After learning a topic, use an analogy to examine the similarities and differences between one system and another. For example, ask students to make comparisons: How was the post-Vietnam War period in Vietnam similar to and different from the post-U.S. Civil War period in the United States? How is the post-Soviet Union period in Russia today similar to and different from the United States post-Revolutionary War period?

- **Metacognition.** When solving problems, ask students to investigate ways of approaching the solutions and discuss the advantages and disadvantages of each. For example, what solutions are there to meet the increased demand for electrical power in a densely populated area? What power sources could be used and which would be safest, most economical, most practical, etc.? What are the ways in which governments could regionalize to improve their effectiveness and economy of services? What impact might this have on local government and the democratic process? After applying their solutions, the students discuss how well their approaches worked and how they might change their approaches next time to improve their success.

The Brooklyn Bridge

Bridging: Invoking transfer by connecting what the learner knows to other new learning and contexts. Select a concept (e.g., energy, democracy, equilibrium, allegory) and use the strategies below to link that concept to the learner's past knowledge. Look at the **Practitioner's Corner** on concept mapping in Chapter 5, p. 200 for help with this task. *Brainstorming* (applying new learning in other situations):

_____

_____

Analogies (examining similarities and differences):

The Analogy Map could help here (see p. 202).

_____

_____

_____

Metacognition (solving problems by investigating advantages and disadvantages of alternative solutions):

Advantages	Disadvantages

PRACTITIONER'S CORNER

Teaching for Transfer: Hugging

Hugging, suggested by Perkins and Salomon (1988), uses similarity to make the new learning situation more like future situations to which transfer is desired. This is a lower form of transfer and relies on an almost automatic response from the learner when the new situation is encountered. Teachers should ensure that the similarity of a situation actually involves the student using the skill or knowledge to be transferred. When students use a word search puzzle to identify certain French verbs written forward or backward, this does not mean that they will be able to understand these verbs in written or spoken French. *Hugging* means keeping the new instruction as close as possible to the environment and requirements that the students will encounter in the future. Here are a few ways to design hugging:

- **Simulation Games.** These are useful in helping students practice new roles in diverse situations. Debates, mock trials, and investigating labor disputes are ways that students can experiment with various approaches to solving complex legal and social issues.

- **Mental Practice.** When a student is unable to replicate an upcoming situation, it is very useful for the student to mentally practice what that situation could be like. The student reviews potential variations of the situation and devises mental strategies for dealing with different scenarios. Suppose a student is to interview a political candidate for the school newspaper. In addition to the prepared questions, what other questions could the student ask, depending on the candidate's response? What if the candidate is reticent or changes the course of the questioning?

- **Contingency Learning.** Here the learner asks what other information or skill must be acquired to solve a problem, and then learns it. For example, if the student is building a model to demonstrate gas laws, what else must the student learn in order to design and construct the apparatus at a reasonable cost so that it shows the desired gas relationships effectively?

Hugging: Invoking transfer by making the new learning situation more like future situations to which transfer is desired. Select a concept (or the same one you chose in Bridging) and use the strategies that follow to show how the concept can be useful in future circumstances.

Simulation games (practicing new roles in diverse situations):

_____

_____

_____

Be prepared to present the simulation to the group.

Mental practice (devising mental strategies for dealing with different scenarios):

_____

_____

_____

Contingency learning (secondary learnings needed to accomplish primary learning):

_____

_____

_____

PRACTITIONER'S CORNER

Using Metaphors to Enhance Transfer

Metaphors can convey meaning as well and as rapidly as literal language. They are usually rich in imagery, are useful bridging strategies, and can apply to both content and skill learnings. West, Farmer, and Wolff (1991) suggest a seven-step process for using metaphors in lesson design.

1. **Select the Metaphor.** The criteria for selecting the appropriate metaphor center on goodness of fit (how well the metaphor explains the target concept or process), degree or richness of imagery, familiarity that the students will have with it, and its novelty.

2. **Emphasize the Metaphor.** The metaphor must be emphasized consistently throughout the lesson. Students should be alerted to interpret the metaphor figuratively and not literally.

3. **Establish Context.** Proper interpretation of the metaphor requires that the teacher establish the context for its use. Metaphors should not be used in isolation, especially if the students lack the background to understand them.

4. **Provide Instructions for Imagery.** Provide students with the instructions they will need to benefit from the rich imagery usually present in metaphors. "Form a mental picture of this" is good advice (See the **Practitioner's Corner** on imagery in Chapter 6, p. 237).

5. **Emphasize Similarities and Differences.** Because the metaphor juxtaposes the similarities of one known object or procedure with another, teachers should emphasize the similarities and differences between the metaphor and the new learning.

6. **Provide Opportunities for Rehearsal.** Use rote and elaborate rehearsal strategies to help students recognize the similarities and differences between the metaphor and the new learning, and to enhance their depth of understanding and types of associations.

7. **Beware Mixed Metaphors.** Because metaphors are such powerful learning devices, make sure you choose them carefully. Mixed metaphors cause confusion and lead to inaccuracy.

We used metaphors in designing the Information Processing Model (See the **Practitioner's Corner** in Chapter 2 on redesigning the model, p. 56) to help remember the important stages in the process. Now, let's practice it with a different concept.

Directions: Working with a partner, select a concept and decide what metaphor(s) would help you or your students remember it.

Concept:_____

Metaphor(s):

_____

_____

_____

_____

_____

_____

_____

_____

PRACTITIONER'S CORNER

Using Journal Writing to Promote Transfer and Retention

Journal writing can be a very effective strategy to promote positive transfer and increase retention. It can be done in nearly all grade levels and subject areas and is particularly effective when used as a closure activity.

Teachers may be reluctant to use this technique because they believe it takes up too much class time while adding more papers for them to evaluate. However, this strategy takes just three to five minutes, two or three times a week. That is, the teacher only spot checks journals periodically. The gain in student understanding and retention will be well worth the small amount of time invested. Here are some suggestions for using journal writing for maximum effectiveness:

- Students should keep a different journal for each class or subject area.

- To use this as a closure activity, ask students to write down their responses to these three questions:

  1. **"What did we learn today about** . . . (insert here the *specific* learning objective)?" Avoid questions like, "Write down what we did today," because younger students are likely to focus on activities rather than on the learning. This question helps to establish *sense*.

  2. **"How does this connect or relate to what we already know about** . . . (insert here some past learning that will help students with positive transfer)?" It is permissible to give hints to guide student thinking. After all, we want to facilitate accuracy. This question can help the learner *chunk* new learning into existing networks.

  3. **"How can this help us, or how can we use this information/skill in the future?"** Give hints if necessary. This question aids in finding *meaning*.

- You can use one day's journal entry as a prefocus activity for the following day, provided the new day's lesson is related.

Chapter 4—The Power of Transfer

Key Points to Ponder

Jot down on this page key points, ideas, strategies, and resources you
want to consider later. This sheet is your personal journal summary and
will help to jog your memory.

_____

_____

_____

_____

_____

_____

_____

_____

_____

_____

Chapter 5

Brain Specialization and Learning

Despite myriad exceptions, the bulk of split-brain research has revealed an enormous degree of lateralization—that is, specialization in each of the hemispheres.

—Michael Gazzaniga,
The Split Brain Revisited

Chapter Highlights: This chapter explores the research on how the brain is specialized to perform certain tasks. It examines hemispheric specialization, debunks some myths, and allows you to determine your hemispheric preference. The chapter also examines how we learn to speak and read, and the implications of this research for classroom instruction and for the curriculum and structure of schools.

I t may seem strange at a point this late in the book to introduce another chapter that focuses on brain function—in this case, how brain areas are specialized. But this functional specialization has led to the development of traits that are uniquely human, such as different learning styles and sophisticated spoken and written languages. These remarkable traits rely heavily on memory systems and transfer. Thus, I thought a review of how memory and transfer work was needed first in order to understand better the nature and impact of brain specialization on learning.

BRAIN LATERALIZATION

One of the intriguing characteristics of the human brain is its ability to integrate disparate and seemingly disconnected activities going on in specialized areas of the brain into a unified whole. Brain scans reveal how certain areas of the brain get involved in processing and performing specific tasks. For example, the auditory cortex responds to sound input, the frontal lobe to cognitive rehearsal, and sections of the left hemisphere to spoken language. The ability of certain areas of the brain to perform unique functions is known as cerebral *specialization*. If the activity is mainly limited to one hemisphere, it is called cerebral *lateralization*.

As evidence continues to accumulate regarding specialized brain areas, neuroscientists have had to modify their theories of brain organization accordingly. Researchers are now endorsing the idea that the brain is a set of modular units that carry out specific tasks. According to this *modular model*, the brain is a collection of units that supports the mind's information-processing requirements (e.g., a speech module, a numerical computation module, a face recognition module, etc.) and not a singular unit whose every part is capable of any function (Gazzaniga,1998a; Gazzaniga et al., 2002; Pinker, 1994; Rose, 2005).

The first indications of brain lateralization were discovered long before scanning technologies were developed. During the late 1950s, neurosurgeons decided that the best way to help patients with severe epileptic seizures was to sever the *corpus callosum* (Figure 1.2), the thick cable of 200 million nerve fibers that connects the two cerebral hemispheres. This last-ditch approach isolated the hemispheres so that seizures in the damaged hemisphere would not travel to the other side. The surgery had been tried on monkeys with epilepsy, and the results were encouraging. By the early 1960s, surgeons were ready to try the technique on human beings. One of the pioneers was Dr. Roger Sperry of the California Institute of Technology. Between 1961 and 1969, surgeons Joseph Bogen and Phillip Vogel successfully performed several operations under Sperry's guidance.

Although the operations resulted in a substantial reduction or elimination of the seizures, no one was sure what effect cutting this bridge between the hemispheres would have on the "split-brain" patients. Sperry and his student Michael Gazzaniga conducted experiments with these patients and made a remarkable discovery. Splitting the brain seemed to result in two separate domains of awareness. When a pencil was placed in the left hand (controlled by the right hemisphere) of a blindfolded patient, the patient could not name it. When the pencil was shifted to the right hand, however, the patient named it instantly. Neither hemisphere seemed to know what the other was doing and they acted, as Sperry said, "each with its own memory and will, competing for control."

As the tests progressed, Sperry charted the characteristics each hemisphere displayed. He concluded that each hemisphere seems to have its own separate and private sensations; its own perceptions; and its own impulses to act. This research showed that the right and left hemispheres have distinctly different functions that are not readily interchangeable. It also solved the mystery of the corpus callosum. Its purpose is largely to unify awareness and allow the two hemispheres to share memory and learning. Sperry won the 1981 Nobel Prize in medicine in part for this work.

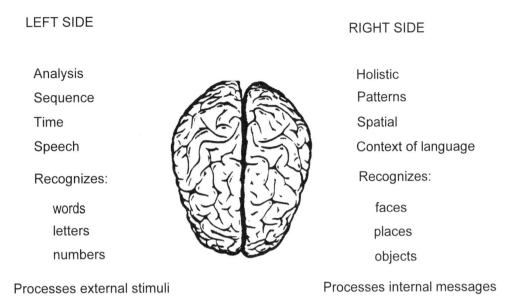

LEFT SIDE

Analysis
Sequence
Time
Speech

Recognizes:

words
letters
numbers

Processes external stimuli

RIGHT SIDE

Holistic
Patterns
Spatial
Context of language

Recognizes:

faces
places
objects

Processes internal messages

Figure 5.1 The left and right hemispheres of the brain are specialized and process information differently. However, in complex tasks, both hemispheres are engaged.

Left and Right Hemisphere Processing (Laterality)

Continued testing of split-brain patients and brain scans of normal (whole-brained) individuals have revealed considerable consistency in the different ways the two halves of the brain store and process information. This cerebral separation of tasks was earlier called *hemisphericity,* but is now more widely referred to as *laterality.* The results of numerous studies on laterality continue to provide more insights into the kind of processing done by each hemisphere and expand our understanding of this remarkable division of labor. Figure 5.1 summarizes and Table 5.1 shows more specifically the functions that the hemispheres carry out as they deal with the vast amount of new and past information that must be assessed every second.

Left Hemisphere

The left brain monitors the areas for speech. It understands the literal interpretation of words, and recognizes words, letters, and numbers written as words. It is analytical, evaluates factual material in a rational way, and detects time and sequence. It also performs simple arithmetic computations. Arousing attention to deal with outside stimuli is another specialty of the left hemisphere.

Right Hemisphere

The right brain gathers information more from images than from words, and looks for patterns. It interprets language through context—body language, emotional content, and tone of voice—rather

Table 5.1   Functions of the Left and Right Cerebral Hemispheres

Left Hemisphere Functions		Right Hemisphere Functions
Connected to right side of the body	**C**	Connected to the left side of the body
Processes input in a sequential and analytical manner	**O** **R**	Processes input more holistically and abstractly
Time-sensitive	**P** **U**	Space-sensitive
Generates spoken language	**S**	Interprets language through gestures, facial movements, emotions, and body language
Does invariable and arithmetic operations	**C** **A**	Does relational and mathematical operations
Specializes in recognizing words and numbers (as words)	**L** **L**	Specializes in recognizing faces, places, objects, and music
Active in constructing false memories	**O**	More truthful in recall
Seeks explanations for why events occur	**S** **U**	Puts events in spatial patterns
Better at arousing attention to deal with outside stimuli	**M**	Better at internal processing

Sources: Carter (1998); Gazzaniga (1998a,1998b); Gazzaniga, Ivry, & Mangun (2002)

than through literal meanings. It specializes in spatial perception, recognizes places, faces, and objects, and focuses on relational and mathematical operations, such as geometry and trigonometry.

What Causes Specialization?

No one knows exactly why the brain is specialized, although it does seem that such a capacity enables it to deal with a great amount of sensory data without going on overload. Why would we need two speech centers or face recognition areas? It would seem that as soon as one area of the brain acquired a specialization, there would be no need for it to be duplicated in the other hemisphere. How it *becomes* specialized is another question. The key to answering this may lie in the brain's structure and wiring. There is general agreement among neuroscientists now that the brain is hardwired for certain functions, such as spoken language, and that this hardwiring is localized.

Another possibility may center around the time it takes for signals to move in the brain. James Ringo and his colleagues (Ringo, Doty, Demeter, & Simard, 1994) used a neural network model that offered an possible explanation for hemispheric specialization. The researchers pointed out that nerve fibers within a hemisphere are shorter than the nerve fibers in the corpus callosum that run between hemispheres. As a result, nerve signals move faster *within* a hemisphere than *between* hemispheres. It would seem, then, that the brain has developed so that each hemisphere can have rapid access to information within itself, but a slower and more limited response to tasks that require communication back and forth across the corpus callosum. The time delays associated with communication between the hemispheres can limit the degree of their cooperation and encourage the development of hemispheric specialization.

Another factor may be that left and right hemispheres are physically different. The hemispheres are made up of the cortex (the thin but tough surface) called *gray matter* and the support tissue below it called *white matter*. The left hemisphere has more gray matter, while the right has more white. The left hemisphere's more tightly-packed neurons are better able to handle intense, detailed work. The right hemisphere's white matter contains neurons with longer axons that can connect with modules farther away. These long-range connections help the right to come up with broad but rather vague concepts. The information from each hemisphere is then pooled by sending signals across the corpus callosum (Carter, 1998).

Specialization Does Not Mean Exclusivity

The research data support the notion that each hemisphere has its own set of functions in information processing and thinking. However, these functions are rarely *exclusive* to only one hemisphere, and in even some simple tasks, it is possible for both hemispheres to be involved. Many tasks can be performed by either hemisphere, although one may be better at it than the other.

In a typical individual, the results of the separate processing are exchanged with the opposite hemisphere through the corpus callosum. There is harmony in the goals of each, and they complement one another in almost all

> *Although each hemisphere has specialized functions, both usually work together when learning.*

activities. Thus, the individual benefits from the integration of the processing done by both hemispheres and is afforded greater comprehension of whatever situation initiated the processing. For example,

- Logic is not confined to the left hemisphere. Some patients with right-brain damage fail to see the lack of logic in their thinking when they propose to take a walk even though they are completely paralyzed.
- Creativity or intuition is not solely in the right hemisphere. Creativity can remain, though diminished, even after extensive right-hemisphere damage.
- Because the two hemispheres do not function independently in a normal brain, it is impossible to educate only one hemisphere.
- Specialization does not mean **exclusivity**. There is no evidence that people are purely left or right brained. One hemisphere may be more active in most people, but only in varying degrees.
- Both hemispheres are capable of synthesis, that is, putting pieces of information together into a meaningful whole.

Hemispheric Preference: A Question of Learning Style

Since the work of Sperry, case studies and additional testing procedures have enabled researchers to understand more about the functions of each hemisphere. These tests include anesthetizing one hemisphere, PET imaging scans, electroencephalographs (which record electrical impulses), and hemisphere-specific vision and hearing tests. The research shows that most people have a preferred (or dominant) hemisphere, and that this preference affects personality, abilities, and learning style. Why this preference? No one knows for sure, any more than we know what causes handedness. It may be that if one hemisphere is more efficient than the other at developing within-hemisphere networks and processing, then that hemisphere contributes more during cognitive processing. As a result, hemispheric preference emerges.

> *Most people have a preferred hemisphere. This preference affects their personality, abilities, and learning style.*

Hemispheric preference is largely a matter of processing style. Just as some people prefer more visual than auditory information when learning, people with strong but opposite hemispheric preferences will interact and interpret their worlds differently. Hemispheric preference runs the gamut from neutral (no preference) to strongly left or right. Those who are left-hemisphere preferred tend to be more verbal, analytical, and able to solve problems. Right-hemisphere-preferred individuals paint and draw well, are good at math, and deal with the visual world more easily than with the verbal (Springer & Deutsch, 1998).

Once again, the preference for either hemisphere does not mean that we do not use both hemispheres. In doing a simple task, we use more the hemisphere which specializes in that task. When we are faced with a task that is more complex, the preferred hemisphere will take the lead, although the nonpreferred hemisphere will likely get involved as well, contributing in its specialized manner (Weisman & Banich, 2000).

Preference and Consciousness

One of the more fascinating revelations from the continued studies of split-brain patients is the realization that their left and right hemispheres can give different answers to questions about themselves. It is as though they have a distinct consciousness residing in each hemisphere. For example, the inventive left hemisphere's consciousness surpasses that of the right. But the mind-boggling suggestion here is that even though our consciousness reflects that of the preferred hemisphere, another—and perhaps very different—consciousness lurks hidden in the nonpreferred hemisphere (Gazzaniga, 1998b). Sperry, himself, suspected as much of his split-brain patients. He wrote, "Everything we have seen indicates that the surgery has left these people with two separate minds . . . that is, two separate spheres of consciousness" (Sperry, 1966).

Examples of Preference

Suppose you are right-handed. A pen is on the table just next to your left hand, and someone asks you to pass the pen. Because this is a simple task, you will pick up the pen with your left hand in a smooth motion and pass it. You are not likely to stretch your right hand across your body or twist your torso to hand it over. If the person asks you to throw the pen, however, you will probably use your right hand because this task is more difficult.

During learning, both hemispheres are engaged, processing the information or skill according to their specializations and exchanging the results with the opposite hemisphere through the corpus callosum. So if someone were to toss a pen to you, your likelihood of successfully catching it would increase greatly if you used *both* hands, not just the right (dominant) hand.

Knowing the difference between how the left and right hemispheres process information explains why we succeed with some tasks but not with others, especially when we are trying to do them simultaneously. For instance, most of us can carry on a conversation (left-hemisphere activity) while driving a car (right-hemisphere and cerebellar activity). In this case, each task is controlled by different hemispheres. However, trying to carry on a conversation on the telephone while talking to someone in the room at the same time is very difficult because these are functions of the same (left) hemisphere and can interfere with each other.

Implications of Preference for Teachers

Hemispheric preference is just one component of learning style. Because teachers tend to teach the way they learn, they need to know as much about their own learning style as possible. Besides telling them something about themselves, this knowledge also helps them to understand learners with very different styles. To determine your hemispheric preference, see the **Practitioner's Corner** at the end of this chapter on p. 191.

So What? Cautions About Interpreting Hemispheric Preference

Perhaps no single piece of brain research has received so much attention and controversy as the notion that the two hemispheres of the brain process information differently. Although a substantial body of evidence suggests that each hemisphere has its specialized abilities, we should not jump to the conclusion that normal people have two brains or are functioning with only half a brain. The differences are not all-or-nothing. Quite the contrary, normal people have one integrated and magnificently differentiated brain that generates a single mind and self.

Unfortunately, some people have misused this research, referring to themselves, or worse, to students as "too left-brained" or "too right-brained." What is important to remember is that the two hemispheres work together as an integrated whole, sharing their different stimuli through the corpus callosum. Nevertheless, misinformation about the specialization of the hemispheres and several popular myths persist.

Some Myths About Hemispheric Preference

Several myths connecting hemispheric preference to other variables have evolved and endured during the past two decades. The myths have obscured the benefit of this research and undermined its value to the teaching and learning process. Here are two common myths we can debunk.

Handedness (lateral preference). Because the hemispheres of the brain control the opposite sides of the body, many have speculated that hemispheric preference is directly connected to handedness, or lateral preference. There is evidence that more right-hemisphere-preferred individuals are left-handed than right-handed. Scanning evidence also shows that most right-handers (about 93 to 95 percent) have left-hemisphere language preference (Knecht et al., 2000), whereas only 70 percent of left-handers have left-hemisphere language preference; the other 30 percent have language preference in the right or in both hemispheres (Carter, 1998). However, no direct cause-and-effect connection between handedness and hemispheric preference has been established. Thus, it is incorrect to assume that most right-handed people are left-hemisphere preferred and vice versa.

Handedness is established in the fetus by the fifteenth week of gestation. Despite all the sophisticated brain research of modern times, the cause of handedness has still escaped explanation. With nearly 90 percent of people right-handed, this would seem to be the outcome of the logical left hemisphere's control. Is left-handedness, then, pathological? Explanations run from simple genetic determination to some pre-natal disturbance that may have upset the left-brain/right-hand connection, such as unusually high testosterone levels. The mystery continues.

Intelligence. There is no research to support the notion that those with one hemispheric preference are any more or less intelligent than those with the opposite preference. Individuals who are strongly and oppositely preferred will exhibit vastly different personalities and learning styles, but this has no connection to intelligence or the ability to learn.

The Gender Connection

Scientists have known for years that there are structural and developmental (Table 5.2) as well as performance differences (Table 5.3) between male and female brains. Studies begun in the early 1970s and subsequent studies by other researchers have shown some gender differences in brain characteristics and capabilities. PET scans and fMRIs, for instance, indicate that males and females use different areas of their brains when accomplishing similar tasks (Cahill, 2005; Diamond & Hopson, 1998; Kimura, 1992; Yegger, 2002). Let's see what those differences are before we discuss what they mean. Keep in mind that research studies deal with groups of males and females. It is not always valid to assign characteristics to a specific person because individuals vary widely from one to another.

Structural and Developmental Differences

- Males have a higher percentage of gray matter (the thin cortex layer containing mostly dendrites) in the left hemisphere than females. In females, the percentage of gray matter is the same in both hemispheres. However, females have a higher percentage of total gray matter, whereas males have a higher percentage of white matter (mainly myelinated axons below the cortex layer) and cerebral spinal fluid. The corpus callosum (cable connecting the hemispheres) is proportionately larger and thicker in females than in males (Gazzaniga et al., 2002; Gur et al, 1999). All of these differences could be further evidence to support the idea that female brains are better at communicating between hemispheres and male brains within those hemispheres.

- For most males and females, the language areas are in the left hemisphere. But females also have an active language processor in the right hemisphere (Figure 5.2). Females possess a greater density of neurons in the language areas than males (Gazzaniza et al., 2002; Gur et al., 2000; Shaywitz, 2003; Shaywitz, Shaywitz, & Gore, 1995).
- The amygdala (which responds to emotional stimulation), loaded with testosterone receptors, grows more rapidly in teenage boys than in teenage girls, and

Figure 5.2 While processing language, fMRI scans show that male brains (left) use left hemisphere regions and that female brains activate regions in both hemispheres (white areas).

Table 5.2 Structural and Developmental Differences Between Female and Male Brains

	Females	**Males**	**Sources**
Gray matter	Higher percentage than males, with same amount in both hemispheres.	Lower percentage than females, with more in left hemisphere than right.	Gur et al., 1999
White matter	Lower percentage than males.	Higher percentage than females, with same amount in both hemispheres	Gur et al., 1999
Cerebral spinal fluid	Lower percentage than men, with same amount in both hemispheres	Higher percentage than females, with more in right hemisphere than left	Gur et al., 1999
Corpus callosum	Larger and thicker than in males	Smaller and thinner than in females	Gazzaniga et al., 2002; Gur et al, 1999
Language areas	Main areas in left hemisphere, with additional processing areas in right hemisphere. Density of neurons in language areas greater than in males.	Located almost exclusively in left hemisphere. Density of neurons in language areas less than in females.	Cahill, 2005; Gazzaniga et al., 2002; Gur et al., 2000; Shaywitz, 2003
Amygdala	Grows slower in teenage girls than in boys, and final size is smaller than in males. Only left amygdala activated by emotional stimulation.	Grows faster in teenage boys than in girls, and final size is larger than in females. Only right amygdala activated by emotional stimulation.	Cahill, 2005; Kreeger, 2002
Hippocampus	Grows faster in teenage girls than in boys, and final size is larger than in males	Grows slower in teenage boys than in girls, and final size is smaller than in females	Kregger, 2002

Table 5.3   Performance Differences Between Female and Male Brains

	Females	**Males**	**Sources**
Testing	No different from males in overall cognitive performance, but better than males on tests of perceptual speed, verbal fluency, determining the placement of objects (sequence), identifying specific attributes of objects, precision manual tasks, and arithmetic calculations.	No different from females in overall cognitive performance, but better than females on spatial tasks, such as mentally rotating three-dimensional objects, at target-directed motor skills, at spotting shapes embedded in complex diagrams, and in mathematical reasoning.	Cahill, 2005; Gazzaniga et al., 2002; Gur et al., 2000; Kimura, 1997; Njemanze, 2005
Facial recognition and expressions	Use more of their left hemisphere	Use more of their right hemisphere	Baron-Cohen, 2003; Everhart, Shucard, Quatrin, & Shucard, 2001

its final size is larger in men than in women. This is at least a partial explanation of why males tend to demonstrate more overt aggressive behavior than females. PET scans reveal that during emotional stimulation, females tend to activate only the amygdala in the left hemisphere while males tend to activate the amygdala only in the right hemisphere. Follow-up studies noted that females remembered the details of an emotional event (a typical left hemisphere function) better than males, whereas the males remembered better the central aspects, or gist, of the situation (Cahill, 2005; Kreeger, 2002).

- Meanwhile, the hippocampus (responsible for memory formation and consolidation), filled with estrogen receptors, grows more rapidly in girls than boys during adolescence (Kreeger, 2002). This could explain why preadolescent girls are generally better at language, arithmetic computations, and tasks involving sequence because all these depend on efficient memory processing.

Performance Differences

- There is no significant difference in overall cognitive performance between the sexes. However, on specific skills, more females perform better on tests of perceptual speed, verbal fluency, determining the placement of objects (sequence), identifying specific attributes of objects, precision manual tasks, and arithmetic calculations. More males perform better on spatial tasks, such as mentally rotating three-dimensional objects, at target-directed motor skills, at spotting shapes embedded in complex diagrams, and in mathematical reasoning

(Cahill, 2005; Gazzaniga et al., 2002; Gur et al., 2000; Neubauer, Grabner, Fink, & Neuper, 2005; Njemanze, 2005).

- When recalling emotions, females use a larger portion of their limbic system than do males. Females are also better at recognizing different types of emotions in others (Baron-Cohen, 2003).
- In face recognition and expression tasks, boys use more of their right brain while girls use more of their left (Everhart, Shucard, Quatrin, & Shucard, 2001).

The results of these and other studies further indicate that more females are left-hemisphere preferred and more males are right-hemisphere preferred. Why is this so? To what extent do nature (genetic makeup) and nurture (environment) contribute to these structural and performance differences? Although no one knows for sure, the research evidence suggests that the influence of prenatal hormones, natural selection, and environment could explain these results.

Possible Causes of Gender Differences

The Effects of Hormones. One possibility is that hormones, such as testosterone and androgen, influence brain development differently in the sexes. As they bathe the fetal brain, these substances direct the wiring and organization of the brain and stimulate the growth and density of neurons in specific areas. Testosterone, for instance, seems to delay the development of the left hemisphere in boys. Thus, girls get a head start in using the left hemisphere; boys are forced to rely more on their right hemisphere (this might also explain why more males are left-handed than females). The early exposure to these hormones seems to alter other brain functions (such as language acquisition and spatial perception) permanently for the individual. The resurgence of hormones with the onset of puberty may further reconfigure the mental organization of teens, especially as new social pressures emerge with their accompanying emotional shifts (Cahill, 2005; Kimura, 1992, 1997; Lutchmaya, Baron-Cohen, & Raggatt, 2002).

The Effects of Natural Selection. A related explanation is that natural selection affected our brain characteristics as we evolved. For thousands of years, the division of labor between the sexes was distinct. In prehistoric times, men were responsible for hunting large game over long distances, making weapons, and defending the group from predators, animal and otherwise. Women took care of the home and the children, prepared food, and made clothing. Such specialization required different cerebral operations from men and women. Men needed more route-finding and spatial abilities and better targeting skills. Women needed more fine-motor and timing skills to maintain the household and language skills to pass on the native language to their offspring. The individual males and females who could perform their respective tasks well survived long enough to pass their genes on to their children. Moreover, any new genetic combinations eventually led to structural changes in the brain—and other parts of the body—that were specific to each gender.

The Impact of the Environment. Another prevailing explanation looks to a combination of the different ways the sexes develop and interact with their environment. First, studies of infant boys and girls demonstrate that the acuity of senses does not develop identically in both genders. That is, hearing and touch (left-hemisphere controlled) develop more quickly in girls. Spatial vision (right-hemisphere controlled), however, develops more rapidly in boys. Second, parents tend to treat baby boys differently from baby girls. And third, boys and girls between the ages of 6 and 12 typically spend their out-of-school time quite differently as they are growing up. Girls are more likely to spend their free time indoors. In this structured environment, girls are exposed to more language through radio and television, and they are more conscious of time because of clocks, media, and other family members who may be coming home. This environment, psychologists argue, enhances left-hemisphere processes. On the other hand, more boys spend their free time outdoors. In this unstructured environment, boys rely more on space (location) than time, design their own games, use more visual than verbal skills during play, and use little language and only in context to accomplish a task. This behavior enhances right-hemisphere processes.

The Empathizing Female and Systemizing Male. Simon Baron-Cohen (2003) has summarized the essential laterality differences by proposing that female brains are predominantly wired for empathy, and that male brains are predominantly wired for systemizing, that is, understanding and building systems. According to his intriguing theory, a person (whether female or male) can be one of three brain types. An individual who is stronger at empathizing than systemizing is Type E. Those who are stronger at systemizing are Type S, and those who are equally strong at both are Type B (for balanced). Baron-Cohen believes that the effects of hormones during prenatal and early postnatal development are largely responsible for these sex differences. He does, however, admit that genetic traits and the environment also exert their influence.

> *The brains of males and females organize differently from very early in their development through their formative years, leading to different preferences in learning.*

Baron-Cohen rightly points out something we should all remember as we study differences in the human brain: sex does not solely determine how an individual's brain is organized. Some males will have brains organized more like females, and some females will have brains organized more like males. Individuals of any brain type can be successful in any endeavor.

The evidence suggests that we no longer think in terms of nature versus nurture. Rather, we should see the relationship of these forces as more circular. Genes influence behavior, and behavior can influence how genes function as a child grows and develops. Thus, a combination of nature and nurture factors causes the brains of males and females to organize differently from very early in their development through their formative years, leading, among other things, to different preferences in learning and how they interact with their world.

> *More girls than boys are left-hemisphere preferred; more boys than girls are right-hemisphere preferred. The reasons are not as important as our response.*

However, during the past decade, technology, such as video games and computers, has had significant impact on how and where children occupy their spare time. It is possible that this impact has already begun to narrow the current differences in the hemispheric preferences of the genders and will continue to do so in the coming years.

Regardless of the source of these preferences, **we should avoid using hemispheric preference to stereotype individuals**, to assume that one preference is better than another, or that persons cannot accomplish certain tasks because of their preference. The cause of hemispheric preference, for all practical purposes, is not relevant. It is our response that really matters. We can use this research to understand better how hemispheric preference affects learning and what teachers can do about it in their classrooms.

Schools and Hemispheric Preference

Recognizing that hemispheric preference is a contributor to learning style, the question arises as to whether school climate and classroom instruction are designed to embrace different styles so that all learners can succeed. Is it possible that schools may be designed inadvertently to favor one type of learning style over another?

Left-Hemisphere Schools?

Take a moment to think about the entire schooling process that takes place from kindergarten through grade 12. During this mental review, look again at the list of left- and right-hemisphere functions. Is K–12 schooling best described by the characteristics listed for the left hemisphere, the right hemisphere, or both equally? Most educators readily admit that schools are predominantly left-hemisphere oriented, especially in the elementary grades. Schools are structured environments that run according to time schedules, favor facts and rules over patterns, and offer predominantly verbal instruction, especially at the secondary level.

This means that left-hemisphere preferred learners (mainly girls) feel more comfortable in this environment. The stronger the left-hemisphere preference, the more successful these learners can be. Conversely, right-hemisphere preferred learners (mainly boys) are not comfortable; the stronger the right-hemisphere preference, the more hostile the learning environment seems. This could explain why most teachers admit that they have many more discipline problems with boys than with girls. Maybe what this research

> *Most K–12 public schooling inadvertently favors left-hemisphere-preferred learners.*

is saying is that boys (more accurately, right-hemisphere-preferred learners) are not born with a "mean gene," but are too often placed in uncomfortable learning environments where they react rebelliously. This might also partially explain why over twice as many boys as girls are in remedial and special education programs nationally. Curiously, there are over 11 percent more girls than boys enrolled in gifted and talented programs (USDOE, 2000).

The currently popular notion of differentiating instruction should recognize that young female and male brains do not mature at the same time. More boys, then, may succeed in schools that recognize different learning styles and individualize instruction accordingly. All students will achieve more when teachers purposefully plan strategies that teach to the whole brain by addressing the strengths and weaknesses of both genders. See the **Practitioner's Corner** at the end of this chapter on strategies for teaching to the whole brain, starting on page 194.

Impact on Mathematics and Science Programs

A major storm erupted in 2005 when the president of Harvard University suggested that males may have more intrinsic aptitude for science (and presumably higher mathematics) than females. Male and female brains deal differently with numbers and computation. However, scanning studies indicate that gender differences in computational processing are more pronounced in preadolescence and become much less important when the brain encounters higher mathematics (Dehaene, Spelke, Pinel, Stanescu, & Tsivkin, 1999). In other words, the genetic (nature) component is less significant than we once thought. It seems more likely that social and cultural forces have had greater influence. Boys in secondary schools are encouraged by their parents and teachers to take more mathematics and science, their experiences in such classes are more compatible with their hemispheric preferences, and they thus score better on tests in these areas. Girls, on the other hand, often encounter a stereotype that presumes females are poor performers in mathematics. One study showed that female performance on mathematics tests was lower than males just because of the existence of this stereotype, and that female performance improved once the stereotype threat was removed (Spencer, Steele, & Quinn, 1999).

The good news is that the gender gap is narrow. The percentage of girls taking various mathematics and science courses is close to or exceeds that of boys, and their test scores on a national average are only a few points lower and not statistically significant (NCES, 2003). This is an encouraging trend. In part, the explanation for this outcome may be the use of computers in the classroom. Both boys and girls are on a level playing field. Computer lessons are not closely linked with past successes or failures, representing a new set of skills that both boys and girls are learning at a very early age. Moreover, computers are patient and fun, contributing to novelty and the fulfillment of expectations of success.

Our job now is to ensure that educators and parents recognize that boys may have some different learning preferences from girls, but that both genders have similar *capabilities* to succeed in mathematics and science. To that end, we need to curb the cultural and social forces that would feed past stereotypes about whether students of a certain gender should take only certain subjects. There is plenty of evidence that when girls are encouraged and motivated, they can excel at science and mathematics. It is worth repeating here that scientific studies tell us about averages within groups and nothing about how any particular individual will succeed or fail in any subject area.

SPOKEN LANGUAGE SPECIALIZATION

Many animals have developed ways to communicate with other members of their species. Birds and apes bow and wave appendages; honeybees dance to map out the location of food; and even one-celled animals can signal neighbors by emitting an array of different chemicals. By contrast, human beings have developed an elaborate and complex means of spoken communication that many say is largely responsible for our place as the dominant species on this planet. Spoken language is truly

Some Specialized Areas of the Brain

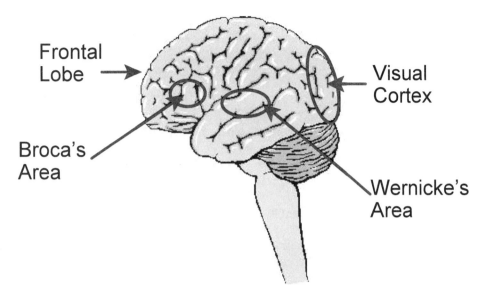

Figure 5.3   Broca's area and Wernicke's area, located in the left hemisphere, are the two major language processing centers of the brain. The visual cortex across the back of both hemispheres, processes visual stimuli, including reading.

a marvelous accomplishment for many reasons. At the very least, it gives form to our memories and words to express our thoughts. The human voice can pronounce all the vowel and consonant sounds that allow it to speak any of the estimated 6,500 languages that exist today. With practice, the voice becomes so fine-tuned that it makes only about one sound error per million sounds and one word error per million words (Pinker, 1994).

Long before the advent of scanning technologies, scientists explained how the brain produced spoken language on the basis of evidence from injured brains. In the 1860s, French surgeon Paul Broca noted that damage to the left frontal lobe induced language difficulties generally known as *aphasia,* wherein patients muttered sounds or lost speech completely. Broca's area (just behind the left temple) is about the size of a quarter. A person with damage to Broca's area (Figure 5.3) could understand language but could not speak fluently.

Later, in the 1870s, German neurologist Carl Wernicke described a different type of aphasia— one in which patients could not make sense out of words they spoke or heard. These patients had damage in the left temporal lobe. Wernicke's area (above the left ear) is about the size of a silver dollar. Those with damage to Wernicke's area could speak fluently, but what they said was quite meaningless. The inferences, then, were that Broca's area processed vocabulary, grammar, and probably syntax of one's native language, while Wernicke's area was the site of native language sense and meaning.

But more recent research, using scanners, indicates that spoken language production is a far more complex process than previously thought. When preparing to produce a spoken sentence, the brain uses not only Broca's and Wernicke's areas, but also calls on several other neural networks scattered

Spoken Language Development

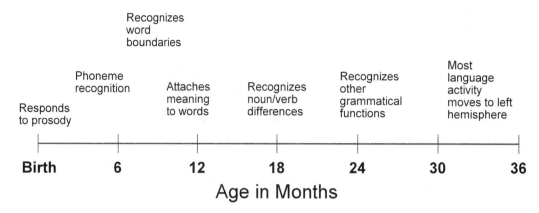

Figure 5.4 An average timeline of spoken language development during the child's first 3 years. There is considerable variation among individual children.

throughout the left hemisphere. Nouns are processed through one set of patterns; verbs are processed by separate neural networks. The more complex the sentence structure, the more areas that are activated, including the right hemisphere, although more so in females than in males.

Learning Spoken Language

Although early language learning begins in the home, schools are largely responsible for enhancing the spoken language of children and teaching them to read. How quickly and successfully the brain learns to read is greatly influenced by the spoken language competence the child has developed. Therefore, it is important to understand what cognitive neuroscience has revealed about how the brain acquires and processes spoken words. Figure 5.4 presents a general timeline for spoken language development during the first three years of growth. The chart is a rough approximation. Obviously, some children will progress faster or slower than the chart indicates. Nonetheless, it is a useful guide for parents and teachers to show the progression of skills acquired during the process of learning language (Sousa, 2005).

Learning Sounds Called Phonemes

The neurons in a baby's brain are capable of responding to the sounds of all the languages on this planet. At birth (some say even before birth) babies respond first to the *prosody*—the rhythm, cadence, and pitch—of their mothers' voice, not the words. Spoken language consists of minimal units of sound, called *phonemes*, which combine to form syllables. For example, in English, the consonant sound "t" and the vowel sound "o" are both phonemes that combine to form the syllable *to-* as in *tomato*. Different languages have different numbers of phonemes. It can be as few as 15 in some languages to well over 40 in English. The total number of phonemes in all

> **The neurons in a baby's brain are capable of responding to the sounds of all the languages on this planet.**

the world's languages is around 90, which represents the maximum number of sounds that the human voice apparatus can create (Beatty, 2001).

Although the infant's brain can perceive the entire range of phonemes, only those that are repeated get attention, as the neurons reacting to the unique sound patterns are continually stimulated and reinforced. By the age of 10 to 12 months, the toddler's brain has begun to distinguish and remember phonemes of the native language and to ignore foreign sounds. For example, one study showed that at the age of 6 months, American and Japanese babies are equally good at discriminating between the "l" and "r" sounds, even though Japanese has no "l" sound. However, by age 10 months, Japanese babies have a tougher time making the distinction, while American babies have become much better at it. During this and subsequent periods of growth, the ability to distinguish native sounds improves, while one's ability to distinguish nonnative speech sounds diminishes (Cheour et al., 1998).

From Phonemes to Words

The next step for the brain is to detect words from the stream of sounds it is processing. This is not an easy task because people don't pause between words when speaking. Yet the brain has to recognize differences between, say, *green house* and *greenhouse*. Remarkably, babies begin to distinguish word boundaries by the age of 8 months even though they don't know what the words mean (Van Petten & Bloom, 1999). Before they reach the age of 12 months, many babies can learn words in one context and understand them in another (Schafer, 2005). They begin to acquire new vocabulary words at the rate of about 8 to 10 a day. At the same time, memory and Wernicke's areas are becoming fully functional so the child can now attach meaning to words. Of course, learning words is one skill; putting them together to make sense is another, more complex skill.

Learning Grammar

In the 1950s, MIT linguist Noam Chomsky argued that all languages contain some common rules that dictate how sentences are constructed, and that the brain has preprogrammed circuits that respond to these rules. Modern linguists think that the brain may not be responding so much to basic language rules as to statistical regularities heard in the flow of the native tongue. They soon discern that some words describe objects while others describe actions. Toddlers detect patterns of word order—person, action, object—so they can soon say, "I want cookie." Other grammar features emerge, such as tense, and by the age of 3, over 90 percent of sentences uttered are grammatically correct. Errors are seldom random, but usually result from following perceived rules of grammar.

If "I batted the ball" makes sense, why shouldn't "I holded the bat" also make sense? Regrettably, the toddler has yet to learn that nearly 200 of the most commonly used verbs in English are irregularly conjugated (Pinker, 1994).

During the following years, practice in speaking and adult correction help the child decode some of the mysteries of grammar's irregularities and a sophisticated language system emerges from what once was babble. No one knows how much grammar a child learns just by listening, or how much is pre-wired. What is certain is that the more children are exposed to spoken language in the early years, the more quickly they can discriminate between phonemes and recognize word boundaries.

> *Although toddlers may be attracted to the rapidly changing sounds and images on a television, there is little or no language development in progress. Television may actually impair a toddler's brain development.*

Just letting the toddler sit in front of a television does not seem to accomplish this goal, probably because the child's brain needs live human interaction to attach meaning to the words. Moreover, television talk is not the slow, expressive speech that parents use with their infants, which infants like and want to hear. Although toddlers may be attracted to the rapidly changing sounds and images on a television, little or no language development is in progress. There is further evidence that prolonged television watching can impair the growth of young brains. A recent longitudinal study indicated that the more television toddlers had watched before the age of 3 years, the lower their scores on later tests of reading achievement and number manipulation (Zimmerman & Christakis, 2005).

Language Delay

Most toddlers begin to speak words around the age of 10 to 12 months. In some children, there is a delay and they may not speak coherent words and phrases until nearly 2 years of age. There is evidence that this language delay to 2 years is inherited, and thus represents a distinct disorder not easily remedied by environmental interventions. This revelation diminishes the claim some people make that mainly environmental influences cause language delay (Dale et al., 1998).

Implications

Given the evidence that the brain's ability to acquire spoken language is at its peak in the early years, parents should create a rich environment that includes lots of communication activities, such as talking, singing, and reading. In schools, it means addressing any language-learning problems quickly to take advantage of the brain's ability to rewire improper connections during this important period of growth. It also means that parents and teachers should not assume that children with language-learning problems are going to be limited in cognitive thought processes as well.

Learning a Second Language

The power of a young child's brain to learn spoken languages is so immense that it can learn several languages at one time. But by the age of 10 to 12 months, the brain is already beginning to lose its ability to discriminate sounds between its native language and nonnative languages. The implication here is that if we wish children to acquire a second language, it makes sense to start that acquisition during the early years when the brain is actively creating phonemic sound and syntactic networks.

> *Proficiency in learning a second language depends not on how long nonnatives have been speaking the language, but on how early in life they began learning it.*

Studies show that proficiency in learning a second language depends not on *how long* non-natives have been speaking the language, but on *how early in life* they began learning it. Researchers Jacqueline Johnson and Elissa Newport found that immigrants who started speaking English at ages 3 to 7 spoke like natives and with no discernible accent. Those who started speaking between ages of 8 and 10 had about 80 percent of the proficiency of native speakers; those who started between ages 11 and 15 spoke with only half the proficiency, and those who started after age 17 had only about 15 percent of the proficiency of the average person born in America (Johnson & Newport, 1991). This indicates that the window of opportunity (see Chapter 1) for language acquisition slides down in the preteen years so that learning a second language later is certainly possible, but more difficult.

Why Is It More Difficult to Learn a Second Language Later?

For most people, the brain areas primarily involved in language acquisition are not very responsive to foreign sounds after the preteen years. Thus, additional areas of the brain must be programmed to recognize, distinguish, and respond to foreign phonemes. Furthermore, scanning studies using fMRIs show that second languages acquired in adulthood show some spatial separation in the brain from native languages. However, when acquired in the preteen years, native and second languages are represented in the same frontal areas (Broca's area). Hence, younger and older brains react to second language learning very differently (Kim, Relkin, Lee, & Hirsch, 1997; Perani & Abutalebi, 2005; Silverberg & Samuel, 2004).

> *Although young brains are naturally adept at language learning, this research should not be interpreted to discourage adolescents and adults from pursuing second language study.*

Although it seems that younger brains are more adept at language learning, this research should not be interpreted to discourage adolescents and adults from pursuing second language study. Nor should it be assumed that youngsters will become fluent solely by studying a second language a few hours a week in the primary grades. Like learning any skill, continuous practice is needed for fluency. Further, the difficulties facing adults learning a second language are very different from those of children. For example, the phonemes, grammar, and syntax rules of the native language are likely to interfere somewhat (an example of negative transfer) with learning those of the second language (Iverson et al., 2003). If these difficulties are properly addressed, then learning a second language as an adult can be a rewarding experience, although it may require more focus, more effort, and greater motivation. See the **Practitioner's Corner** on p. 204 at the end of this chapter on acquiring a second language.

LEARNING TO READ

Let's take a little time now to discuss the one area where neuroscience has made its most important contribution to teaching and learning to date—understanding how the brain learns to read. The more scientists learn about the neural systems required for successful reading, the more they realize how complicated the process is and how much can go wrong. My purpose here is to present a quick description of how we believe the brain learns to read and to mention a few common reading problems. For a much more extensive discussion on reading and teaching strategies, see Sousa (2005) and Shaywitz (2003).

Is Reading a Natural Ability?

Not really. The brain's ability to acquire spoken language with amazing speed and accuracy is the result of genetic hardwiring and specialized cerebral areas that focus on this task. But there are no areas of the brain that specialize in reading. In fact, reading is probably the most difficult task we ask the young brain to undertake. Reading is a relatively new phenomenon in the development of humans. As far as we know, the genes have not incorporated reading into their coded structure, probably because reading—unlike spoken language—has not emerged over time as a survival skill.

Many cultures (but not all) do emphasize reading as an important form of communication and insist it be taught to their children. And so the struggle begins. To get that brain to read, here's what

> *There are no areas of the brain that specialize in reading. Reading is probably the most difficult task we ask the young brain to undertake.*

we are saying, for example, to the English-speaking child: "That language you have been speaking quite correctly for the past few years can be represented by abstract symbols we invented called letters of the alphabet. We are going to disrupt that sophisticated spoken language network you have already developed and ask you to reorganize it to accommodate these letters, which, by the way, are not very reliable. You see, although it takes more than about 44 different sounds to speak English, we have only 26 letters to represent them. That means some sounds have more than one letter and some letters stand for more than one sound. Seem like fun? Plus, there are lots of exceptions, but you'll just have to adjust." Female brains are already relishing the adventure while male brains are wondering how they ever got into this mess.

Once exposed to formal instruction, about 50 percent of children make the transition from spoken language to reading with relative ease. For the other 50 percent, reading is a much more formidable task, and for about 20 to 30 percent, it definitely becomes the most difficult cognitive task they will ever undertake in their lives.

Learning to read successfully requires three neural systems and the development of specific skills that will work together to help the brain decode abstract symbols into meaningful language. We will first look at the neural systems involved because that will help clarify what skills an individual needs to develop to learn to read.

Neural Systems Involved in Reading

Researchers using fMRIs are getting a clearer picture of the cerebral processes involved in reading. For successful reading to occur, three neural systems are required to work together. Figure 5.5 illustrates those systems. Visual processing begins when the eyes scan the letters of the printed word (in this example, *d-o-g*), and the visual signals travel to the visual cortex located in the occipital lobes at the rear of the brain (see also Figure 5.2). The word's signals are decoded in an area on the left side of the brain called the *angular gyrus*, which separates it into its basic sounds, or phonemes. This process activates the language areas of the brain located in the left hemisphere near and in the temporal lobe, where auditory processing also occurs. The auditory processing system sounds out the phonemes in the head, *duh-awh-guh*. Broca's and Wernicke's areas supply information about the word from their mental dictionaries, and the frontal lobe integrates all the information to provide meaning—a furry animal that barks.

The three systems can prompt each other for more information (represented by the double arrows). For instance, if auditory processing is having difficulty sounding out the word, it might prompt the visual system to rescan the print to ensure that it read the letters correctly. Similarly, the frontal lobe may prompt another visual scan or auditory rehearsal if it is having difficulty attaching meaning to the information. All this occurs in a fraction of a second. The actual process is a little more complicated than described here, but this is essentially what neuroscientists believe happens.

Although the process outlined in Figure 5.5 appears linear and singular, it is really bidirectional and parallel, with many phonemes being processed at the same time. That the brain learns to read at all attests to its remarkable ability to sift through seemingly confusing input and establish patterns and systems. For a few children, this process comes naturally, but most have to be taught.

Skills Involved in Reading

In order for this complex integration of neural systems to result in successful reading, an individual must develop specific skills and possess certain information. Specifically,

- **Phonological and phonemic awareness.** *Phonological awareness* is the recognition that oral language can be divided into smaller components, such as sentences into words, words into syllables and, ultimately, into individual sounds. This recognition includes identifying

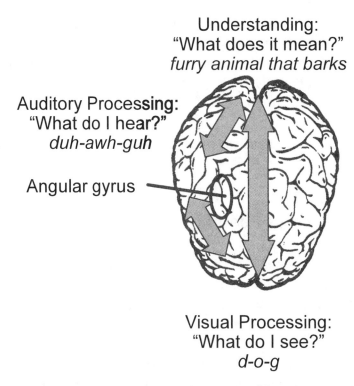

Understanding:
"What does it mean?"
furry animal that barks

Auditory Processing:
"What do I hear?"
duh-awh-guh

Angular gyrus

Visual Processing:
"What do I see?"
d-o-g

Figure 5.5   Three neural systems are involved in reading. The visual processing system scans the printed word, the auditory processing system sounds it out in the head, and the frontal lobe integrates the information to produce meaning. The angular gyrus helps decode the visual word recognition signals for further processing in the left hemisphere's language centers (Broca's and Wernicke's areas).

and manipulating onsets and rimes as well as having an awareness of alliteration, rhyming, syllabication, and intonation. Being phonologically aware means hearing the difference between *bat* and *pat* and between *bat* and *bet*. Before tackling the printed word, children need to be able to recognize that words are made up of individual sounds (phonemes) and that these sounds can be manipulated to create new words. This skill is called *phonemic awareness* (a subdivision of phonological awareness) and includes the ability to isolate a phoneme (first, middle, or last) from the rest of the word, to segment words into their component phonemes, and to delete a specific phoneme from a word.

- **Alphabetic principle and phonics.** The *alphabetic principle* describes the understanding that spoken words are made up of phonemes and that the phonemes are represented in written text as letters. This system of using letters to represent phonemes is very efficient in that a small number of letters can be used to write a very large number of words. Matching just a few letters on a page to their sounds in speech enables the reader to recognize many printed words. *Phonics* is an instructional approach that builds on the alphabetic principle and associates letters and sounds with *written* symbols. To demonstrate phonics knowledge, a child tells the teacher which letter is needed to change *cat* to *can*. Simply learning letter-sound relationships during phonics instruction does not necessarily lead to phonemic awareness.

- **Vocabulary.** Readers must usually posses a word in their mental dictionary in order to recognize it in print. Children learn the meanings of most words indirectly, through everyday experiences with oral and written language. These experiences include conversations with other people, listening to adults read to them, and reading on their own. They learn vocabulary words directly when they are explicitly taught individual words and word-learning strategies. Some vocabulary should be taught directly. Direct instruction is particularly effective for teaching difficult words representing complex concepts that are not part of the children's everyday experiences.

- **Fluency.** Fluency is the ability to read a text orally with speed, accuracy, and proper expression. Children who lack fluency read slowly and laboriously, often making it difficult for them to remember what has been read (recall the limited capacity of working memory) and to relate the ideas expressed in the text to their own experiences. Frequent practice in reading is one of the main contributors to developing fluency. Fluency bridges the gap between word recognition and comprehension. Because fluent readers do not need to spend much time decoding words, they can focus their attention on the meaning of the text. With practice, word recognition and comprehension occur almost simultaneously.

- **Text comprehension.** Comprehension is a complex interactive process that begins with identifying words by using knowledge outside the text, accessing word meaning in context, recognizing grammatical structures, drawing inferences, and monitoring oneself to ensure that the text is making sense. When confronted with several meanings for a word in a sentence, the brain needs to select the one that makes sense in context. Many English words have dozens of meanings, depending on their context. Thus, developing the ability to quickly block irrelevant meanings becomes a necessity for reading fluency and comprehension.

Some of these skills may begin to develop at home during the preschool years as parents read to their children and expose them to print materials. This allows them to hear word sounds, to practice pronunciation and speak more fluently, and to learn new words and their meanings. Thus, the degree to which children experience literacy at home will determine largely whether they begin school not just *able* to learn to read, but *ready* to learn to read. Children from low-income families are not often exposed to print materials and reading at home. Yet, studies show that when parents and school districts make the extra effort to provide these experiences, the acquisition of language and phonological skills for low-income preschool children is greatly enhanced (Poe, Burchinal, & Roberts, 2004).

> *The degree to which children experience literacy at home determines whether they begin school not just able to learn to read, but ready to learn to read.*

Problems in Learning to Read

Reading is so complex that any little problem along the way can slow or interrupt the process. It is small wonder that children have more problems with reading than any other skill we ask them to learn. In recent years, researchers have made significant progress using fMRI scans to understand how the brain reads. Yet, despite these advancements, fMRI scans are not a practical tool at present for diagnosing reading problems in a single individual. That is because the results of fMRI studies are usually reported for groups rather than for individuals. Researchers have found some variations in the activated areas of the brain among individuals within both poor readers and control groups. More research is needed to clarify these differences before fMRI or any other imaging techniques can be used confidently for diagnostic purposes. Until that time, however, researchers can use the information gained from imaging studies to develop other kinds of diagnostic tests that more closely align with our new understanding of reading and reading problems.

For the moment, critical observation of a child's progress in learning to speak, and eventually in learning to read, remains our most effective tool for spotting potential problems. Most difficulties associated with reading do not go away with time. Therefore, the earlier that parents and teachers can detect reading problems in children, the better.

Most research studies on reading have focused primarily on developmental reading problems that scientists refer to as *developmental dyslexia.* In developmental dyslexia, the child experiences unexpected difficulty in learning to read despite adequate intelligence, environment, and normal senses. It is a spectrum disorder, varying from mild to severe. Neuroimaging studies have established that there are significant differences in the way normal and dyslexic brains respond to specific spoken and written language tasks. Furthermore, there is now strong evidence that these differences may weaken with appropriate instructional interventions (Shaywitz, 2003).

Scientists have long been searching for the causes of reading problems. This has not been an easy task because of the large number of sensory, motor, and cognitive systems that are involved in reading. Struggling readers may have impairments in any one or more of these systems, but not all struggling readers have dyslexia. Specifically, dyslexia seems to be caused by deficits in the neural regions responsible for language and phonological processing or by problems in nonlinguistic areas of the brain.

The following is a brief description of some of the causes of difficulties when learning to read. Most reading problems can be divided into linguistic and nonlinguistic causes. Parents and teachers should consult other resources, such as NAEYC (1998), Shaywitz (2003), and Sousa (2005), for an in-depth discussion of these problems and how to deal with them,.

Linguistic Causes

- **Phonological deficits.** The readers have difficulty sounding out the sounds of the phonemes in their heads.
- **Differences in auditory and visual processing speeds.** When learning to read, the visual and auditory processing systems work at similar speeds to decode letters into sounds. Research studies of poor readers have revealed that some of them have a slower than normal auditory processing speed. Consequently, the visual system may already be processing the third letter of a word while the auditory system is still processing the first letter's sound. As a result, the brain incorrectly associates the sound of the first letter with the symbol of the third letter. For example, in reading the word *dog,* the visual system may already be processing the *g,* but the slower auditory system is still processing the *duh* sound associated

with the letter *d*. This reader's brain, then, mistakenly associates the letter *g* with the sound *duh*.

- **Structural differences in the brain.** MRI studies have found that the brain of people diagnosed with dyslexia are structurally different from non-dyslexic brains. These differences could contribute to the deficits associated with dyslexia.

- **Phonological memory deficits.** Some poor readers have difficulty retaining phonemes in working memory and are thus unable to remember a sequence of words long enough to generate a sentence.

- **Genetics and gender.** There is a strong association between dyslexia and genetic mutations in twins and families. Dyslexia is a chronic problem and not just a "phase." The stereotype that nearly all dyslexics are boys is not true, although it probably persists because boys are more likely to show their frustration with reading by acting out. In fact, Shaywitz (2003) found that boys tend to be over-identified as having reading problems, while girls are often under-identified.

- **Brain lesions in the word processing areas.** PET scans have shown that some people with developmental dyslexia have lesions in the areas on the left side of the brain responsible for processing and decoding written words.

- **Word-blindness.** Word-blindness is the inability to read words even though the person's eyes are optically normal. It results from either a congenital defect or trauma to the word processing areas of the brain.

Nonlinguistic Causes

- **Perception of sequential sounds.** Some poor readers are unable to detect and discriminate sounds presented in rapid succession. This deficit is related to auditory processing in general, not just to distinguishing phonemes.

- **Sound-frequency discrimination.** Some individuals with reading disorders are impaired in their ability to hear differences in sound frequency. This auditory defect can affect the ability to discriminate tone and pitch in speech.

- **Detection of target sounds in noise.** The inability to detect tones within noise is another recently discovered nonlinguistic impairment. When added to the findings in the two deficits mentioned just above, this evidence suggests that auditory functions may play a much greater role in reading disorders than previously thought.

- **Motor coordination and the cerebellum.** Several imaging studies show that many dyslexic readers have processing deficits in the cerebellum of the brain. The cerebellum is located at the rear of the brain just below the occipital lobe. It is mainly responsible for coordinating learned motor skills. Deficiencies in this part of the brain could result, according to researchers, in problems with reading, writing, and spelling.

- **Attention-deficit hyperactivity disorder (ADHD).** Attention-deficit hyperactivity disorder (ADHD) is a developmental disorder characterized by difficulty in focusing and sustaining attention. Children with ADHD are often assumed to also have developmental reading problems. But that is not usually the case. ADHD and developmental dyslexia are separate disorders, and less than 25 percent of ADHD children also have dyslexia.

Several computer programs, including *Fast ForWord* (Scientific Learning Corp.) and *Earobics Literacy Launch* (Cognitive Concepts, Inc.), have had considerable success in helping struggling readers overcome some of these difficulties. See the **Resources** section for more information.

Implications for Teaching Reading

Teaching children to read is no easy task, especially in primary classrooms where teachers welcome children from an ever-increasing variety of home situations, culture, and native languages. Given these variables, successful teachers of reading are flexible rather than rigid in their approach, and they know through experience what they need to do to make learning to read exciting and meaningful. They also acknowledge that the findings of scientific studies are clear: effective reading programs must contain components that support phonemic awareness, the alphabetic principle, vocabulary building, comprehension, and fluency. Developmentally appropriate literature complements this process to provide relevant and enjoyable reading experiences. See the **Practitioner's Corner** on p. 207 for suggestions on teaching reading.

What's Coming Up?

In too many schools, budget constraints and anxiety over high-stakes testing are reducing the amount of time that students are exposed to the arts and physical education. Yet, scientific evidence continues to accumulate about the positive impact that music, visual arts, and movement have on brain growth and development. The next chapter discusses some of that evidence and argues why we must preserve the arts and physical education if schools are to be truly brain-compatible.

PRACTITIONER'S CORNER

Testing Your Hemispheric Preference

There are many instruments available to help individuals assess their hemispheric preference. The one below takes just a few minutes. The results are only an indication of your preference and are not conclusive. You should use additional instruments to collect more data before reaching any firm conclusion about your hemispheric preference.

Directions: From each pair below, circle A or B corresponding to the sentence that **best describes you.** Answer all questions. There are no right or wrong answers.

1. A. I prefer to find my own way of doing a new task.
    B. I prefer to be told the best way to do a new task.

2. A. I have to make my own plans.
    B. I can follow anyone's plans.

3. A. I am a very flexible and occasionally unpredictable person.
    B. I am a very stable and consistent person.

4. A. I keep everything in a particular place.
    B. Where I keep things depends on what I am doing.

5. A. I spread my work evenly over the time I have.
    B. I prefer to do my work at the last minute.

6. A. I know I am right because I have good reasons.
    B. I know when I am right, even without reasons.

7. A. I need a lot of variety and change in my life.
    B. I need a well-planned and orderly life.

8. A. I sometimes have too many ideas in a new situation.
    B. I sometimes don't have any ideas in a new situation.

9. A. I do easy things first and the important things last.
    B. I do the important things first and the easy things last.

10. A. I choose what I **know** is right when making a hard decision.

B. I choose what I **feel** is right when making a hard decision.

11. A. I plan my time for doing my work.

B. I don't think about the time when I work.

12. A. I usually have good self-discipline.

B. I usually act on my feelings.

13. A. Other people don't understand how I organize things.

B. Other people think I organize things well.

14. A. I agree with new ideas before other people do.

B. I question new ideas more than other people do.

15. A. I tend to think more in **pictures.**

B. I tend to think more in **words.**

16. A. I try to find the one best way to solve a problem.

B. I try to find different ways to solve a problem.

17. A. I can usually **analyze** what is going to happen next.

B. I can usually **sense** what is going to happen next.

18. A. I am not very imaginative in my work.

B. I use my imagination in nearly everything I do.

19. A. I begin many jobs that I never finish.

B. I finish a job before starting a new one.

20. A. I look for new ways to do old jobs.

B. When one way works well, I don't change it.

21. A. It is fun to take risks.

B. I have fun without taking risks.

Scoring:

Count the number of "A" responses to questions
1, 3, 7, 8, 9, 13, 14, 15, 19, 20, and 21. Place that
number on the line to the right.   A._____

Count the number of "B" responses to the remaining
questions. Place that number on the line to the right.   B._____

Total the "A" and "B" responses you counted.   Total_____

The total indicates your hemispheric preference according to the following scale:

0–5	Strong left hemisphere preference
6–8	Moderate left hemisphere preference
9–12	Bilateral hemisphere balance (little or no preference)
13–15	Moderate right hemisphere preference
16–21	Strong right hemisphere preference

Reflection:

A. Did your score surprise you? Why or why not?

B. Describe here what your score may tell you about your teaching.

C. What implications do your answers in B above have for your students?

PRACTITIONER'S CORNER

Teaching to the Whole Brain: General Guidelines

Although the two hemispheres process information differently, we learn best when both are engaged in learning. Just as we would catch more balls with both hands, we catch more information with both hemispheres processing and integrating the learning. Teachers should design lessons that include activities directed at both hemispheres so that students can integrate the new learning into a meaningful whole. In doing so, students get opportunities to develop both their strong and weak learning style preferences. Here are some ways to do that in daily planning:

- **Deal With Concepts Verbally *and* Visually.** When teaching new concepts, alternate discussion with visual models. Write key words on the board that represent the critical attributes of the concept, then use a simple diagram to show relationships among the key ideas within and between concepts. This helps students attach both auditory and visual cues to the information, increasing the likelihood that sense and meaning will emerge, and that they will be able to accurately retrieve the information later. When using a video presentation, show the *smallest* segment with *maximum* meaning, then stop the tape and have students discuss what was shown.

- **Design Effective Visual Aids.** How we position information on a visual aid (e.g., overhead transparency, board, easel pad, video screen) indicates the relationships of concepts and ideas, which are processed by the right hemisphere. Vertical positioning implies a step or time sequence, or hierarchy. Thus, writing

    Delaware

    Pennsylvania

    New Jersey

is appropriate to indicate the order of these states' admission into the Union (chronology). Writing them horizontally

    Delaware, Pennsylvania, New Jersey

implies a parallel relationship that is appropriate to identify any three populous eastern states. Avoid writing information in visual aids in a haphazard way whenever a parallel or hierarchical relationship among the elements is important for students to remember.

- **Discuss Concepts Logically and Intuitively.** Concepts should be presented to students from different perspectives that encourage the use of both hemispheres. For example, if you are teaching about the Civil War, talk about the factual (logical) events, such as major causes, battles, and the economic and political impacts. When the students understand these, move on to more thought-provoking (intuitive) activities, such as asking what might have happened if Lincoln had not been assassinated, or what our country might be like now if the Confederate states had won the war.

  After teaching basic concepts in arithmetic, ask students to design a number system to a base other than 10. This is a simple and interesting process that helps students understand the scheme of our decimal number system. In literature, after reading part of a story or play, ask students to write a plausible ending using the facts already presented. In science, after giving some facts about the structure of the periodic table of the elements, ask students to explain how they would experiment with a new element to determine its place in the table.

- **Avoid Conflicting Messages.** Make sure that your words, tone, and pacing match your gestures, facial expressions, and body language. The left hemisphere interprets words literally, but the right hemisphere evaluates body language, tone, and content. If the two hemispheric interpretations are inconsistent, a conflicting message is generated. As a result, the student withdraws internally to resolve the conflict and is no longer focused on the learning.

- **Design Activities and Assessments for Both Hemispheres.** Students of different hemispheric preference express themselves in different ways. Give students options in testing and in completing assignments so they can select the option best suited to their learning styles. For example, after completing a major unit on the U.S. Civil War, students could write term papers on particular aspects of the war, draw pictures, create and present plays or write songs of important events, or construct models that represent battles, the surrender at Appomattox, and so on. Simulations, role-playing, designing computer programs, and building models are all effective assessment tools in addition to the tradition paper-and-pencil tests.

PRACTITIONER'S CORNER

Strategies for Teaching to the Whole Brain

Students learn best when teachers use strategies that engage the whole brain. Although current research shows that both hemispheres work together in many processing activities, it is still useful to know teaching strategies that involve the skills inherent in—but not necessarily limited to—each hemisphere. *Remember that we cannot educate just one hemisphere.* Rather, we are ensuring that our daily instruction includes activities that stimulate the whole brain. Here are some teaching strategies to consider (Key, 1991).

Teaching Strategies That Activate Left-Hemisphere Functions

- **Efficient Classroom Organization.** Have an efficient work area. Distribute the talkers around the room; they will spark discussions when needed.

- **Relevant Bulletin Boards.** Organize bulletin boards to be relevant to the current content and easily understood.

- **Clean the Board.** Make clean erasures on the board. This reduces the chance that previous and unrelated word cues will become associated with the new topic under discussion.

- **Use a Multisensory Approach.** Let students read, write, draw, and compute often in all subject areas.

- **Use Metaphors.** Create and analyze metaphors to enhance meaning and encourage higher-order thinking.

- **Encourage Punctuality.** Stress the importance of being on time. Encourage students to carry agendas.

- **Encourage Goal Setting.** Teach students to set study goals for themselves, stick to their goals, and reward themselves when they achieve them.

- **Stimulate Logical Thinking.** Ask "what if?" questions to encourage logical thinking as students consider all possibilities for solving problems.

Teaching Strategies That Activate Right-Hemisphere Functions

- **Give Students Some Options.** For example, allow them to do oral or written reports. Oral reports help students piece concepts together while requiring fewer mechanics than written work. Some students may prefer to present a short play or skit.

- **Use Visual Representations.** Use the board and overhead projector to show illustrations, cartoons, charts, timelines, and graphs that encourage students to visually organize information and relationships. Have students create or collect their own visual representations of the new concepts.

- **Help Students Make Connections.** Tying lessons together and using proper closure (Chapter 3) allow the brain to compare new information to what has already been learned.

- **Encourage Direct Experiences.** Facilitate direct experiences with new learning through solving authentic problems and involvement in real-world situations.

- **Allow for Student-to-Student Interaction.** Students need time to interact with each other as they discuss the new learnings. Remember, whoever explains, learns.

- **Teach for Transfer.** Teach students to use generalities and perceptions. Have them use metaphors and similes to make connections between unlike items. This is an important function for future transfer of learning.

- **Incorporate Hands-On Learning.** Provide frequent opportunities for experiential and hands-on learning. Students need to realize that they must discover and order relationships in the real world.

Use the chart below to decide what types of classroom strategies would work best with students whose hemisphere and sensory preferences are as indicated. Use the **bridging** and **hugging** strategies you learned in Chapter 4 to help you with this.

Modality	Left-Hemisphere Preference	Right-Hemisphere Preference
Visually Preferred		
Kinesthetically Preferred		
Auditorily Preferred		

Reflection:

A. What are your hemispheric and sensory preferences?

Hemispheric Preference:_____

Sensory Preference(s):_____

B. How did your preferences in A influence the strategies you designed in the chart for this activity? Jot down the results of your analysis here. Were there any surprises?

_____

_____

_____

_____

_____

_____

_____

_____

_____

_____

PRACTITIONER'S CORNER

Concept Mapping—General Guidelines

Concept mapping consists of extracting ideas and terms from curriculum content and plotting them visually to show and name the relationships among them. The learner establishes a visual representation of relations between concepts that might have been presented only verbally. Integrating visual and verbal activities enhances understanding of concepts whether they be abstract, concrete, verbal, or nonverbal. The key to concept mapping is the clear indication of the relationship that one item has to another. West et al. (1991) summarize nine types of cognitive relationships:

Name	**Relationship**	**Example**
1. Classification	A is an example of B	A cat is a mammal.
2. Defining/subsuming	A is a property of B	All mammals have hair.
3. Equivalence	A is identical to B	$2(a + b) = 2(b + a)$
4. Similarity	A is similar to B	A donkey is like a mule.
5. Difference	A is unlike B	A spider is not an insect.
6. Quantity	A is greater/less than B	A right angle is greater than an acute angle.
7. Time sequence	A occurs before/after B	In mitosis, prophase occurs before metaphase.
8. Causal	A causes B	Combustion produces heat.
9. Enabling	A enables/allows B	A person must be at least 18 years old to vote.

Concept mapping uses graphic diagrams to organize and represent the relationships between and among the components. These diagrams are also called *graphic* and *visual organizers*. Studies show that graphic organizers are particularly effective with students who have learning disabilities (Kim, Vaughn, Wanzek, & Wei, 2004) and with students who are English language learners (Chularut & DeBacker, 2004). Students should discuss these different types of relationships and give their own examples before attempting to select a concept map. There are dozens of possible organizers (Bromley, Irwin-DeVitis, & Modlo, 1995; Hyerle, 1996, 2004). Below are three common types. In each, the relationship between items is written as a legend (for a few examples) or next to the line connecting the items (when there are many examples).

- **Spider maps** best illustrate classification, similarity, and difference relationships.

- **Hierarchy maps** illustrate defining and/or subsuming, equivalence, and quantity relationships.

- **Chain maps** illustrate time sequence, causal, and enabling relationships.

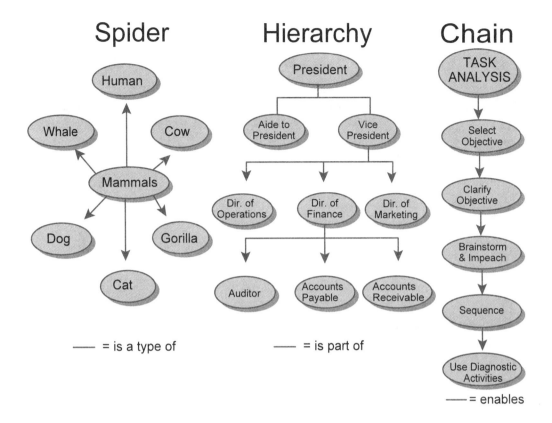

More types of concept maps:

- **Story maps** are useful for classifying main ideas with supporting events and information from the story. These are particularly helpful for readers who have difficulty finding the main idea in a piece of writing.

- **Analogy maps** illustrate similarities and differences between new and familiar concepts. This map can help teachers determine whether two concepts are too similar to each other and should, therefore, be taught at different times (see Chapter 4).

- **K-W-L maps** illustrate the degree of new learning that will be needed. The "K" is for what we already *know*; "W" is for what we *want* to know; and "L" is for what we *learned*. This map is a useful device for lesson closure (see Chapter 2).

More types of concept maps:

- **Venn diagrams** map the similarities and differences between two concepts. Like analogy maps, these help teachers determine if two concepts are too similar to each other to be taught in the same lesson.

- **Plot diagrams** are used to find the major parts of a novel.

- **A brace map** shows subsets of larger items.

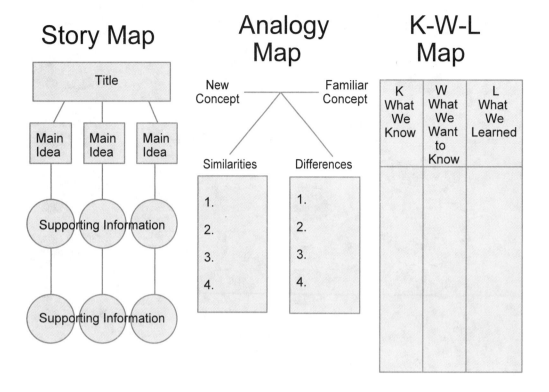

Story Map

Title

Main Idea | Main Idea | Main Idea

Supporting Information

Supporting Information

Analogy Map

New Concept | Familiar Concept

Similarities
1.
2.
3.
4.

Differences
1.
2.
3.
4.

K-W-L Map

K What We Know	W What We Want to Know	L What We Learned

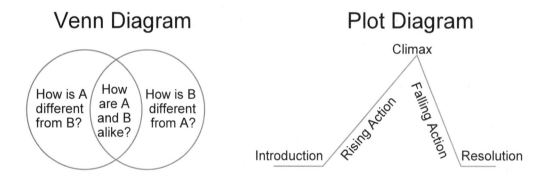

Venn Diagram

How is A different from B? | How are A and B alike? | How is B different from A?

Plot Diagram

Climax

Rising Action | Falling Action

Introduction | Resolution

A Brace Map

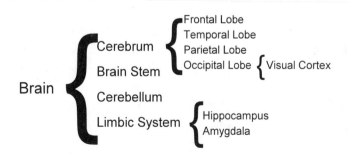

Brain
- Cerebrum
  - Frontal Lobe
  - Temporal Lobe
  - Parietal Lobe
  - Occipital Lobe — Visual Cortex
- Brain Stem
- Cerebellum
- Limbic System
  - Hippocampus
  - Amygdala

Directions: Time for practice. Select a broad curriculum concept, such as energy, time, or forms of government. Draw an appropriate graphic organizer in the box below and fill it in with the major parts of the concept. Present your work to other participants.

PRACTITIONER'S CORNER

Acquiring Another Language

When Should Children Learn Another Language? Although the brain maintains its ability to learn throughout life, it is quite clear from the research described earlier in this text that language learning occurs most easily during the first ten years or so. We should take advantage of this window of opportunity if we offer additional languages in schools.

Why Learn Another Language? In addition to knowing our native language, we benefit from learning another language as well. Language instruction should start as soon as possible. Here are some reasons for learning another language at an early age:

- Enriches and enhances a child's mental development.

- Gives students more flexibility in thinking, greater sensitivity to language, and a better ear for listening. (The brain learns to respond to phonemes that are different from the native language.)

- Improves understanding of a child's native language. (Unless a language or hearing difficulty exists, research does not support the claim that learning a second language early will interfere with learning the native language.)

- Gives a child the ability to communicate with people he or she would otherwise not have the chance to know.

- Opens the door to other cultures and helps a child understand and appreciate people from other countries. (This is important as our country becomes increasingly multicultural.)

- Gives a student a head start in language requirements for college.

- Increases job opportunities in many careers where knowing another language is a considerable asset.

What Are Barriers to Primary-Grade Second Language Programs? The two most common objections are that it is too expensive and that it might interfere with native language development. Primary-grade programs need not cost much at all. Volunteer parents can be the source of native speakers, and the materials come at low cost. As for interference, no research evidence supports this contention. Rather, several studies show that strategies used to acquire another language often help children understand and speak their native language better (DeHouwer, 1999).

What Are the Characteristics of an Effective K–6 Additional Language Program?

- **All students** have access to the program regardless of race/ethnic origin, learning styles, home language, or future academic goals.

- **Program goals** are consistent with the time devoted to additional language instruction. In the primary grades, the main goal is to hear the sounds, flow, and syntax of another language. There are different types of K–6 second language programs that achieve different levels of language proficiency and require different time commitments.

- **Sequence** of language instruction should be available through the K–12 school years. Acquisition of another language requires consistent practice, so a K–12 sequence is crucial to mastery. For this reason, instruction in other languages is often exempted from block scheduling formats that limit classes to one semester per year.

- **Systematic curriculum development** in content of another language is part of the school plan. Look for ways to include these language experiences across the curriculum.

- **Native speakers** must be used for the primary-grade instruction to ensure that the young brain hears authentic language sounds.

- **Connections between language and culture** are made explicit so that the learners understand the development of the additional language in the context of its culture.

Teaching Strategies for Acquiring Another Language

Teaching strategies for instruction in another language vary with the age of the learner who is beginning the study. Primary-grade teaching focus is mainly on recognizing, discriminating, and practicing the phonemes of the other language, as spoken by native speakers. Grammar is not taught per se, but implied through extensive student conversation. In the intermediate and later grades (including adult levels), the main goal is to develop communication competencies so that the student feels comfortable speaking, writing, and thinking the other language. Thus, teachers of other languages and of English Language Learners (ELL) should follow a sequence that begins with young learners. This sequence aims to do the following:

- **Develop Communication Competence.** One of the primary goals of learning another language is to gain competence in communication. This involves acquiring four major competencies, requiring integration of the verbal and nonverbal aspects of language as well as right- and left-hemisphere processing. Teachers should keep these four competencies in mind as they select their instructional strategies:

Grammatical Competence. The degree to which a student has mastered the formal linguistic code of the language including vocabulary, rules of punctuation, word formation, and sentence structure. This entails the analytic and sequential processing of the left hemisphere.

Sociolinguistic Competence. The ability to use grammatical forms appropriately in contexts that range from very informal to very formal styles. It includes varying the choice of verbal and nonverbal language to adapt the speech to a specific person or social context, and this requires sensitivity to individual and sociocultural differences. This is essentially the right hemisphere's ability to contextualize language.

Discourse Competence. The ability to combine form and thought into a coherent expression. It involves knowing how to use conjunctions, adverbs, and transitional phrases to achieve continuity of thought. This requires the integration of both hemispheres; the analytic ability of the left hemisphere to generate the grammatical features, and the use of the right hemisphere to synthesize them into meaningful, coherent wholes.

Strategic Competence. The ability to use verbal and nonverbal communication strategies, such as body language and circumlocution, to compensate for the user's imperfect knowledge of the language, and to negotiate meaning.

This research points out the need for teachers to ensure that the nonverbal form of intellect is not neglected in second language acquisition. In planning lessons, teachers should:

- Not rely heavily on grammar, vocabulary memorization, and mechanical translations, especially during the early stages of instruction.

- Do more with contextual language, trial and error, brainstorming of meaning, visual activities, and role-playing.

- Give students the opportunity to establish the contextual networking they need to grasp meaning, nuance, and idiomatic expressions.

When these skills are in place, shift to more work on enlarging students' vocabulary and knowledge of grammar.

PRACTITIONER'S CORNER

Considerations for Teaching Reading

Reading is the result of a complex process that relies heavily on previously acquired spoken language, but also requires the learning of specific skills that are not innate to the human brain. Because of the many steps involved in learning to read, challenges can occur anywhere along the way. Children often devise strategies to overcome problems but may need help in getting to the next step. As with learning any skill, reading requires practice.

The scientific research suggests that reading instruction include a balance between the development of phonemic awareness and the use of enriched texts to help learners with syntax and semantics. Here are some basic points to consider when teaching reading. For more specific teaching strategies, see NRP (2000), Shaywitz (2003), and Sousa (2005).

Basic Guidelines for a Balanced Approach.

- **No one reading program is best for all children.** Successful teachers of reading have developed activities that differentiate among their students according to their current level of readiness to read.

- **Developing phonemic awareness.** The brain reads by breaking words into sounds. Children first need to be taught the 44 basic sounds (phonemes) in the English language and be able to manipulate these sounds successfully. This is known as phonemic-awareness training. The more difficulty a learner has in beginning reading, the more likely the need for concentrated practice on phonemic awareness.

- **Mastering the Alphabetic Principle (Decoding).** Beginning readers need to be able to recognize the sounds represented by the letters of the alphabet. The better that a learner can *sound out* words, the faster the brain learns to match what it sees to what it hears. Therefore, readers should be taught to discern the individual sounds within words as they read them, and to say them aloud. *Dog* is "duh-awh-guh," and *bat* is "bah-ah-tuh." This practice helps the brain remember the decoding process of sight-to-sound so crucial to accurate and fast reading. However, problems develop when the reader's eyes move faster than the sound processing system can decode the phonemes. In this case, slow down the visual speed by having the student move a finger under each letter (grapheme). This also ensures that readers keep their eyes moving across the page, not fixating them into a stare, which also retards the reading process.

- **Phonics are important.** Phonics is the instructional approach that helps students master the alphabetic principle. It is an important component of learning to read but should not be taught as a separate unit through drill and rote memorization. Students lose interest and motivation to read. It is more effective to teach phonics as a means of developing spelling strategies and word analysis skills.

- **Practice for Comprehension.** Once the alphabetic principle is learned, practice in reading aloud is needed to develop speed and accuracy so that learners can comprehend what they are reading and get a sense of the language's syntax. This also helps teachers hear how accurately the student has matched the visual grapheme with the auditory phoneme.

- **Read With the Learners.** Teachers should read aloud as learners follow along in the text. This helps students with prosody—hearing the flow, rhythm, and tonal changes of the language. Have students move a finger under the words to show that they are correctly matching what they hear the teacher say with what they see on paper.

- **Read to the Learners.** Read literature slightly advanced for the learner while students listen, even with their eyes closed, to absorb the richness, rhythm, imagery, sound, and feeling of language in different contexts.

- **Introduce Literature.** Move on to interesting books and other forms of literature for practice and motivation to read. At this point, it is important to emphasize the contextual nature of the English language. Most meaning and pronunciation comes from *how* words are used in relation to all other words in the sentence (the context). Compare, for example, "The boy picked up the *lead* weight" to "The boy had a *lead* part in the school play."

- **Avoid** asking new readers to guess the sounds of words if they have not had phonemic-awareness training. Without the training, they have no clue how the word should sound, and mispronouncing the word will only reinforce the incorrect association between the grapheme and the phoneme. Remember that practice makes permanent, not necessarily perfect.

The chart on the next page is a reasonable hierarchy to be considered for teaching reading based on a deeper scientific understanding of the complexity of how the brain reads. In this hierarchy, emphasis is placed on ensuring accurate phonemic awareness at the very beginning of reading instruction. More evidence is emerging from brain scans of children reading that problems arise when there is poor phonemic awareness, thus confusing the decoding system.

EXAMPLE OF A HIERARCHY FOR TEACHING READING

Note: This procedure for teaching reading reflects the research on how the brain learns to read. It balances the early need for solid phonemic awareness with the later introduction of literary samples illustrating the more complex semantic and syntactic elements of language.

Semantic Level: The learners recognize that the meaning of words can change in different contexts. The teacher selects a variety of literature examples to illustrate contextual variations of language.	Students are likely to master these skills with literary texts that are rich with writing that contains syntactic and semantic variations.
Syntax Level: The learners create more complex sentences with correct grammatical structure. The teacher reads stories aloud to help learners develop a sense of syntax by listening to the phrasing and word positions in sentences. They recognize that in the sentences, "The dog chased the boy" and "The boy was chased by the dog," the syntax has changed but not the meaning. Having students read aloud allows the teacher to check pronunciation.	
Discourse Level: The learners construct and connect simple sentences in a logical sequence. Their spoken language has already developed some sentence patterns intuitively, such as subject-predicate-object, as in "I want a cookie" or "He throws the ball." Prefixes and suffixes are introduced and practiced.	Students are likely to master these skills faster if they use texts with the words that contain the phonemes being taught. These are called decoded texts.
START HERE: **Phonological Level:** This level focuses on developing phonological awareness and mastering the alphabetic principle. Learners are processing the basic sound elements of language. Students read aloud to ensure that the correct connections are made between the 44 English phoneme sounds and the 26 letters of the alphabet. Then practice with rhyming, word recognition, and meaning.	

PRACTITIONER'S CORNER

Reading Guidelines for All Teachers

To some extent, all teachers are teachers of reading. Beyond the primary grades, students read to learn, and teachers place heavy reliance on their students' ability to acquire information through reading. Because this reliance increases substantially in the upper grades, reading ability is a major determinant of student success in high school. Reading in all subject areas is likely to be more successful when teachers help students use reading skills efficiently and effectively. Here are some strategies to consider (Sousa, 2005).

- **Use direct instruction** to clearly identify important concepts in the reading and explain why we are learning them. Ask students to summarize the main points you just made. This helps the students determine sense and meaning. The amount of reading assigned should be just enough to accomplish the task. Don't overwhelm students with non-essential reading, especially in subject areas where they lack confidence.

- **Conquer vocabulary** by defining any new words or words used in an unfamiliar context. This should be done *before* assigning the reading.

- **Help with comprehension** by advising students to scan for key words and phrases that aid in comprehension, and to ask themselves questions like: How much do I need to read in this sitting? Why am I reading this? What's the main point? Why is it important? What else is this like that I've already learned? Can I summarize in my own words what I just read?

- **Talk, Talk, and Talk Some More.** You will remember that talk is a very powerful learning and memory tool. When working together, students should ask each other questions about the text they are reading, summarize main points, and clarify anything they did not understand. Cooperative learning groups is an effective strategy to accomplish this sharing, especially in classes that have a wide range of student abilities, including reading.

- **Use Graphic Organizers.** Have students use or design their own graphic organizers and concept maps to help understand the major points in their reading. This is particularly useful in textbooks and nonfiction reading that is full of detail.

- **Add Novelty.** Add novelty (Chapter 3) so that students don't see reading as drudgery. For example, get students to speculate on what might happen next in a story, or have them write their own plausible endings. Consider giving them the option to write a song or a poem or a short skit to illustrate some of the story's main events or characters. Let them create their own stories, plays, or publications, which they can read or perform for other students.

- **Incorporate supplemental textbooks** that cover the same material as the course text but are written at a lower reading level. This may require several books because it is unlikely that one book will cover all the course content.

- **Establish in-class vertical files** of magazine and newspaper articles about subjects found in the course text. Update the files periodically and encourage students to contribute to the files when they come across an appropriate article.

- **Use audiovisual aids.** These are a great help to students who have reading problems. Many students have become acclimated to a multimedia environment. Whenever possible, use videotapes, audiotapes, computer programs, television, overhead transparencies, and other technology to supplement and accompany direct instruction.

Chapter 5—Brain Specialization and Learning

Key Points to Ponder

Jot down on this page key points, ideas, strategies, and resources you want to consider later. This sheet is your personal journal summary and will help to jog your memory.

_____

_____

_____

_____

_____

_____

_____

_____

_____

_____

Chapter 6

The Brain
and the Arts

The quality of civilization can be measured through its music, dance, drama, architecture, visual art, and literature. We must give our children knowledge and understanding of civilization's most profound works.

—Ernest L. Boyer

Chapter Highlights: This chapter discusses how recent brain imaging studies are helping us understand the role and importance of music, the visual arts, and movement in brain growth and cognitive function. It suggests ways to incorporate artistic activities into lessons at all grade levels and in all subject areas.

We have never discovered a culture on this planet, past or present, that doesn't have art. Yet there have been a number of cultures—even today—that don't have reading and writing. Why is that? One likely explanation is that the activities represented by the arts—dance, music, drama, and visual arts—are basic to the human experience and necessary for survival. If they weren't, why would they have been part of every civilization from the Cro-Magnon cave dwellers to the urban citizens of the 21st century?

213

THE ARTS ARE BASIC TO THE HUMAN EXPERIENCE

As we learn more about the brain, we continue to find clues as to why the activities required for the arts are so fundamental to brain function. Music: It seems that certain structures in the auditory cortex respond only to musical tones. Dance: A portion of the cerebrum and most of the cerebellum are devoted to initiating and coordinating all kinds of movement, from intense running to the delicate sway of the arms. Drama: Specialized areas of the cerebrum focus on spoken language acquisition and call on the limbic system to provide the emotional component. Visual arts: The internal visual processing system can recall reality or create fantasy with the same ease.

> *We have never discovered a culture on this planet—past or present—that doesn't have music, art, and dance.*

These cerebral talents did not develop by accident. They are the result of many centuries of interaction between humans and their environment, and the continued existence of these talents must indicate they contribute in some way to our survival. In those cultures that do not have reading and writing, the arts are the media through which that culture's history, mores, and values are transmitted to the younger generations and perpetuated. They also transmit more basic information necessary for the culture's survival, such as how and what to hunt for food and how to defend the village from predators.

Consequently, art is an important force behind group survival. For example, about 1,000 of the 6,500 languages on this planet are spoken in just one place—New Guinea! Each language is totally unrelated to any other known language in New Guinea (or elsewhere) and is spoken by a tribe of just a few thousand people living within a ten-mile radius. Even more astonishing is that each tribe has its own music, visual arts, and dance (Diamond, 1992).

In modern cultures, the arts are rarely thought of as survival skills, but rather as frills—the esthetic product of a wealthy society with lots of time to spare. In fact, people pay high ticket prices to see the arts performed professionally, leading to the belief that the arts are highly valued. This cultural support is often seen in high schools, which have their choruses, bands, drama classes, and an occasional dance troupe.

Yet seldom do public elementary schools enjoy this continuous support, precisely when the young brain is most adept at refining the skills needed to develop artistic talent (Several private school initiatives have been the exception, most notably the Montessori schools and the Waldorf schools). Furthermore, when school budgets get tight, elementary grade art and music programs are among the first to be reduced or eliminated. Now, pressure from the No Child Left Behind Act to improve reading and mathematics achievement is prompting elementary schools to trade off instruction in the arts for more classroom preparation for the Act's high-stakes testing.

WHY TEACH THE ARTS?

The basic arguments I make here are these:

- The arts play an important role in human development, enhancing the growth of cognitive, emotional, and psychomotor pathways.

- Schools have an obligation to expose children to the arts at the earliest possible time and to consider the arts as fundamental—not optional—curriculum areas.
- Learning the arts provides a higher quality of human experience throughout a person's lifetime.

The Arts and the Young Brain

In Chapter 1, we discuss the explosive growth of dendrites and synaptic connections during the brain's early years. Much of what young children do as play—singing, drawing, dancing—are natural forms of art. These activities engage all the senses and help wire the brain for successful learning. When children enter school, these art activities need to be continued and enhanced. The cognitive areas are developed as the child learns songs and rhymes, and creates drawings and finger paintings. The dancing and movements during play develop gross motor skills, and the sum of these activities enhances emotional well-being.

The arts also contribute to the education of young children by helping them realize the breadth of human experience, see the different ways humans express sentiments and convey meaning, and develop subtle and complex forms of thinking (Eisner, 2002a).

The Arts Develop Cognitive Growth

Although the arts are often thought of as separate subjects, like chemistry or algebra, they really are a collection of skills and thought processes that transcend all areas of human engagement. When taught well, the arts develop cognitive competencies that benefit learners in every aspect of their education and prepare them for the demands of the 21st century. Elliot Eisner (2002b) of Stanford University identifies these eight competencies:

- **The perception of relationships.** Creating a work in music, words, or any other art discipline helps students recognize how parts of a work influence each other and interact. For example, this is the kind of skill that enables an executive to appreciate the way a particular system affects every other subsystem in an organization.
- **An attention to nuance.** The arts teach students that small differences can have large effects. Great amounts of visual reasoning go into decisions about nuance, form, and color to make an art work satisfying. In writing, similarly, great attention to detail in use of language is needed to employ allusion, innuendo, and metaphor.
- **The perspective that problems can have multiple solutions, and questions can have multiple answers.** Good things can be done in different ways. Schools often emphasize learning focused on a single correct answer. In business and in life, most difficult problems require looking at multiple options with differing priorities.
- **The ability to shift goals in process.** Work in the arts helps students recognize and pursue goals that were not thought of at the beginning. Too often in schools, the relationship of means to ends is oversimplified. Arts help us see that ends can shift in process.

- **The permission to make decisions in the absence of a rule.** Arithmetic has rules and measurable results, but many other things lack that kind of rule-governed specificity. In the absence of rules, it is personal judgment that allows one to assess what feels right and to decide when a task is well done.
- **The use of imagination as the source of content.** Arts enhance the ability to visualize situations and use the mind's eye to determine the rightness of a planned action.
- **The acceptance of operating within constraints.** No system, whether linguistic, numerical, visual, or auditory covers every purpose. Arts give students a chance to use the constraints of a medium to invent ways to exploit those constraints productively.
- **The ability to see the world from an aesthetic perspective.** Arts help students frame the world in fresh ways—like seeing the Golden Gate Bridge from a design or poetic angle.

It is encouraging that more states have recently promoted the arts in their curriculum through policies, such as including the arts as part of high school graduation requirements, standards, and assessments. Although the extent of commitment varies, some states have developed more extensive programs in the arts for schools and created partnerships with state arts councils and local arts organizations. The Education Commission of the States is sponsoring a two-year initiative (2004 to 2006) to ensure that every child has the opportunity to learn about, enjoy, and participate in the arts.

My point is that the arts should be taught for the arts' sake, and one should not have to suggest that we teach the arts only because they enhance the learning of other academic subjects. Nonetheless, I am a realist, and I recognize that it is important, nonetheless, to document any spillover effects that learning the arts can have on learning other subjects. That is because of the risk that the arts will fall by the wayside as schools are held more accountable for improving achievement in language arts and mathematics, despite strong public support for arts programs.

The Sciences Need the Arts

Few people will argue against studying the natural sciences in the elementary and middle schools, and support remains strong for the sciences—including Advanced Placement courses—in high schools. When budgets get tight, some people even view music and other arts courses as a drain on the funds needed to preserve science and mathematics courses. Others often see science and the arts as polar opposites. The sciences are thought of as objective, logical, analytical, reproducible, and useful; the arts are supposed to be subjective, intuitive, sensual, unique, and frivolous. In the competition between the arts and sciences in U.S. society, the arts have frequently lost. Typically, more public and private funds are given to any single technical or scientific discipline than all the arts combined.

But scientists and mathematicians know that the arts are vital to their success and use skills borrowed from the arts as scientific tools. These include the ability to observe accurately, to think spatially (how does an object appear when I rotate it in my head?) and perceive kinesthetically (how does it move?). These skills are not usually taught as part of the science curriculum but are at home in writing, drama, painting, and music.

Indeed, the arts often inform the sciences (Root-Bernstein, 1997). For example:

- Buckminster Fuller's geodesic domes can describe soccer balls and architectural buildings, as well as the structure of viruses and some recently discovered complex and enormous molecules.
- NASA employs artists to design displays that present satellite data so that it is accurate, yet understandable.
- A biochemist looks at the fiber folds in her weaving cloth as another way of explaining protein folding.
- Computer engineers code messages to the frequencies of a specific song to prevent interception or blocking of the message, unless the decoder knows the song.
- Genetic researchers convert complex data into musical notation to facilitate analysis of the data, as for example, decoding the sequence of genes in a chromosome.

Thus, playing the piano, writing a poem, or creating a painting sharpen observations, hone details, and put things into context. These are the same tools needed by a good scientist. The study of the arts not only allows students to develop skills that will improve the quality of their lives but also sustains the same creative base from which scientists and engineers seek to develop their innovations and breakthroughs of the future.

IMPACT OF THE ARTS ON STUDENT LEARNING AND BEHAVIOR

Arts Education and Arts Integration

Numerous research studies show that well-designed arts experiences produce positive academic and social effects as well as assist in the development of critical academic skills, basic and advanced literacy, and numeracy. The studies look at both stand-alone arts programs as well as programs that integrate concepts and skills from the arts into the many areas of study. One intriguing and important revelation of these studies is that the most powerful effects are found in programs that *integrate* the arts with subjects in the core curriculum.

Researchers speculate that arts integration causes both students and teachers to rethink how they view the arts and generates conditions that educational researchers and cognitive scientists say are ideal for learning. The arts are not just expressive and affective, they are deeply cognitive. They develop essential thinking tools: pattern recognition and development; mental representations of what is observed or imagined; symbolic, allegorical, and metaphorical representations; careful observation of the world; and abstraction from complexity. Studies repeatedly show that in schools where arts are integrated into the core curriculum (Rabkin & Redmond, 2004):

- Students have a greater emotional investment in their classes
- Students work more diligently and learn from each other
- Cooperative learning groups turn classrooms into learning communities
- Parents become more involved
- Teachers collaborate more
- Art and music teachers become the center of multi-class projects
- Learning in all subjects becomes attainable through the arts
- Curriculum becomes more authentic, hands-on, and project-based
- Assessment is more thoughtful and varied
- Teachers' expectations for their students rise

The following research studies are but a few of the many that have accumulated in recent years about the effects of art instruction on student learning. They include results from both stand-alone and arts integration programs.

SAT Scores

The association between students taking arts courses and their SAT scores is one of the largest studies of its kind. It included over several years more than 10 million American high schoolers who responded to a questionnaire indicating the number of years of arts classes they took. The results were amazingly consistent (Vaughn & Winner, 2000).

- Students who took arts classes had higher math, verbal, and composite SAT scores than students who did not take arts classes.
- SAT scores increased linearly with the addition of more years of arts classes, that is, the more years of arts classes, the higher the SAT scores.
- The strongest relationship with SAT scores was found with students who took four or more years of arts classes.
- The correlations with mathematics scores were consistently smaller than those for verbal scores.
- Acting classes had the strongest correlation with verbal SAT scores. Acting classes and music history, theory, or appreciation had the strongest relationship with math SAT scores. However, all classifications of arts classes were found to have significant relationships with both verbal and math SAT scores.

It is important to note that although enrollment in arts courses is positively correlated with higher SAT verbal and mathematics scores, it does not prove that one caused the other. Perhaps there are other variables involved. Nonetheless, it is difficult to challenge the strength of this relationship, given the magnitude of the study.

Disaffected Students

The arts reach students who are not otherwise being reached. Arts sometimes provide the only reason that certain students stay in touch with school. Without the arts, these young people would be left with no access to a community of learners. A ten-year ongoing study in the Chicago public schools shows test scores rising faster on the Iowa Test of Basic Skills reading section than a matched population (for neighborhood, family income, and academic performance) of sixth graders in the regular schools. A study of the Minneapolis schools showed that arts integration had positive effects on all students, but much more so with disadvantaged students (Rabkin & Redmond, 2004). In Florida, 41 percent of potential dropout students said something about the arts kept them in school. Further, these students were more engaged in their art classes than in academic classes (Barry, Taylor, & Walls, 2002).

Different Learning Styles

Ample research evidence indicates that students learn in many different ways. This research also notes that some students can become behavior problems if conventional classroom practices are not engaging them. Success in the arts is often a bridge to successful learning in other areas, thereby raising a student's self-concept. Table 6.1 shows how students involved in arts-based youth organizations have a better self-concept than a standard student population. These numbers are particularly significant considering that students in the arts organizations are twice as likely to have stressful home situations involving parents getting a divorce, going on and off welfare, or losing a job. The students in this sample noted how the arts allowed them to express pent-up feelings and to gain some distance from these problems by talking about them, thinking, and listening (Fiske, 1999).

Table 6.1	Percentage of Students in Standard School Population and in Arts-Based Youth Organizations Reporting a Positive Perception of Self		
		Standard School Population	**Arts-Based Youth Organizations**
Student feels good about him/herself.		76.2	92.3
Student feels s/he is a person of worth.		75.9	90.9
Student is able to do things as well as others.		76.2	88.8
Student, on the whole, is satisfied with self.		70.0	84.6
Source: Fiske (1999)			

Personal and Interpersonal Connections

The arts connect students to themselves and each other. Creating art is a personal experience, as students draw upon their own resources to produce the result. This is a much deeper involvement than just reading text to get an answer. Studies indicate that the attitudes of young people toward one another improve through their arts learning experiences. For instance, more than 2,400 elementary and middle school students from 18 public schools participated in a study that showed students in arts-rich schools scoring higher in creativity and several measures of academic self-concept than students in schools without that level of arts instruction (Burton, Horowitz, & Abeles, 2000).

School and Classroom Climate

The arts transform the environment for learning. Schools become places of discovery when the arts are the focus of the learning environment. Arts change the school culture, break down barriers between curriculum areas, and can even improve the school's physical appearance. Because administrators and teachers determine a school's climate, a study of 29 arts-rich New York City schools compared some indicators of school climate to the remaining, non-arts schools. In the arts-rich schools, administrators encouraged teachers to take risks, broaden the curriculum, and learn new skills. The teachers had a significantly higher degree of innovation in their instruction, were more supportive of students, and had greater interest in their own professional development. Once again, the arts-rich program had a much greater impact on these results than did the students' socioeconomic status (Fiske, 1999).

Gifted and Talented Students

The arts provide new challenges for students already considered successful. Students who outgrow their learning environment usually get bored and complacent. The arts offer a chance for unlimited challenge. For instance, older students may teach and mentor younger ones who are learning to play musical instruments, and some advanced students may work with professional artists.

The World of Work

The arts connect learning experiences to the world of everyday work. The adult workplace has changed. The ability to generate ideas, bring ideas to life, and communicate them to others are keys to workplace success. Whether in a classroom or in a studio as an artist, the student is learning and practicing future workplace behaviors.

Let's take a look at the three major forms of artistic expression—music, visual arts, and dance and drama—and observe what brain research is telling us. What impact will these studies have on student learning and success?

MUSIC

Music exerts a powerful effect on the brain through intellectual and emotional stimulation. It can also affect our body by altering our heart rate, breathing, blood pressure, pain threshold, and muscle movements. These responses result from the activation of neural networks that include the frontal cortex, the amygdala, and other limbic areas involved in motivation and reward.

Is Music Inborn?

Many researchers now believe that the ability to perceive and enjoy music is an inborn human trait. But is there any credible evidence to support this biological basis of music? First of all, any behavior thought to have a biological foundation must be universal. Even though the uses of music may vary across past and current cultures, all cultures do sing and associate certain meanings and emotions with music.

> *Compelling evidence suggests that the brain's response to music is innate and has strong biological roots.*

Second, biologically based behaviors should reveal themselves early in life. Researchers have shown that infants of just three months old can learn and remember to move an overhead crib mobile when a certain song is played. Thus, infants can use music as a retrieval cue. In addition, the memory of the specific song lasted more than seven days (Fagan et al., 1997). Babies can also differentiate between two adjacent musical tones and can recognize a melody when it is played in a different key (Weinberger, 2004). At the age of seven months, infants can categorize rhythmic and melodic patterns on the basis of underlying meter (Hannon & Johnson, 2005). Moreover, preschool children spontaneously use music in their communication and play.

Third, if music has a strong biological component, then it should exist in other animals. Monkeys, for example, can form musical abstractions, such as determining harmonic patterns. Although many animals use musical sounds to attract mates and signal danger, only humans have developed a sophisticated and unlimited musical repertoire.

Fourth, if music has biological roots, we might expect the brain to have specialized areas for music—and it does. For example, areas in the auditory cortex are organized to process pitch. Furthermore, the brain's ability to respond emotionally to music is connected to biology and culture. The biological aspect is supported by the fact that the brain has specialized areas that respond only to music, and these areas are able to stimulate the limbic system, provoking an emotional response. PET scans show that the neural areas stimulated depend on the type of music—melodic tunes stimulate areas that evoke pleasant feelings, whereas dissonant sounds activate other limbic areas that produce unpleasant emotions (Blood, Zatorre, Bermudez, & Evans, 1999; Menon & Levitin, 2005).

Effects of Listening to Music Versus Creating Instrumental Music

No one arts area has gained more notoriety in recent years than the impact of music on the brain. Numerous books are on the market touting the so-called "Mozart Effect" and promising that music can do all sorts of things from relieving pain, to increasing a child's IQ, to improving mathematics skills. To what degree are these claims backed by credible scientific evidence? As

> *How the brain responds when listening to music is very different from how it responds when creating music.*

with most claims of this nature, there is a growing body of scientific data, followed by media attention and a lot of hype. Let's try to sort out what the research in music is saying so that we can reap its benefits while making informed decisions about the validity of the assertions.

Research on the effects of music on the brain and body can be divided into the effects of *listening* to music, and the effects of *creating* or *producing* music on an instrument, especially an acoustic rather than an electronic one. The brain and body respond differently in these two situations. Unfortunately, not enough attention has been paid to this crucial distinction. Consequently, people have mistakenly assumed that the results of studies that involved creating music would be repeated when listening to music. If educators want to use the research on the effects of music to benefit students, then it is important that they differentiate the studies on listening from those on creating music.

How the Brain Listens to Music

The sounds of music are transmitted to the inner ear and are broken down according to the specific frequencies that make up the sounds (Figure 6.1). Different cells in the *cochlea* respond to different frequencies, and their signals are mapped out in the auditory cortex, especially in the right hemisphere in which perceptions of pitch, melody, timbre, and harmony emerge. This information is then transmitted to the frontal lobe where the music can be linked to emotion, thoughts, and past experiences. Over time, the auditory cortex is "retuned" by experience so that more cells become sensitive to important sounds and musical tones. This sets the stage for the processing of the more complex music patterns of melody, harmony, and rhythm.

Each hemisphere of the brain contains areas that respond to both music and language. But, as mentioned in Chapter 5, the left hemisphere also contains regions of specialization that respond only to language, and the right hemisphere has areas devoted exclusively to music perception. This explains why some people can be extraordinarily talented in language skills but have difficulty humming a melody. The reverse situation occurs in the brains of individuals with savant syndrome, who are talented musicians despite severe language retardation.

The discovery that the auditory cortex (located in the temporal lobes) in the right hemisphere has regions that respond only to music came from studies comparing patients who have damage to their left or right temporal lobes. Patients with right temporal lobe damage have lost the ability to

How the Brain Hears Music

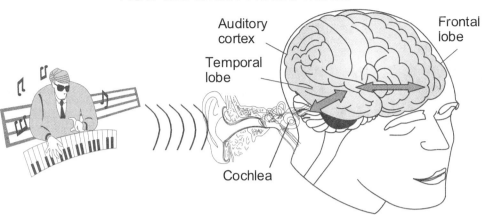

Figure 6.1   Sound entering the ear is converted into nerve impulses in the cochlea. These impulses are transmitted to the auditory cortex in the temporal lobe in which specialized regions, especially in the right hemisphere, analyze pitch and timbre. Information from the auditory cortex is transmitted to the frontal lobe, which associates the sound of music with thought and stimulates emotions and past experiences.

recognize familiar songs, a condition known as *amusia.* However, only the response to music is affected. The patients can still recognize human voices, traffic sounds, and other auditory information.

Music can also be imagined because people have stored representations of songs and the sounds of musical instruments in their long-term memory. When a song is imagined, the brain cells that are activated are identical to those used when a person actually hears music from the outside world. But when a song is imagined, brain scans show that the visual cortex is also stimulated so that visual patterns are imaged as well. The mechanism that triggers musical imagery is not yet understood, but it is not uncommon for people to have songs running through their heads when they get up in the morning.

The Benefits of Listening to Music

Therapeutic Benefits. For many years, medical researchers and practitioners have reported on the therapeutic effects of music to relieve stress, diminish pain, and treat other more severe disabilities, such as mental retardation, Parkinson's disease, Alzheimer's disease, and visual and hearing impairments. Other studies have shown that listening to music can boost immune function in children and that premature babies exposed to lullabies in the hospital went home earlier. The sheer volume of studies and positive results attest to music's therapeutic benefits.

How does music work this magic? That is still a mystery, but there are some important hints. Researchers have known for a long time that music can directly influence blood pressure, pulse, and the electric activity of muscles. Newer evidence shows that music may even help build and strengthen connections between brain cells in the cortex. This effect is important, and some doctors are already using music to help rehabilitate stroke patients. Some stroke patients who have lost their ability to speak retain their ability to sing. By getting patients to sing what they want to say, their fluency improves, and therapists can use existing pathways to retrain the speech centers of the brain.

Educational Benefits. The notion that music could affect cognitive performance catapulted from the research laboratory to the television talk shows in 1993 when Frances Rauscher and Gordon Shaw conducted a study using 84 college students. They reported that the students' spatial-temporal reasoning—the ability to form mental images from physical objects, or to see patterns in time and space—improved after listening to Mozart's Sonata for Two Pianos in D Major (K.448) for 10 minutes. But the students' improved abilities faded within an hour (Rauscher, Shaw, & Ky, 1993).

The results of this study, promptly dubbed "The Mozart Effect," were widely publicized and soon reinterpreted to incorrectly imply that listening to a Mozart sonata would enhance intelligence by raising IQ. In fact, the study reported that the music improved only spatial-temporal reasoning (one of many components of total IQ) and that the effect quickly faded. But the results did encourage the researchers to go further and test whether *creating* music would have a longer-lasting effect.

Shaw was convinced that listening to the complex melodic variations in Mozart's sonata (K.448) stimulated the frontal cortex more than simpler music. He and several colleagues tested this idea by having subjects take turns listening to Mozart's sonata (K.448), Beethoven's *Für Elise*, and popular piano music. The fMRIs showed that both the popular and the Beethoven piano music activated only the auditory cortex in all subjects. The Mozart sonata, however, activated the auditory as well as the frontal cortex in all of the subjects, leading Shaw to suggest that there *is* a neurological basis for the "Mozart Effect" (Muftuler, Bodner, Shaw, & Nalcioglu, 1999).

> *Recent studies confirm that the Mozart effect is real, and that it can occur with other kinds of music beside Mozart.*

Subsequent studies confirm that listening to Mozart enhances various types of spatial and temporal reasoning tasks, especially problems requiring a sequence of mental images to correctly reassemble objects. The data suggest that the effect is real, yet it can occur with other kinds of music besides Mozart. However, researchers do not yet know conclusively *why* the effect occurs. Nonetheless, the effect is important to educators because it shows that passive listening to music appears to stimulate spatial thinking, and that neural networks normally associated with one kind of mental activity can readily share the cognitive processes involved in a different activity. So learning or thinking in one discipline may not be completely independent of another (Hetland, 2000a).

Several studies have shown that listening to certain music can stimulate the parts of the brain that are responsible for memory recall and visual imagery (Nakamura et al., 1999). Researchers have also found that listening to background music enhances the efficiency of those working with their hands. In a study of surgeons, for example, background music enhanced their alertness and concentration (Restak, 2003). This explains why background music in the classroom helps many students stay focused while completing certain

> *Listening to background music can enhance recall, visual imagery, attention, concentration, and dexterity.*

learning tasks. However, one must exercise caution in selecting the *type* of background music. Several studies show that overly stimulating music serves more as a distraction and interferes with cognitive performance (Hallam, 2002). See the **Practitioner's Corner** on page 235 on using background music in the classroom.

Creating Music

Although passive listening to music does have some therapeutic and short-term educational benefits, the making of music seems to provide many more cerebral advantages. Learning to play a musical instrument challenges the brain in new ways. In addition to being able to discern different tone patterns and groupings, new motor skills must be learned and coordinated in order to play the instrument. These new learnings cause profound and seemingly permanent changes in brain structure. For example, the auditory cortex, the motor cortex, the cerebellum, and the corpus callosum are larger in musicians than in non-musicians.

This raises an interesting question: Are the brains of musicians different because of their training and practice in music, or did these differences exist before they learned music? The answer came when researchers trained non-musicians to listen for small changes in pitch and similar musical components. In just three weeks, their brains showed increased activation in the auditory cortex. This suggests that the brain differences in highly skilled musicians are more likely the result of training and not inherited (Restak, 2003). In support of this notion, another study compared 5- to 7-year-olds who were beginning piano or string lessons with a similar group not beginning instrument training. The researchers found no pre-existing neural, cognitive, motor, or musical differences between the two groups, and no correlations between music perceptual skills or visual-spatial measures. As in previous studies, correlations were found between music perceptual skills and phonemic awareness (Norton et al., 2005). No doubt some genetic traits enhance music learning, but it seems that most musicians are made, not born.

> *No doubt some genetic traits enhance music learning, but it seems that most musicians are made, not born.*

Benefits of Creating Music

The effects of learning to play an instrument can begin at an early age. One major study involved 78 preschoolers from three California preschools, including one serving mostly poor, inner-city families. The children were divided into four groups. One group (Keyboard) took individual, 12- to 15-minute piano lessons twice a week along with singing instruction. Another group (Singing) took 30-minute singing lessons five days a week, and a third group (Computer) trained on computers. The fourth group received no special instruction. All students took tests before the lessons began to measure different types of spatial-reasoning skills.

Spatial-Temporal Task

Figure 6.2 The graph shows the results of a spatial-temporal task performed by the preschool students before and after piano keyboard training, group singing, training on the computer, and no lessons. National standard age scores for all ages are 10, showing that these were average children before training.

After six months, the children who received six months of piano keyboard training had improved their scores by 34 percent on tests measuring spatial-temporal reasoning (Figure 6.2). On other tasks, there was no difference in scores. Furthermore, the enhancement lasted for days, indicating a substantial change in spatial-temporal function. The other three groups, in comparison, had only slight improvement on all tasks (Rauscher et al., 1997). Subsequent studies continue to show a strong relationship between creating music with keyboards and the enhancement of spatial reasoning in young children (Hetland, 2000b; Rauscher & Zupan, 2000).

Why did piano keyboard training improve test performance by 34 percent while the computer keyboard training didn't? Remember that the study measured spatial-temporal improvements only. As this and other studies show, music training seems to specifically influence neural pathways responsible for spatial-temporal reasoning, and that effect is more noticeable in the young brain. This may be due to the combination of tactile input from striking the piano keys, auditory input from the sounds of the notes, and the visual information of where one's hand is on the keyboard. This is a much more complex interaction than from the computer keyboard. Computers, of course, are very valuable teaching tools, but when it comes to developing the neural pathways responsible for spatial abilities, the piano keyboard is much more effective.

Creating Music Benefits Verbal Memory

Numerous studies have shown that musical training improves verbal memory. Researchers in one study administered memory tests to 90 boys between the ages of 6 and 15. Half belonged to their school's strings program for one to five years, while the other half had no musical training. The musically trained students had better verbal memory, but showed no differences in visual memory. Apparently, musical training's impact on the left temporal lobe seems to improve the ability of that region (where Broca's and Wernicke's areas are located) to handle verbal learning. Furthermore, the memory benefits of musical training are long-lasting. Students who dropped out of the music training group were tested a year later and found to retain the verbal memory advantage they had gained earlier (Ho, Cheung, & Chan, 2003).

Does Creating Music Affect Ability in Other Subjects?

Research studies continue to look for the impact that music instruction can have on learning in other subject areas. Two subject areas of particular interest are mathematics and reading.

Music and Mathematics

Of all the academic subjects, mathematics seems to be most closely connected to music. Music relies on fractions for tempo and on time divisions for pacing, octaves, and chord intervals. Here are some mathematical concepts that are basic to music.

- **Patterns.** Music is full of patterns of chords, notes, and key changes. Musicians learn to recognize these patterns and use them to vary melodies. Inverting patterns, called counterpoint, helps form different kinds of harmonies.
- **Counting.** Counting is fundamental to music because one must count beats, count rests, and count how long to hold notes.
- **Geometry.** Music students use geometry to remember the correct finger positions for notes or chords. Guitar players' fingers, for example, form triangular shapes on the neck of the guitar.
- **Ratios and Proportions, and Equivalent Fractions.** Reading music requires an understanding of ratios and proportions, that is, a whole note needs to be played twice as long as a half note, and four times as long as a quarter note. Because the amount of time allotted to one beat is a mathematical constant, the duration of all the notes in a musical piece are relative to one another on the basis of that constant. It is also important to understand the rhythmic difference between 3/4 and 4/4 time signatures.
- **Sequences.** Music and mathematics are related through sequences called intervals. A mathematical interval is the difference between two numbers; a musical interval is the ratio of their frequencies. Here's another sequence: Arithmetic progressions in music correspond to geometric progressions in mathematics.

Because of the many common mathematical concepts that underlie music, scientists have long wondered how these two abilities are processed in the brain. Several recent fMRI studies have shown that musical training activated the same areas of the brain (mainly the left frontal cortex) that are also activated during mathematical processing. It may be, then, that early musical training begins to build the very same neural networks that will later be used to complete numerical and mathematical tasks (Schmithhorst & Holland, 2004).

Keyboard Training. Motivated by the studies showing that music improved spatial-temporal reasoning, Gordon Shaw set out to determine whether this enhancement would help young students learn specific mathematics skills. He focused on proportional mathematics, which is particularly difficult for many elementary students, and which is usually taught with ratios, fractions, and comparative ratios. Shaw and his colleagues worked with 136 second-grade students from a

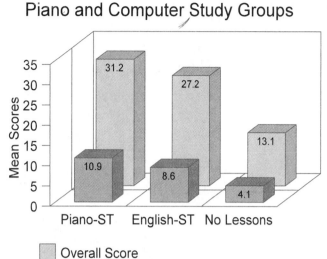

Piano and Computer Study Groups

Mean Scores

	Piano-ST	English-ST	No Lessons
Overall	31.2	27.2	13.1
Sub-test	10.9	8.6	4.1

☐ Overall Score
◼ Fractions and Proportions Sub-test

Figure 6.3 The mean overall, and fraction and proportions sub-test scores of the group that had piano and computer training with special software (Piano-ST), the group with computer and software (English-ST), and the group with no lessons.

low socioeconomic neighborhood in Los Angeles. One group (Piano-ST) was given four months of piano keyboard training, as well as computer training and time to play with a newly designed computer software to teach proportional mathematics. The second group (English-ST) was given computer training in English and time to play with the software; the third group (No Lessons) had neither music nor specific computer lessons, but did play with the computer software.

The Piano-ST group scored 27 percent higher on proportional math and fractions subtests than the English-ST students, and 166 percent higher than the No Lessons group (Figure 6.3). These findings are significant because proportional mathematics is not usually introduced until fifth or sixth grade, and because a grasp of proportional mathematics is essential to understanding science and mathematics at higher levels (Graziano, Peterson, & Shaw, 1999).

Strings Training. Begun in 2000, the Newark (NJ) Early Strings Program created a partnership with the New Jersey Symphony Orchestra to provide Suzuki-based string instruction to students in Newark's elementary schools, starting in second grade. A recent assessment showed that students in the program in grades two through four performed significantly better on standardized tests in language arts and mathematics than their peers. The program also had a positive effect on the students' self-esteem and self-discipline, and increased parent involvement in the schools (Abeles & Sanders, 2005).

A 1998 study showed how creating music can make a difference for students from low socioeconomic status. The low socioeconomic students who took music lessons from eighth through twelfth grade increased their test scores in mathematics and scored significantly higher than those low socioeconomic students who were not involved in music. Mathematics scores more than doubled, and history and geography scores increased by 40 percent (Catterall, Chapleau, & Iwanga, 1999).

The creating of instrumental music seems to provide the greatest cerebral advantages.

A subsequent review of studies involving more that 300,000 secondary school students confirmed the strong association between music instruction and achievement in mathematics. Of particular interest is an analysis of six experimental studies that revealed a causal relationship between music and mathematics performance, and that the relationship had grown stronger in recent years (Vaughn, 2000). Isn't this something that educators should consider in planning the core curriculum? If numeracy is so important, perhaps every student should learn to play a musical instrument.

Music and Reading

Several studies confirm a strong association between music instruction and standardized tests of reading ability. Although we cannot say that this is a causal association (that taking music instruction *caused* improvement in reading ability), this consistent finding in a large group of studies builds confidence that there is a strong relationship (Butzlaff, 2000). Researchers suggest that this strong relationship may result because of positive transfer occurring between language and reading. Their rationale is as follows:

- Although music and written language use highly differentiated symbol systems, both involve similar decoding and comprehension reading processes, such as reading from left to right, sequential ordering of content, etc.
- There are interesting parallels in the underlying concepts shared between music and language reading skills, such as sensitivity to phonological or tonal distinctions.
- Reading music involves the simultaneous incorporation and reading of written text with music.
- Learning in the context of a highly motivated social context, such as music ensembles, may lead to a greater desire for academic responsibility and performance that enhances reading achievement.

Studies done with 4- and 5-year-old children revealed that the more music skills children had, the greater their degree of phonological awareness and reading development. Apparently, music perception taps and enhances auditory areas that are related to reading (Anvari, Trainor, Woodside, & Levy, 2002).

THE VISUAL ARTS

The human brain has the incredible ability to form images and representations of the real world or sheer fantasy within its mind's eye. Solving the mystery of DNA's structure, for example, required Watson and Crick in the early 1950s to imagine numerous three-dimensional models until they hit on the only image that explained the molecule's peculiar behavior—the spiral helix. This was an incredible marriage of visual art and biology that changed the scientific world forever. Exactly how the brain performs the functions of imagination and meditation may be uncertain, but no one doubts the importance of these valuable talents, which have allowed human beings to develop advanced and sophisticated cultures.

Imagery

For most people, the left hemisphere specializes in coding information verbally whereas the right hemisphere codes information visually. Although teachers spend much time talking (and sometimes have their students talk) about the learning objective, little time is given to developing visual cues. This process, called *imagery*, is the mental visualization of objects, events, and arrays related to the new learning and represents a major way of storing information in the brain. Imagery can take place in two ways: *imaging* is the visualization in the mind's eye of something that the person has actually experienced; *imagining* depicts something the person has not yet experienced and, therefore, has no limits.

A mental image is a pictorial representation of something physical or of an experience. The more information an image contains, the richer it is. Some people are more capable of forming rich images than others, but the research evidence is clear: Individuals can be taught to search their minds for images and be guided through the process to select appropriate images that, through hemispheric integration, enhance learning and increase retention. When the brain creates images, the same parts of the visual cortex are activated as when the eyes process real world input. Thus, the powerful visual processing system is available even when the brain is creating internal pictures in the mind's eye (Kosslyn et al., 1999; Mazard, Laou, Joliot, & Mellet, 2005).

The human brain's ability to do imagery with such efficiency is likely due to the importance of imagery in survival. When confronted with a potentially life-threatening event—say, a car speeding toward you in the wrong traffic lane—the brain's visual processing system and the frontal lobes process several potential scenarios in a fraction of a second and initiate a reflex reaction that is most likely to keep you alive. As students today engage with electronic media that produce images, they are not getting adequate practice in generating their own imaging and imagining, skills that not only affect survival but also increase retention and, through creativity, improve the quality of life.

> *Imagery not only affects survival, but increases retention and improves the quality of life.*

Training students in imagery encourages them to search long-term memory for appropriate images and to use them more like a movie than a photograph. For example, one recalls the house one lived in for many years. From the center hall with its gleaming chandelier, one mentally turns left and "walks" through the living room to the sun room beyond. To the right of the hall is the paneled dining room and then the kitchen with the avocado green appliances and oak cabinets. In the back, one sees the flagstone patio, the manicured lawn, and the garden with its variety of flowers. The richness of the image allows one to focus on just a portion of it and generate additional amounts of detail. In this image, one could mentally stop in any room and visualize the furniture and other decor. Imagery should become a regular part of classroom strategies as early as kindergarten. In the primary grades, the teacher should supply the images to ensure accuracy.

Imagery can be used in many classroom activities, including notetaking, cooperative learning groups, and alternative assessment options. Mindmapping is a specialized form of imagery that originated when the left-brain/right-brain research emerged in the 1970s. The process combines language with images to help show relationships between and among concepts, and how they connect to a key idea. Buzan (1989) and Hyerle (2004) illustrate different ways in which mind maps can be drawn.

Research on Visual Arts and Learning

A review of the research literature shows a serious lack of studies that examine the impact of the visual arts and imagery on learning. One reason is the difficulty in determining which aspects of visual arts training (apart from imagery) are at work in programs that integrate visual art into core curriculum subjects.

Most studies in this area relate to imagery in sports. Coaches have known for a long time that athletes who use imagery to mentally rehearse what they intend to do perform better than if they do not use imagery. Studies reveal that the more time and intensity devoted to imagery, the better the athletic performance (Cumming & Hall, 2002; Harwood, Cumming, & Hall, 2003).

Apart from sports, one meta-analysis did look at imagery and creativity. Data from nine studies involving nearly 1,500 students were analyzed and showed a statistically significant association between imagery and creativity. Not surprisingly, students who used more imagery during learning displayed more creativity in their discussions, modeling, and assessments (LeBoutillier & Marks, 2003).

MOVEMENT

The mainstream educational community has often regarded thinking and movement as separate functions, assigning them different priorities. Activities involving movement, such as dance, theater, and occasionally sports, are often reduced or eliminated when school budgets get tight. But as brain studies probe deeper into the relationship between body and mind, the importance of movement to cognitive learning becomes very apparent.

Movement and the Brain

A New Role for the Cerebellum

In earlier chapters, we discussed the long-known role of the cerebellum in coordinating the performance of motor skills. For several decades, neuroscientists assumed that the cerebellum carried out its coordinating role by communicating exclusively with the cerebrum's motor cortex. But this view did not explain why some patients with damage to the cerebellum also showed impaired cognitive function. Recent research using scans centered on the cerebellum shows that its nerve fibers communicate with other areas of the cerebrum as well.

Studies have found that the cerebellum plays an important role in attention, long-term memory, spatial perception, impulse control, and the frontal lobe's cognitive functions—the same areas that are stimulated during learning (Bower & Parsons, 2003). It seems that the more we study the cerebellum, the more we realize that movement is inescapably linked to learning and memory (Figure 6.4).

Autism and ADHD. Further evidence of the link between the cerebellum and cognitive function has come from some studies of autism. Brain images show that many autistic children have

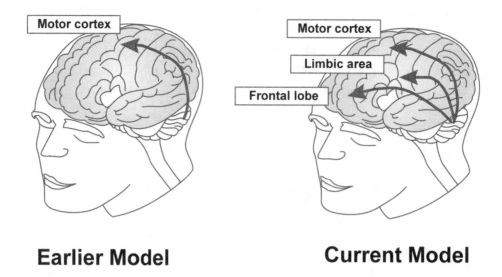

Earlier Model   **Current Model**

Figure 6.4   Researchers earlier thought that the cerebellum's role was limited to coordinating movement with the motor cortex. Recent studies indicate that the cerebellum also acts to support limbic functions (such as attention and impulse control) and cognitive processes in the frontal lobe.

> *The more we study the role of the cerebellum, the more we realize that movement and learning are inescapably linked.*

smaller brain stems and cerebellums and fewer cerebellar neurons. This cerebellar deficit may explain the impaired cognitive and motor functions seen in autism (Courchesne, 1999; Rodier, 2000). Using movement and other intense sensory experiences, therapy centers working with autistic children and those with attention-deficit hyperactivity disorder (ADHD) are reporting remarkable improvement in their ability to focus their attention to complete a task, as well as an increased ability to listen quietly when others share ideas.

Physical Exercise Improves Brain Performance

Even short, moderate physical exercise can improve brain performance. Studies indicate that physical activity increases the number of capillaries in the brain thus facilitating blood transport. It also increases the amount of oxygen in the blood, which the brain needs for fuel. The concentration of oxygen affects the brain's ability to carry out its tasks. Studies confirm that higher concentrations of oxygen in the blood significantly enhanced cognitive performance in healthy young adults. They were able to recall more words from a list and perform visual and spatial tasks faster. Moreover, their cognitive abilities varied directly with the amount of oxygen in the brain (Chung et al., 2004; Scholey et al., 1999).

Despite the realization that physical activity enhances brain function and learning, secondary students spend most of their classroom time sitting. Although enrollment in high school daily physical education classes has risen slightly in recent years, it is only about 25 percent.

Implications for Schools

Armed with the knowledge that movement is connected to cognitive learning, teachers and administrators need to encourage more movement in all classrooms at all grade levels. At some point in every lesson, students should be up and moving about, preferably talking about their new learning. Not only does the movement increase cognitive function, but it also helps students use up some kinesthetic energy—the "wiggles," if you will—so they can settle down and concentrate better later. Mild exercise before a test also makes sense. So does teaching dance to all students in K–8 classrooms. Dance techniques help students become more aware of their physical presence, spatial relationships, breathing, and of timing and rhythm in movement.

> *At some point in most lessons, students should be up and moving around, talking about the new learning.*

Summarizing the research on the interplay of motion and the cognitive functions of the brain, we should consider using movement activities (Patterson, 1997) because they

- Involve more sensory input, which is likely to hold the students' attention for a longer period of time.
- More closely resemble what students would be doing outside of school. Many students are involved with interesting kinesthetic activities after school. Doing these types of activities in school awakens and maintains that interest.
- Engage other cerebral aptitudes, such as music or visual-spatial skills, thus enhancing integration of sensory perception. This process will help students make connections between new and past learnings.
- Are more likely to lead to long-term recall. You can easily recall that time you participated in the school play or other public performance. Your memory is clear because this experience activated your kinesthetic sensory system.
- Stimulate the right hemisphere and help the student perceive concepts in their totality, rather than in the traditional language patterns (left hemisphere) that are so common.

Teachers can find many ways to weave movement into all lessons: act out a social studies lesson; walk through a map of the world or plot out a geometric formula on the gymnasium floor; use a dance to show the motion of molecules in the different states of matter or the planets in the solar system. See **Practitioner's Corner** on pp. 240–241 for some additional suggestions.

What's Coming Up?

Solving the environmental, social, and economic problems of the 21st century will require plenty of creative thinking and imagination. Are schools doing enough to teach students how to analyze problems, judge competing solutions, and create new answers to old problems? Is the strong emphasis on high-stakes testing really advancing the level of thinking or is it merely stressing the acquisition of more facts? How to foster a classroom that genuinely encourages higher-order thinking, while trying to do everything else, is the subject of the next chapter.

PRACTITIONER'S CORNER

Including the Arts in All Lessons

Including arts activities in any subject and at any grade level can be simple and fun. It doesn't need to be additional work and may substitute for some other activity you usually do.

- **Visual Arts.** Are there components of the lesson that students can draw, sketch, color, or paint? Would a visual arts project be acceptable as an alternative assessment to measure student understanding?

  Example: A science teacher has a student draw a chart to illustrate the important steps in an experiment.

- **Music.** Is there an appropriate song or other musical composition that could be incorporated into the lesson or unit? Remember that music is a very effective memory device. Is there a familiar tune that would help students remember important facts about the unit?

  Example: A social studies teacher has students put important facts about the Revolutionary War to a familiar melody.

- **Literary Device.** Could students write a poem, limerick, or play to illustrate major points in the unit? Rhyming is also an excellent memory tool: "In fourteen hundred ninety-two, Columbus sailed the ocean blue . . ."

  Example: A mathematics teachers has students devise limericks to help them remember the mathematical order of operations.

- **Dance and Theater.** Is there a dance that could help students remember some critical events or information? Can students act out a play that other students wrote?

  Example: An English teacher has students write and act out a different but plausible ending to Shakespeare's *Romeo and Juliet*.

- **Community Artists.** Are there community artists who can demonstrate their skills in the classroom? Teachers working with artists receive on-the-job training, and learn techniques that they can use later on their own.

PRACTITIONER'S CORNER

Using Music in the Classroom

Listening to music in the classroom can promote student focus and productivity at all grade levels. Remember that no one musical selection, nor the volume at which it is played, will please *everyone*. Just ensure that the music played enhances rather than interferes with the situation or task. Here are a few guidelines to consider when planning to use music:

- **When to Play the Music.** Music can be played at different times during the learning episode. Be sure to choose the appropriate music for the particular activity. Music can be played:

  - Before class begins (choose music that sets the emotional mood)
  - When students are up and moving about (choose an upbeat tune)
  - When the students are busy doing seat work, either alone or in groups (choose music that facilitates the learning task)
  - At the end of the class (students leave on a positive note, looking forward to returning)

  It is *not* advisable to play music when you are doing direct instruction (unless the music is part of the lesson) because it can be a distraction.

- **Be Aware of Beats Per Minute.** Because music can affect a person's heart rate, blood pressure, and emotional mood, the number of beats per minute in the music is very important. If you are using the music as background to facilitate student work, choose music that plays at about 60 beats per minute (the average heartbeat rate). If the music is accompanying a fast-paced activity, then choose 80 to 90 beats per minute. To calm down a noisy group as, say, in the school cafeteria or commons area, choose music at 40 to 50 beats per minute.

- **With or Without Lyrics?** Using music with or without lyrics depends on the purpose of playing the music. Music played at the beginning or end of class can contain lyrics because the main purpose is to set a mood, not get focus. But if students are working on a learning task, lyrics become a distraction. Some students will try to listen to the lyrics, and others may discuss them—in both instances, they are off the task.

- **Select Familiar or Unfamiliar Music?** Once again, this depends on the music's purpose. Familiar music is fine when setting a mood. However, when working on a specific assignment, you may wish to use music that is unfamiliar. If the students know the background music, some will sing or hum along, causing a distraction. Choose unfamiliar music, such as classical or new age music, and have enough different selections so that they are each played infrequently. Avoid the nature sounds selections as background music because they can be the source of much discussion and controversy. Of course, nature sounds could be used to stimulate discussion in appropriate lesson contexts.

- **Student Input.** Students may ask to bring in their own selections. To maintain a positive classroom climate, tell them that they *can* bring in their music, *provided the selections meet the above criteria.* Explain to them why this is necessary. Some kinds of student music would be appropriate in certain contexts as, for example, to facilitate a student discussion on interpreting music or another art form. In some cases, music may provide just the amount of meaning needed to enhance learning and retention.

- **Suggestions** (from teachers who have tried these, and reported success):

Beginning and end of class:
    Vivaldi – *The Four Seasons*
    Kenny G – Any selection
    Bach – *Brandenburg Concertos*
    Yanni – Most selections
    The Beach Boys
    Chopin – Most selections

Fast-paced activity:
    Rock
    Disco
    Reggae
    Hits from the 1950s
    Hits from the 1960s
    Marches (e.g., Sousa)

Reflection or processing activity:
    Beethoven – *Moonlight Sonata*
    Pachebel – *Canon in D major*
    Mozart – Piano concertos
    Enya (New Age) – Most selections
    Ray Lynch (New Age) – Any selection
    George Winston – *Seasons*
    Gary Lamb (Original) – Any selection

Happy listening!

PRACTITIONER'S CORNER

Using Imagery

Imagery runs the gamut from simple concrete pictures to complex motor learning and multistep procedures. Because imagery is still not a common instructional strategy, it should be implemented early and gradually. These guidelines are adapted from Parrott (1986) and West et al. (1991) for using imagery as a powerful aid to understanding and retention.

- **Prompting.** Use prompts for telling students to form mental images of the content being learned. They can be as simple as "form a picture in your mind of . . ." to more complex directions. Prompts should be specific to the content or task and should be accompanied by relevant photographs, charts, or arrays, especially for younger children.

- **Modeling.** Model imagery by describing your own image to the class and explaining how that image helps your recall and use of the current learning. Also, model a procedure and have the students mentally practice the steps.

- **Interaction.** Strive for rich, vivid images where items interact. The richer the image, the more information it can include. If there are two or more items in the images, they should be visualized as acting on each other. If the recall is a ball and a bat, for example, imagine the bat hitting the ball.

- **Reinforcement.** Have students talk about the images they formed and how it helped their learning. Ensure that they get ample feedback from others on the accuracy and vividness of the images.

- **Add Context.** Whenever possible, add context to the interaction to increase retention and recall. For example, if the task is to recall prefixes and suffixes, the context could be a parade with the prefixes in front urging the suffixes in the rear to catch up.

- **Avoid Overloading the Image.** Although good images are complete representations of what is to be remembered, they should not overload the working memory's capacity in older students of about seven items.

Visualized Notetaking

Visualized notetaking is a strategy that encourages students to associate language with visual imagery. It combines on paper sequential verbal information with symbols and holistic visual patterns. Teachers should encourage students to link verbal notes with images and symbols that show sequence, patterns, or relationships. Here are a few examples:

- **Stickperson.** Use the stickperson symbol to remember information about a person or group of people. The student attaches notes about a person in eight areas to the appropriate spot on the stick figure: ideas to the brain; hopes/vision to the eyes; words to the mouth; actions to the hands; feelings to the heart; movement to the feet; weaknesses to the Achilles tendon; and strengths to the arm muscle.

- **Expository Visuals.** These take many forms. Use a set of flow boxes to help students collect and visualize the cause-effect interrelationships for an event. Causes are written in the boxes on the left, the event in the center box, and effects in the boxes on the right. Creating different designs to visualize other topics is a valuable imaging activity.

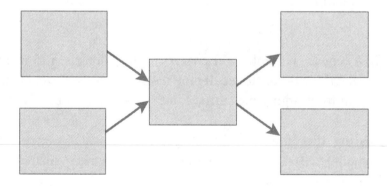

- **Notebook Design.** Even the design of the notebook page can call imagery into play to enhance learning and retention. One variation involves dividing the notebook page into sections for topics, vocabulary, important questions, things to remember, next homework assignment, and next test (see example below). Positioning each area on the page acts as a visual organizer that promotes the use of appropriate symbols.

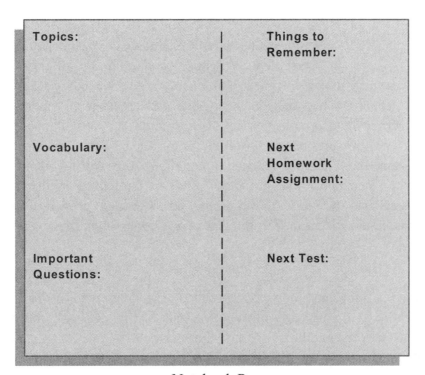

Notebook Pages

- **Mindmapping.** Mind maps are powerful visual tools for remembering relationships between and among parts of a key idea. Using a mind map for notes helps the student see relationships unfolding during the notetaking process. The maps also allow students to look beyond the obvious, make inferences, and discover new knowledge not otherwise possible in the traditional lecture notetaking format. See Buzan (1989) and Hyerle (1996, 2004) for lots of ideas on different ways to draw and use mind maps.

PRACTITIONER'S CORNER

Strategies for Using Movement

Incorporating movement activities into lessons is interesting and fun for the teacher and the students. Although moving around in class is common in the primary grades, it drops dramatically at the secondary level. Middle and high school teachers are understandably concerned about having adequate time to cover the enormous amount of material in the curriculum. But because trading a few minutes of teacher talk for a movement activity can actually increase the amount of learning retained, it could be a very worthwhile investment of time.

Remember that not many students participate in the physical education program. Yet physical activity is essential to promoting the normal growth of mental function, to generating positive emotions, and in learning and remembering cognitive material. Some suggestions are as follows:

- **Energizers.** Use movement activities to energize students who are at low points in their energy levels (e.g., during early morning periods for high school students or during that downtime just past the middle of the day). For example,
  "Measure the room's length in hand spans."
  "Touch seven objects in the room that are the same color."
  "Go to four different sources of information in this room."
  "In your group, make a poster-sized mind map of this unit."
  "Use ball toss games for review, storytelling, and vocabulary building.

- **Acting Out Key Concepts.** This strategy uses the body in a physical way to learn and remember a difficult concept. If the lesson objective is to learn the continents, try this: Stand in front of a world map. Say the continent and point to the assigned body part (Chapman & King, 2000).

North America = left hand	Europe = forehead
Asia = right hand	Africa = waist
South America = left knee	Australia = right knee
Antarctica = a point on the floor between the feet	

Allow time for practice, then remove the map and repeat the activity.
Is there a difficult concept that you teach that could be acted out?

- **Role-Playing.** Do role-plays on a regular basis. For example, students can organize extemporaneous pantomime or play charades to dramatize major points in a unit. Have them develop and act out short commercials advertising upcoming units or to review previously learned material.

- **Vocabulary Building: Act Out the Word**. Look for vocabulary words that lend themselves to a physical movement. Then,

  a. Say the word
  b. Read the meaning
  c. Do the movement (the movement acts out the meaning of the word).

  For example,

  a. *oppugn*
  b. "to oppose or attack"
  c. make body gestures that indicate "opposing" or "attacking."

  Do the three parts (a, b, and c) three times. This places the information in working memory. Now continue rehearsing the word, and use it in context so that it transfers to long-term memory (Chapman, 1993).

- **Verbal to Physical Tug-of-War.** In this activity, students choose a partner and a topic from the unit they have been learning. Each student forms an opinion about the topic and has 30 seconds to convince a partner why his or her own topic is more important (the verbal tug-of-war). After this debate, the partners separate to opposite sides for a physical tug-of-war with a rope.

Chapter 6—The Brain and the Arts

Key Points to Ponder

Jot down on this page key points, ideas, strategies, and resources you want to consider later. This sheet is your personal journal summary and will help to jog your memory.

_____

_____

_____

_____

_____

_____

_____

_____

_____

_____

Chapter 7

Thinking Skills and Learning

Too often children are given answers to remember rather than problems to solve.

—Robert Lewin

Chapter Highlights. This chapter discusses some of the characteristics and dimensions of human thinking. It examines the revised Bloom's Taxonomy, notes its continuing compatibility with current research on higher-order thinking, and explains its relationship to difficulty, complexity, and intelligence.

How can something as tangible as the human brain create such phantom things as ideas? How does it create Beethoven's symphonies, Michelangelo's sculptures, and Einstein's universe? What processes translate the countless neuron firings into thoughts and then into products of magnificent beauty or weapons of destruction? The human brain collects information about the world and organizes it to form a representation of that world. This representation, or mental model, describes *thinking,* a process that an individual human uses to function in that world.

CHARACTERISTICS OF HUMAN THINKING

Thinking is easier to describe than to define. Its characteristics include the daily routine of reasoning where one is at the moment, where one's destination is, and how to get there. It includes developing concepts, using words, solving problems, abstracting, intuiting, and anticipating the future. Other aspects of thinking include learning, memory, creativity, communication, logic, and generalization. How and when we use these aspects often determine the success or failure of our many interactions with our environment. This chapter discusses thinking, explores strategies that attempt to describe the characteristics of various types of thinking, and suggests how they can be used in the classroom to promote higher-order thinking and learning.

Types of Thinking

Can you answer these questions?

- Who was the second president of the United States?
- What are the similarities and differences between the post-Civil War and post-Vietnam War periods?
- Defend why we should or should not have capital punishment.

Each of these questions requires you to think, but the type of thinking involved is not the same. The first question requires you to simply refer to a listing you have in long-term memory that recalls the sequence of presidents. Dealing with the second question is quite different. You must first recall what you have stored about both wars, separate these items into lists, then analyze them to determine which events were similar and which were different. The third question requires the retrieval and processing of large amounts of information about capital punishment, its impact on society, and its effectiveness as a deterrent to crime. Then you need to form a judgment about whether you believe criminals will be influenced by a capital punishment penalty. These three questions require different and increasingly complex thought processes to arrive at acceptable answers. Thus, some thinking is more complex than other thinking. Brain scans indicate that different parts of the brain, particularly in the frontal cortex, are involved as the problem-solving task becomes more complicated (Goldberg, 2001; Jausovec & Jausovec, 2000).

> *Brain scans show that different parts of the brain are involved as the problem-solving task becomes more complicated.*

The brain has evolved different mechanisms for dealing with various situations. Logic is one of those. It recognizes, for example, that if A is equal to B, and B is equal to C, then A must be equal to C. There are other mechanisms, too. Rationality, pattern identification, image making, and approximation are all forms of thinking that serve to help the individual deal with a concept, a problem, or a decision.

Thinking as a Representational System

Although the file cabinets and their ordered system are useful metaphors for explaining the operation of long-term storage in the information processing model (Chapter 2), they do not explain all the situations one encounters when the brain behaves as a representational system. Sometimes we cannot recognize a person's face, but we remember the name and the events that surrounded our first meeting with this person. And just thinking of the word *beach* evokes a complex series of mental events that corresponds to the internal representation we have of all the beaches we have ever encountered. Beaches gleam in the sun, are often hot, create a shoreline, merge with water, are dotted with umbrellas, and recall memories of holiday fun. The word itself is not actually a beach, but it brings forth many associations having to do with beaches. This is an example of a representational system, and it illustrates the diversity of patterns in human thinking. It is this recognition of diversity that has led to the notion of multiple intelligences. That is, an individual's thinking patterns vary when encountering different challenges, and these semiautonomous variations in thinking result in different degrees of success in learning.

Thinking and Emotion

Emotions play an important role in the thinking process. In Chapter 2, we discussed the amygdala's role in encoding emotional messages into long-term memory. We also noted that emotions often take precedence during cerebral processing and can impede or assist cognitive learning. If we like what we are learning, we are more likely to maintain attention and interest and move to higher-level thinking. We tend to probe and ask those "what if?" kinds of questions. When we dislike the learning, we usually spend the least amount of time with it and stay at minimal levels of processing. That's why the classroom's emotional climate is so important.

Students sometimes feel neutral about a new learning topic. Challenging them with activities that require higher-order thinking often sparks an interest that brings forth positive feelings. Recent studies reaffirm that as learners generate positive emotions, their scope of attention broadens and their critical thinking skills are enhanced. Neutral and negative emotions, on the other hand, narrow the scope of attention and thinking (Fredrickson & Branigan, 2005). When students recognize the power of their own thinking, they use their skills more and solve problems for themselves rather than just waiting to be told the answers.

THE DIMENSIONS OF HUMAN THINKING

Designing Models

Cognitive psychologists have been designing models for decades in an effort to describe the dimensions of thinking and the levels of complexity of human thought. The models have generally divided thought into two categories, *convergent* or lower-order thinking and *divergent* or higher-order thinking. Other multidimensional frameworks have appeared that attempt to describe all aspects of thinking in detail. Of course, a model is only as good as its potential for achieving a desired goal (in this case, encouraging higher-order thinking in students) and the likelihood that teachers feel sufficiently comfortable with the model to make it a regular part of their classroom practice. In examining the models that describe the dimensions of thinking, most include the following major areas:

- **Basic processes** are the tools we use to transform and evaluate information, such as:
  Observing: includes recognizing and recalling.
  Finding patterns and generalizing: includes classifying, comparing and contrasting, and identifying relevant and irrelevant information.
  Forming conclusions based on patterns: includes hypothesizing, predicting, inferring, and applying.
  Assessing conclusions based on observations: includes checking consistency, identifying biases and stereotypes, identifying unstated assumptions, recognizing over- and under-generalizations, and confirming conclusions with facts.

The consistency with which these basic processes appear in most models results from the recognition that they allow us to make sense of our world by pulling together bits of information into understandable and coherent patterns. Further, these processes support the notion that conclusions should be based on evidence. From these conclusions, we form patterns that help us to hypothesize, infer, and predict.

- **Domain-specific knowledge** refers to the knowledge in a particular content area that one must possess in order to carry out the basic processes described above.
- **Critical thinking** is a complex process that is based on objective standards and consistency. It includes making judgments using objective criteria and offering opinions with reasons.
- **Creative thinking** involves putting together information to arrive at a whole new concept, idea, or understanding. It often involves four stages that include preparation (gathering and examining the needed information), incubation (mulling over the idea and making connections to other experiences), illumination (the "Aha!" when the new idea comes to light), and verification (methods for testing the idea).
- **Metacognition** is the awareness one has of one's own thinking processes. It means that students should know when and why they are using the basic processes, and how these functions relate to the content they are learning. Metacognition consists of two processes occurring simultaneously: monitoring progress while learning, and making appropriate changes when problems occur during learning.

Are We Teaching Thinking Skills?

The ordinary experience of thinking about that sunny beach raises intriguing questions about how the brain is organized to think with increasing complexity. What skills does the human brain need to maneuver through simple and complex thoughts? Can these skills be learned and, if so, how and when should they be taught?

Most humans are born with a brain that has all the sensory components and neural organization necessary to survive successfully in its environment. The neural organization changes dramatically, of course, as the child grows and learns, resulting in the expansion of some networks and the elimination of others. Even the most superficial look at human information processing reveals a vast system of magnificent neural networks that can learn language, recognize one face among thousands, and infer an outcome by rapidly analyzing data. Every bit of evidence available suggests that the human brain is *designed* for a broad range of thinking patterns. So if the brain is capable of higher-order thinking, why do we see so little of it in the normal course of student discussion and performance?

It just may be that the reason our students are not thinking critically is that we have not exposed them consistently to models or situations in school that require them to do so. Schooling, for the most part, still demands little more than several levels of convergent thinking. Its practices and testing focus on content acquisition through rote rehearsal, rather than the processes of thinking for analysis and synthesis. Even those teachers who have worked conscientiously to include activities requiring higher-order thinking are confronted with the realities of preparing students

> *We do not teach the brain to think. We can, however, help learners to organize content to facilitate more complex processing.*

for high stakes testing that usually focuses on recall and application. Repeating the answer becomes more important than the process used to get the answer. Consequently, students and teachers frequently deal with learning at the lower levels of complexity.

What we are trying to do now is recognize these limitations, rewrite curriculum, retrain teachers, and encourage students to use their innate thinking abilities to process learning at higher levels of complexity. In other words, we need to work harder at teaching them *how to organize content in such a way that it facilitates and promotes higher-order thinking.*

Modeling Thinking Skills in the Classroom

Teachers serve as valuable and authentic role models when they use creative and critical reflection to improve their practice. Students are more likely to learn thinking skills in classrooms where teachers nurture a love for learning and establish a setting that is conducive to creative and critical thought. Such a positive learning climate emerges when teachers:

- Exhibit genuine interest and commitment to learning
- Analyze their own thinking processes and classroom practices and explain what they do
- Change their own positions when the evidence warrants it
- Are willing to admit a mistake
- Allow students to participate in setting rules and making decisions related to learning and assessment

- Encourage students to follow their own thinking and not just repeat the teacher's views
- Allow students to select assignments and activities from a range of appropriate choices
- Prepare and present lessons that require higher-order thinking to achieve learning objectives

Having established a classroom environment that fosters higher-level thinking, the teacher's next task is to select a practical and easily understood model for teaching students the skills they need for creative, critical, and divergent thinking. Of all the current models available, let's look at a very workable and effective design that has stood the test of time—Bloom's Taxonomy.

REVISITING BLOOM'S TAXONOMY OF THE COGNITIVE DOMAIN

What model can teachers use that, when properly implemented, promotes thinking, has been successful in the past, and holds the promise of success for the future? My suggestion is to start with the taxonomy of the cognitive domain developed about 50 years ago by Benjamin Bloom, and see if we can adapt it to the needs of the modern era. Some readers may be thinking "Oh, no, not Bloom again!" Perhaps some newer teachers are asking, "Who's Bloom?" Regardless of your response, I hope you will bear with me to learn why this model may continue to form the basis for successful classroom activities that promote higher-order thinking.

Why do I continue to propose this type of model? In recent years, I have seen the spread of state-adopted curriculum standards, the mandates of the No Child Left Behind Act, a greater emphasis on state and national testing, and an intense public insistence that school and teacher accountability be measured in test scores. Consequently, teachers who are under pressure to teach to the test are not likely to implement overly complicated, multi-level thinking skills programs. That is why I am comfortable proposing that we reexamine this familiar model and decide how, with some adjustments, it can still serve our needs. My aim is to convince you of its value in aiding less able students experience the excitement of higher-order thinking and the exhilaration of greater achievement.

Why Start With This Model?

One of the more enduring and useful models for enhancing thinking was developed by Benjamin Bloom and his colleagues in the 1950s. Bloom's system of classification, or taxonomy, identifies six levels of complexity of human thought (Bloom, Engelhart, Furst, Hill, & Krathwohl, 1956). I believe that with some revisions, this framework can upgrade the quality of teacher instruction and student learning for the following reasons:

- It is familiar to many prospective and practicing teachers.
- It is user-friendly and simple when compared to other models.
- It provides a common language about learning objectives that cuts across subject matter and grade levels.

- It requires only modest retraining for teachers to understand the relationship between the difficulty and complexity components.
- It helps teachers recognize the difference between difficulty and complexity, so they can help slower learners improve their thinking and achievement significantly.
- It can be implemented in every classroom immediately without waiting for major reform or restructuring.
- It is inexpensive in that teachers need only a few supplementary materials to use with the current curriculum.
- It motivates teachers because they see their students learning better, thinking more profoundly, and showing more interest.
- With revisions, it can reflect fairly well the latest research on brain functions.

I know that Bloom's Taxonomy has been standard fare in preservice and inservice teacher training for many years. Yet I suspect, as Bloom himself had conjectured, that the taxonomy's value as a model for moving all students to higher levels of thinking has not been fully explored. In fact, my experience recently has been that, although most teachers remember this model, they have little enthusiasm for it in the current atmosphere that emphasizes preparing students for high stakes tests at the expense of promoting higher-order thinking and learning. Moreover, as we

> *With revisions, Bloom's Taxonomy can still be a useful tool for moving students, especially slower learners, to higher levels of thinking.*

will discuss later, the taxonomy's connection to student ability has been largely misunderstood and misapplied. This situation is regrettable because the model is easy to understand and, when used correctly, can accelerate learning and elevate student interest and achievement, especially for slower learners.

The Model's Structure and Revision

Bloom's original taxonomy contained six levels that many readers can no doubt recite from memory. Moving from the least to the most complex, they are: knowledge, comprehension, application, analysis, synthesis, and evaluation (Figure 7.1). From 1995 through 2000, a group of educators worked to revise the original taxonomy based on more recent understandings about learning. The group published the results of their work in 2001 and the basic revision is shown in Figure 7.2 (Anderson et al., 2001).

Revising the taxonomy provided the opportunity to rename three categories and interchange two of them, as well as change the names of all levels to the

Levels of Bloom's Taxonomy

Original Version (1956)

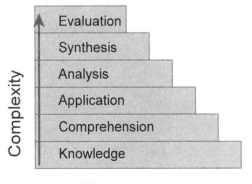

Figure 7.1 Bloom's original taxonomy had six levels from knowledge (lowest complexity) to evaluation (highest complexity).

Levels of Bloom's Taxonomy

Revised Version (2001)

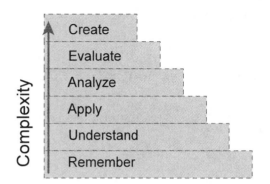

Figure 7.2 The revised taxonomy retains the six levels but changes the labels to verb form, renames three levels, and interchanges the top two levels. The dotted outline suggests a more open and fluid model, recognizing that an individual may move among the levels during extended processing.

verb form to fit the way they are used in learning objectives. The original *Knowledge* level was renamed *Remember* because it more accurately describes the recall process occurring at this level. Also, knowledge can be acquired at *all* levels. *Comprehension* was renamed *Understand* because that is the term most commonly used when teachers discuss this level. *Application, Analysis,* and *Evaluation* were changed to the verbs *Apply, Analyze,* and *Evaluate.*

Synthesis changed places with *Evaluation* and was renamed *Create.* This exchange was made because the researchers felt that recent studies in cognitive neuroscience suggest that generating, planning, and producing an original product demands more complex thinking than making judgments based on accepted criteria (Table 7.1). Although there are still six separate levels, the hierarchy of complexity is not as rigid, and it recognizes that an individual may move easily among the levels during extended processing.

Below is a review of each level using the story of *Goldilocks* and the bombing of Pearl Harbor as examples of how two differing concepts can be taken through the taxonomy.

Remember. Remember refers to the mere rote recall and recognition of previously learned material, from specific facts to a definition or a complete theory. All that is required is bringing it forth from long-term memory in the form in which it was learned. This is recall of semantic memory. It represents the lowest level of learning in the cognitive domain because there is no presumption that the learner understands what is being recalled. Students in first grade recite the Pledge of Allegiance daily. Do they all comprehend what they are saying? If so, would one fine, patriotic boy have started his pledge with, *I led the pigeons to the flag of the United . . .* ?

Examples: What did Goldilocks do in the three bears' house?
            What was the date of the bombing of Pearl Harbor?

Understand. This level describes the ability to make sense of the material. Understanding may occur by converting the material from one form to another (words to numbers), by interpreting the material (summarizing a story), or by estimating future trends (predicting the consequences or effects). The learning goes beyond mere rote recall and represents the lowest level of comprehension. When a student understands the material, rather than merely recalling it, the material becomes available for future use to solve problems and to make decisions. Questions at this level attempt to determine if the students comprehend the information in a sensible way. When this happens, students may say, "Now I get it."

Table 7.1 Revision of Bloom's Taxonomy of the Cognitive Domain

Below are the levels in decreasing order of complexity with terms and sample activities that illustrate the thought processes at each level.

Level	Terms	Sample Activities
Create	imagine compose design infer	Pretend you were a participant in the Boston Tea Party and write a diary entry that tells what happened. Rewrite *Little Red Riding Hood* as a news story. Design a different way of solving this problem. Formulate a hypothesis that might explain the results of these three experiments.
Evaluate	appraise assess judge critique	Which of the two main characters in the story would you rather have as a friend? Why? Is violence ever justified in correcting injustices? Why or why not? Which of the environments we've studied seems like the best place for you to live? Defend your answer. Critique these two products and defend which one you would recommend to the consumer.
Analyze	analyze contrast distinguish deduce	Which events in the story are fantasy and which really happened? Compare and contrast the post–Civil War period with the post–Vietnam War period. Sort this collection of rocks into three categories. Which of these words are Latin derivatives and which are Greek?
Apply	practice calculate apply execute	Use each vocabulary word in a new sentence. Calculate the area of your classroom. Think of three situations in which we would use this mathematics operation. Use the parts to reassemble this motor correctly.
Understand	summarize discuss explain outline	Summarize the paragraph in your own words. Why are symbols used on maps? Write a paragraph explaining the duties of the mayor. Outline the steps for completing this experiment.
Remember	define label recall recognize	What is the definition of a verb? Label the three symbols on this map. What are the three branches of government? Which object in the picture is a xylophone?

Source: Adapted from Anderson et al., 2001

Examples: Why did Goldilocks like the baby bear's things best?
Why did the Japanese bomb Pearl Harbor?

Apply. This level refers to the ability to use learned material in new situations with a minimum of direction. It includes the application of such things as rules, concepts, methods, and theories to solve problems. The learner activates procedural memory and uses convergent thinking to select, transfer, and apply data to complete a new task. Practice is essential at this level.

Examples: If Goldilocks came to your house today, what things might she do? If you had been responsible for the defense of the Hawaiian Islands, what preparation would you have made against an attack?

Analyze. This is the ability to break material into its component parts so that its structure may be understood. It includes identifying parts, examining the relationships of the parts to each other and to the whole, and recognizing the organizational principles involved. The learner must be able to organize and reorganize information into categories. The brain's frontal lobes are working hard at this level. This stage is more complex because the learner is aware of the thought process in use (metacognition) and understands both the content and structure of the material.

Examples: What things in the Goldilocks story could have really happened?
What lesson did our country learn from Pearl Harbor?

Evaluate. This level deals with the ability to judge the value of material based on specific criteria and standards. The learner may determine the criteria or be given them. The learner examines criteria from several categories and selects those that are the most relevant to the situation. Activities at this level almost always have multiple and equally acceptable solutions. This is a high level of cognitive thought because it contains elements of many other levels, plus conscious judgments based on definite criteria. At this level, learners tend to consolidate their thinking and become more receptive to other points of view.

Examples: Do you think it was right for Goldilocks to go into the bears' house without having been invited? Why or why not?
Do you feel that the bombing of Pearl Harbor has any effect on Japanese-American relations today? Why or why not?

Create. This refers to the ability to put parts together to form a plan that is new to the learner. It may involve the production of a unique communication (essay or speech), a plan of operations (research proposal), or a scheme for classifying information. This level stresses creativity, with major emphasis on forming *new* patterns or structures. This is the level where learners use divergent thinking to get an *Aha!* experience. It indicates that being creative requires a great deal of information, understanding, and application to produce a tangible product. Michelangelo could never have created the *David* or the *Pietà* without a thorough comprehension of human anatomy and types of marble, as well as the ability to use polishing compounds and tools with accuracy. His artistry comes from the mastery with which he used his knowledge and skill to carve magnificent pieces. Although most often associated with the arts, this process can occur in all areas of the curriculum (see Chapter 6).

Examples: Retell the story as *Goldilocks and the Three Fishes*.
Retell the story of Pearl Harbor assuming the U.S. armed forces had been ready for the attack.

Test Question No. 10: Bloom's Taxonomy has not changed over the years.

Answer: False. In 2001, a team of researchers and psychologists published a revision of Bloom's Taxonomy that aligned it more closely with current research and usage.

Important Characteristics of the Revised Model

Several points need to be made here about the revision, especially in light of recent discoveries in how the brain processes information.

Loosening of the Hierarchy

Bloom's original model held that the six levels were cumulative, that is, each level above the lowest required all the skills of lesser complexity. To Bloom, a learner could not comprehend material without mentally possessing it. Similarly, one could not correctly apply a learning to new situations without understanding it. However, because the 2001 revision gives much greater weight to teacher choice and usage, the strict hierarchy has been loosened to allow levels to overlap one another. For example, certain forms of explaining, usually associated with *Understand,* might be more complex than executing, which is associated with *Apply.*

Moreover, this loosening is more consistent with recent evidence from brain research showing that different brain areas are used to solve different types of problems. One study using PET scans found that problems requiring deductive reasoning activated areas in the right hemisphere while problems involving inductive reasoning stimulated areas in the left hemisphere (Parsons & Osherson, 2001). Another study using EEG found that different cerebral regions were involved in solving problems of logic and sequence rather than in solving open-ended problems with multiple answers (Jausovec & Jausovec, 2000). This evidence tends to weaken Bloom's basic notion that one type of thinking is dependent on the prior activation of lower level thinking. But cognitive psychologists have long suspected that thinking skills at the upper levels were a lot more fluid than Bloom's rigid hierarchy suggested. Nonetheless, the experimental findings support the notion that there are different types of thinking which the revised taxonomy accurately describes.

Cognitive and Emotional Thinking

It is important to remember that this is a model to describe the *cognitive* processing of information that poses no immediate danger to the learner. It is *not* intended to describe *emotional* thinking, which often occurs without cognitive input. For example, when a stranger walks near you on a dark street, the amygdala in your brain immediately evaluates the environmental stimuli to determine if a threat exists. The amygdala reacts to a threatening voice or menacing look, often triggering a fight-or-flight reaction. In this situation, the individual's brain is evaluating without the benefit of conscious thought. There is no time for remembering, understanding, applying, or analyzing. Let's just get out of here! The taxonomy is not appropriate here because it addresses conscious and deliberate cognitive thought, not survival behavior.

Other Ways to View the Levels

To align the revised taxonomy more with recent studies on cognitive processing, it is helpful to look at other ways of describing the levels. For example, the lower three levels (*Remember, Understand,* and *Apply*) describe a *convergent* thinking process whereby the learner recalls and focuses what is known and comprehended to solve a problem through application. The upper three levels (*Analyze, Evaluate,* and *Create*) describe a *divergent* thinking process, because the learner's processing results in new insights and discoveries that were not part of the original information. When the learner is thinking at these upper levels, thought flows naturally from one to the other and the boundaries disappear.

Another approach is to view *Remember* and *Understand* as skills designed to acquire and understand information and *Apply* and *Analyze* as skills for changing and transforming information through deduction and inference. The skills at *Evaluate* and *Create* generate new information by appraising, critiquing, and imagining. Even here, one must remember that the levels are fluid and overlap.

Testing Your Understanding of the Taxonomy

To determine if you understand the revised taxonomy's six different levels, complete the activity below. Then, look at the answers and explanation following the activity.

Directions. Identify the highest level (remember, the levels are cumulative) of the taxonomy indicated in these learning objectives.

1. Given a ruler to measure the room, find how long the room is.
2. What is the Sixth Amendment to the U.S. Constitution?
3. Given copies of the Articles of Confederation and the Bill of Rights, the learner will write a comparison of the two documents and discuss similarities and differences.
4. Identify and write a question for each level of the taxonomy.
5. Use your own words to explain the moral at the end of the fable.
6. Given two ways to solve the problem, the learner will make a choice of which to use and give reasons.
7. Write your own fairy tale including all the characteristics of a fairy tale.

Answers:

1. *Apply.* The learner must know the measuring system, comprehend the meaning of length, and use the ruler correctly.
2. *Remember.* The learner simply recalls that the Sixth Amendment deals with the rights of the accused.
3. *Analyze.* The learner must separate both documents into their component parts and compare and contrast them for relationships that describe their similarities and differences.
4. *Apply.* The learner knows each level, comprehends its definition, then uses this information to write the question for each level.
5. *Understand.* The learner shows comprehension by explaining the fable's moral.
6. *Evaluate.* The learner chooses between two feasible options and explains the reasons for the choice.
7. *Create.* Using the general characteristics of fairy tales, the learner creates a new one.

The Taxonomy and the Dimensions of Thinking

To what extent does the revision of Bloom's taxonomy address the major areas mentioned earlier that are included within most of the current models describing the dimensions of thinking?

Basic Processes. The six levels of the revised taxonomy cover all the skills included under these processes. *Observing* is contained in the levels of *Remember* and *Understand. Finding patterns* and *generalizing* are skills in the levels of *Remember, Understand,* and *Analyze.* Forming conclusions based on patterns is in *Analyze* and *Create.* Finally, *assessing conclusions* is a characteristic of the taxonomy's *Evaluate* level.

Domain-Specific Knowledge. The revised taxonomy recognizes that the acquisition of knowledge occurs at all levels. It specifically separates this domain into four types of knowledge: factual (names, dates), conceptual (ideas, patterns), procedural (steps, sequences), and metacognitive (reflections on thought processes).

Critical Thinking. The upper levels of the taxonomy require critical thinking in order to analyze, contrast, criticize, and assess information.

Creative Thinking. Students working diligently at the *Create* level are using all the skills associated with creative thinking.

Metacognition. This is the one area that is not explicitly cited in any one of the six levels. Nonetheless, when analyzing or discussing the rationale for selecting from among equally viable choices at the *Evaluate* level, the learner has to reflect on the processes used to arrive at the selection and gather data to defend the choice. This self-awareness of the thinking process used is the essence of metacognition. The other components, such as having a respect for self-monitoring as a valued skill, a positive and personal attitude toward learning, and an attention to learning through introspection and practice, are very likely to result from the accurate, frequent, and systematic use of the taxonomy's upper levels.

The Critical Difference Between Complexity and Difficulty

Complexity and difficulty describe different mental operations, but are often used synonymously. This error, resulting in the two factors being treated as one, limits the use of the taxonomy to enhance the thinking of all students. By recognizing how these concepts are different, the teacher can gain valuable insight into the connection between the taxonomy and student ability. *Complexity* describes the *thought process* that the brain uses to deal with information. In the revision of Bloom's Taxonomy (Table 7.1), it can be described by any of the six words representing the six levels. For example, the question, "What is the capital of Rhode Island?" is at the *Remember* level, while the question "Tell me in your own words what is meant by a state capital" is at the *Understand* level. The second question is more *complex* than the first because it is at a higher level in the taxonomy.

Difficulty, on the other hand, refers to the *amount of effort* that the learner must expend *within* a level of complexity to accomplish a learning objective. It is possible for a learning activity to become increasingly difficult without becoming more complex. For example, the task "Name the states of the Union" is at the *Remember* level of complexity because it involves simple recall (semantic memory) for most students. Similarly, the task "Name the states of the Union and their capitals" is also at the *Remember* level, but is more difficult than the prior question because it

> **Teachers are more likely to increase difficulty, rather than complexity, when attempting to raise student thinking.**

involves more effort to recall additional information. Similarly, the task "Name the states and their capitals in order of their admission to the Union" is still at the *Remember* level, but it is considerably more difficult than the first two. It requires gathering more information and then sequencing it in chronological order.

These are examples of how students can exert great effort to achieve a learning task while processing at the lowest level of thinking. When seeking to challenge students, classroom teachers are more likely (perhaps unwittingly) to increase difficulty rather than complexity as the challenge mode. This may be because they do not recognize the difference between these concepts or that they believe that difficulty is the method for achieving higher-order thinking (Figure 7.3).

Connecting Complexity and Difficulty to Ability

When teachers are asked whether complexity or difficulty is more closely linked to student ability, they more often choose complexity. Some explain their belief that only students of higher ability can carry out the processes indicated in the *Analyze, Evaluate,* and *Create* levels. Others say that whenever they have tried to bring slower students up the taxonomy, the lesson got bogged down. But the real connection to ability is difficulty, not complexity.

The mistaken link between complexity and ability is the result of an unintended but very real self-fulfilling prophesy. Here's how it works. Teachers allot a certain amount of *time* for the class to learn a concept, usually based on how long they think it will take the *average* student to learn it

Levels of Bloom's Revised Taxonomy
Difficulty and Complexity

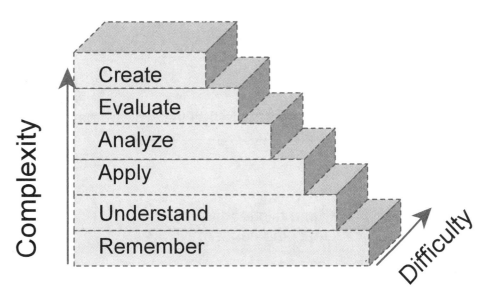

Figure 7.3   Complexity and difficulty are different. Complexity establishes the level of thought while difficulty determines the amount of effort required within each level.

(Figure 7.4). The fast learners learn the concept in less than the allotted time. During the remaining time, their brains often sort the concept's sublearnings into important and unimportant categories, that is, they select the critical attributes for storage and discard what they decide is unimportant. This explains why fast learners are usually fast retrievers: They have not cluttered their memory networks with trivia.

Meanwhile, the slower learners need more than the allotted time to learn the concept. If that time is not given to them, not only do they lose part of the sublearnings but they also do not have time to do any sorting. If the teacher attempts to move up the taxonomy, the fast learners have the concept's more important attributes in working memory to use appropriately and successfully at the higher levels of complexity. The slow learners, on the other hand, have not had time to sort, have cluttered their working memory with all the sublearnings (important and unimportant), and do not recognize the parts needed for more complex processing. For them, it is like taking five big suitcases on an overnight trip, whereas the fast learners have taken just a small bag packed with the essentials. As a result, teachers become convinced that higher-order thinking is for the fast learners and that ability is linked to complexity.

Bloom reported on studies that included slower students for whom the unimportant material was not even taught. The curriculum was sorted from the start, and the focus was on

> *With guidance and practice, slower learners can regularly reach the higher levels of Bloom's revised taxonomy.*

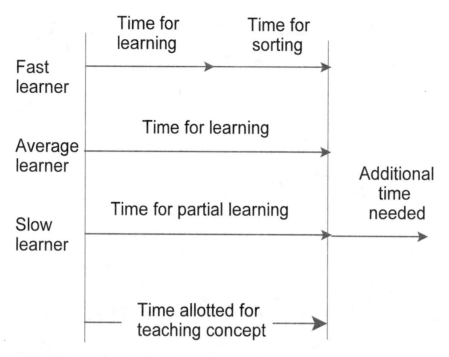

Figure 7.4   The time allotted to learn a concept is usually fixed even though students learn at different rates.

critical attributes and other vital information. When the teacher moved up the taxonomy, these students in some cases demonstrated better achievement than the control groups (Bloom, 1976). When teachers differentiate between complexity and difficulty, a new view of Bloom's Taxonomy emerges, one which promises more success for more students.

The Taxonomy and Constructivism

In their description of the characteristics of constructivist teachers, Brooks and Brooks (1993) noted that these teachers ask open-ended questions and continually encourage students to analyze, evaluate, and create. From this description, it seems evident that teachers who constantly use the upper levels of Bloom's revised taxonomy are demonstrating, among other things, constructivist behaviors.

Curriculum Changes to Accommodate the Taxonomy

The implications from these studies are very significant in that they suggest two important things about using the taxonomy.

- If teachers avoid the self-fulfilling prophecy snare, they can get slower learners to do higher-order thinking successfully and often.

- One way to accomplish this is to review the curriculum and remove the topics of least importance in order to gain the time needed for practice at the higher levels. An effective method for doing this pruning is to list among all the concepts in a curriculum in order of most important to least. Delete the least important bottom 20 to 25 percent, and use the time gained by this sorting and paring to move all students up the taxonomy. Finally, take advantage of the power of positive transfer by integrating these concepts with previously taught material and connecting them to appropriate concepts in other curriculum areas.

Higher-Order Thinking Increases Understanding and Retention

The number of neurons in our brains declines as we age, but our ability to learn, remember, and recall is dependent largely on the number of connections between neurons. The stability and permanency of these connections reflect the nature of the thinking process and the type and degree of rehearsal that occurred during the learning episode.

> *Our students would make a quantum leap to higher-order thinking if every teacher in every classroom correctly and regularly used a model such as Bloom's revised taxonomy.*

As mentioned earlier, PET scans show that elaborative rehearsal, involving higher-order thinking skills, engages the brain's frontal lobe. This engagement helps learners make connections between past and new learning, creates new pathways, strengthens existing pathways, and increases the likelihood that the new learning will be consolidated and stored for future retrieval.

Many teachers recognize the need to do more activities that require elaborate thinking rather than just rote rehearsal. They admit that when they move up through higher levels of Bloom's Taxonomy (or any other thinking skills framework) students demonstrate a much greater depth of understanding. However, they also admit that there are barriers to using this approach regularly because it takes more time. Examples of the barriers they cite are the pressures to cover an ever-expanding curriculum and the tyranny of quick-answer testing of all types. These obstacles will not be overcome easily, but teachers can work toward a compromise—finding ways to engage the novel brain with challenging activities and developing alternative assessment strategies.

Other Thinking Skills Programs

Other thinking skills programs and models exist, and new ones are appearing regularly. My analysis of them is that they can be very useful after extensive teacher training, substantial curricular reform, and sizable investments for new curriculum materials. Some programs assert that even Bloom's revised taxonomy is too restrictive and does not include other important thinking skills. Yet in reviewing these programs, I have not found one thinking skill that cannot be associated with at least one level of the revised taxonomy. In most of these programs, the difference is in how the skills are labeled and organized. Consequently, I am convinced that if every teacher correctly used the revised taxonomy in every classroom and in every subject area, our students would make a quantum leap forward in their ability to do higher-order thinking. And they can do this now while waiting for more comprehensive reform efforts to become reality.

What's Coming Up?

Now that we have looked at important aspects of how the brain learns and remembers, the next step is to consolidate this information into a workable design for planning lessons. What components should be included in a lesson? What questions should teachers be asking when considering content and strategies for instruction? How do teachers get the support they need in their school to try out new techniques and to keep abreast of what we are learning about learning? The answers to these vital questions are coming up in the next chapter.

PRACTITIONER'S CORNER

Understanding Bloom's Revised Taxonomy

Directions: With a partner, explain verbally what the pictorial view below is all about. Then fill in the chart on the next page, using the explanation of the pictures to describe your thought processing at each level of the taxonomy.

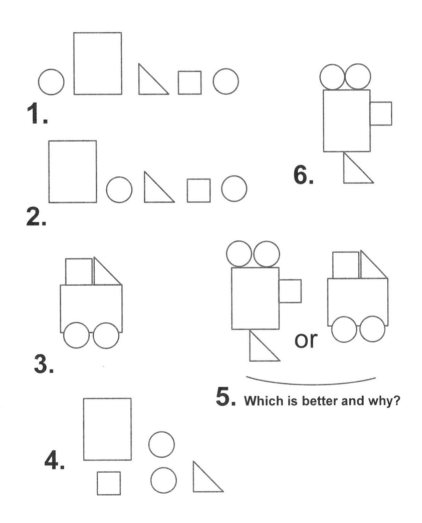

Directions: Write on the lines below the six levels of the revised Bloom's Taxonomy, starting with the least complex at the bottom. Then write a few words next to each level that explain the type of processing that occurs when describing the various pictures on the previous page.

LEVEL	DESCRIPTION of PROCESSING
6.	
5.	
4.	
3.	
2.	
1.	

PRACTITIONER'S CORNER

Take a Concept/Situation Up the Taxonomy!

Directions: Think of a task that you need to accomplish with your own child, parent, colleague, or spouse (e.g., how to use the washing machine with different types of clothes, planning a vacation) and describe questions or activities that move the task up Bloom's revised taxonomy.

CONCEPT/SITUATION:_____

Create (putting ideas together to form a new whole):

Evaluate (judging material using certain criteria):

Analyze (breaking down a concept and looking for relationships):

Apply (using a concept or principle in a new situation):

Understand (translating the material to achieve comprehension):

START HERE: Remember (rote remembering of information):

PRACTITIONER'S CORNER

Tips on Using Bloom's Revised Taxonomy

- **Watch the Behavior of the Learner.** The learner's behavior reveals the level of complexity where processing is taking place. Whenever the brain has the option of solving a problem at two levels of complexity, it generally chooses the less complex level. Teachers can inadvertently design activities that they believe are at one level of complexity that students actually accomplish at a different (usually lower) level.

- **Provide Sufficient Practice at the Lower Levels.** In most instances, students should deal with the new learnings thoroughly and successfully at lower levels before moving to upper levels. It is very difficult to create a product without a solid knowledge base and sufficient practice in applying the learnings.

- **Beware of Mimicry.** Sometimes students seem to be applying their learning to a new situation (*Apply* level) when they are just mimicking the teacher's behavior. Mimicry is usually the *Remember* level. For students to be really at the *Apply* level, they must understand and explain why they are using a particular process to solve *new* problems.

- **Discuss Core Concepts at the Higher Levels.** Not all topics are suitable for processing at the upper levels. There are some areas in which creativity is not desired (e.g., basic arithmetic, spelling, the rules of grammar), but consider taking to the upper levels every concept that is identified as a core learning. This helps students to attach meaning and make connections to past learnings, thereby significantly increasing retention.

- **Choose Complexity Over Difficulty.** Give novel, multisensory tasks to move students progressively up the taxonomy. Limit the exposure to trivial information and discourage students from memorizing it, a process that many find monotonous and meaningless. Instead, give them divergent activities in *Analyze, Evaluate,* and *Create* that are more interesting and more likely to result in a deeper understanding and retention of the learning objectives. For example, Raths (2002) suggests that a discussion of tourists, migrants, and immigrants could ask students to *analyze* these concepts in the context of rights and obligations of nonresidents and noncitizens, *evaluate* proposals for dealing with social problems such as illegal immigrants, and *create* policies that solve specific social problems without causing other problems (e.g., dealing with immigrants without negatively affecting tourism).

PRACTITIONER'S CORNER

Bloom's Taxonomy: Increasing Complexity

Examples become more complex from bottom to top, and more difficult from left to right.

BLOOM'S LEVEL	INCREASING LEVEL OF DIFFICULTY ⟶	
CREATE	Rewrite the story from the point of view of the dog.	Rewrite the story from the points of view of the dog *and of the cat.*
EVALUATE	Compare the *two* main characters in the story. Which would you rather have as a friend and why?	Compare the *four* main characters in the story. Which would you rather have as a friend and why?
ANALYZE	What were the similarities and differences between this story and the one we read about the Civil War hero?	What were the similarities and differences between this story, the one we read about the Civil War hero, *and the one about the Great Depression*?
APPLY	Think of another situation that could have caused the main character to behave that way.	Think of at least *three* other situations that could have caused the main character to behave that way.
UNDERSTAND	Write a paragraph that describes the childhood of any one of the main characters.	Write a paragraph that describes the childhood of each of the *four* main characters.
REMEMBER	Name the major characters in this story.	Name the major characters and the *four locations* in this story.

The left-hand side of the table shows the vertical label: INCREASING COMPLEXITY

PRACTITIONER'S CORNER

Understanding the Difference Between Complexity and Difficulty

First, let's try a real-life application.

1. Select a partner and decide who is Partner A and who is Partner B.

2. Each partner performs, in turn, the activities for each situation in the Table X below.

3. When both partners have completed the three situations, discuss whether complexity or difficulty was changed **in each situation** when moving from A's to B's activity.

	Table X. Deciding Whether Complexity or Difficulty Is Increased		
Situation	**Partner A's Activity**	**Partner B's Activity**	**Complexity or Difficulty Changed? How?**
1	Tell your partner the month of your birth and the city and state where you were born.	Tell your partner the make of your current automobile.	
2	Roll a piece of paper into a ball. Stand 10 feet from your partner. Ask your partner to stand and to form his/her arms into a ring in front (as though to hug someone). Now toss the ball five times and try to get all five tosses through the ring formed by your partner's arms.	Repeat what your partner just did, except stand facing away from your partner and toss the paper ball over your head five times, still aiming for your partner's ringed arms.	
3	Fanfold a piece of paper. Then explain to your partner three uses for the folded paper.	After listening to your partner's explanation of the uses, choose one you think is best and explain why.	

Now, let's try a school situation. Examine how each teacher in Table Y below changes Activity A to Activity B. Then decide if the teacher has increased that activity's level of complexity or difficulty.

	Table Y. Deciding Whether Complexity or Difficulty Is Increased		
Teacher	**Activity A**	**Activity B**	**Increased Complexity or Difficulty?**
1	Make an outline of the story you just read.	Make an outline of the last two stories you read.	
2	Compare and contrast the personalities of Julius Caesar and Macbeth.	After reading three acts of *Macbeth*, write a plausible ending.	
3	Choose one character in the story you would like to be and explain your choice.	Choose two characters in the story you would like to be and explain why.	
4	Name the three most common chemical elements on Earth.	Describe in your own words what is meant by a chemical element.	

Reflections:

Is complexity or difficulty more closely related to intelligence?

How will understanding that difference affect my teaching?

Summary: Increasing the *difficulty* of a task adds to the students' efforts without increasing the level of their thinking processes. Think of it as moving *horizontally* within a level of the revised Bloom's Taxonomy. Strategies such as repetition and drill tend to increase difficulty. Jot down below some other strategies that increase difficulty. For what types of learning would it be important to use strategies to increase difficulty?

_____

_____

_____

_____

_____

Increasing the *complexity* of a task causes the students to change the way they mentally process the task. Think of it as moving *vertically* up the taxonomy from one level to a higher one. Strategies that cause students to compare and contrast, or to choose among options and defend their choice, are examples of increasing complexity. Jot down below some other strategies that increase complexity. For what types of learning would it be important to use strategies to increase complexity?

_____

_____

_____

_____

PRACTITIONER'S CORNER

Questions to Stimulate Higher-Order Thinking

Incorporate these questions into lesson plans to stimulate higher-order thinking. Be sure to read the guidelines for using the Bloom's revised taxonomy to ensure the maximum effectiveness of these questions. Remember to provide adequate wait-time. Students should become accustomed to this type of questioning in every study assignment.

What would you have done? Why do you think this is the best choice?

What are some of the things you wondered about while this was happening?

Could this ever really happen? What might happen next?

What do you think might happen if . . . ? What do you think caused this?

How is it different from . . . ? Can you give an example?

Where do we go next? Where could we go for help on this?

Have we left out anything important?

Can we trust the source of this material?

In what other ways could this be done? How can you test this theory?

How many ways can you think of to use . . . ?

Do you agree with this author/speaker? Why or why not?

Can you isolate the most important idea?

How could you modify this? How would changing the sequence affect the outcome?

How can you tell the difference between . . . and . . . ?

PRACTITIONER'S CORNER

Activities to Stimulate Higher-Order Thinking

The following activities help teachers encourage higher-order thinking in their classrooms:

- Encourage students to use analogies and metaphors when describing and comparing new concepts, theories, and principles.

- Have students attempt to solve real life problems (e.g., energy crisis, environmental pollution) where there is a possibility of more than one adequate solution.

- Ask questions that foster higher-order thinking, such as those with multiple answers or several equally correct answers.

- Involve students in debates and discussions that tackle more than one side of an issue, and require students to support their arguments with evidence.

- Get students in role plays or simulations of historical events where people held conflicting views (e.g., drafting the U.S. Constitution, women's right to vote).

- Supplement regular textbooks with additional materials (including audio/visual content) that provide a wider variety of perspectives about a particular idea.

- Encourage students to watch television programs, attend community meetings, and read newspaper articles that express different viewpoints. Follow this with an analysis of the relative strengths and weaknesses of the arguments, including an analysis of the possible motives underlying the various positions.

- Have students analyze the content of popular media (e.g., television, movies, music) for their accuracy and completeness of its portrayals of everyday life. For example, do commercials glorifying the acquisition of expensive personal goods balance with the existence of poverty in the community. Do the media perpetuate stereotypes?

- Explore with students the methods used to develop knowledge in a particular field. For example: What technologies help us look inside the living human brain?

Chapter 7—Thinking Skills and Learning

Key Points to Ponder

Jot down on this page key points, ideas, strategies, and resources you want to consider later. This sheet is your personal journal summary and will help to jog your memory.

_____

_____

_____

_____

_____

_____

_____

_____

_____

Chapter 8

Putting It All Together

In the world of the future, the new illiterate will be the person who has not learned to learn.

—Alvin Toffler

Chapter Highlights. This chapter focuses on how to use the research presented in this book to plan daily lessons. It suggests guidelines and a format for lesson design, and mentions support systems to maintain expertise in the techniques and continuous professional growth.

The preceding chapters discussed some of the major strides that research is making in exploring how the brain processes information and learns. Suggestions are offered in each chapter's **Practitioner's Corners** on how to translate these new discoveries into practical classroom strategies that can improve the efficacy of teaching and learning. But this information is of value to students only if teachers can incorporate it into their classroom practice so that it becomes part of their daily instructional behavior. The question now is: How do we use this large amount of information when planning our daily lessons?

DAILY PLANNING

General Guidelines

Start by keeping the following general thoughts in mind while planning:

- Learning engages the entire person (cognitive, affective, and psychomotor domains).
- The human brain seeks patterns in its search for meaning.
- Emotions affect all aspects of learning, retention, and recall.
- Past experience always affects new learning.
- The brain's working memory has a limited capacity.
- Lecture usually results in the lowest degree of retention.
- Rehearsal is essential for retention.
- Practice does not make perfect.
- Each brain is unique.

Daily Lesson Design

To use this research in daily planning, we need a lesson plan model as a framework. The type of lesson plan that a teacher uses depends to a large degree on the instructional method the teacher decides to use. The following are examples of some instructional methods (Moore, 2005):

- **Direct Teaching.** The teacher lectures, does much of the work, and can present a great deal of information in a short period of time. Extent of student participation varies from none to considerable. Still the most common teaching method in secondary schools and higher education.
- **Demonstration.** Teacher shows something, tells what is happening, and asks the students to discuss the demonstration.
- **Concept Attainment.** Students figure out the attributes of a group or category (provided by the teacher) by comparing and contrasting examples that possess the attributes and examples that do not. Through discussion, students develop a definition or hypothesis about the concept (lesson objective).
- **Socratic Method.** This lesson draws information from students through a series of carefully designed questions that eventually help students achieve the lesson objective.
- **Cooperative Learning.** Students work together in heterogeneous groups to accomplish a specific task.
- **Simulations and Games.** The lesson centers around a problem situation that represents reality. Role-playing is used to help students understand the motives and behaviors of people. Educational games involve students in decision-making roles.
- **Individualized Instruction.** These methods include differentiated instruction, mastery learning, and independent study.
- **Drill and Practice.** This lesson specifically targets the recall and improvement of certain skills to enhance accuracy and speed.

No single lesson plan format fully addresses every aspect of every possible teaching method. But I do think one comes very close. The format I propose evolved from Madeline Hunter's (2004) work at UCLA in the 1970s. Hunter was a clinical psychologist who was a pioneer in recognizing the need to include strategies from cognitive science in teaching. Despite its age, the format is based on sound principles of brain-compatible learning while being flexible enough to use with a variety of instructional methods.

I have made minor modifications to Hunter's original format by expanding it to include some of the more recent strategies. The nine components of the design are:

1. *Anticipatory Set.* This strategy captures the students' focus. Almost any technique to get their initial attention can be valuable. Vary the initial attention-getter to provide novelty, and remember the power of humor in getting attention and setting a positive emotional climate for the lesson to follow. Once you get their initial attention, the rest of the set is most effective when it

   (a) allows students to remember an experience that will help them acquire the new learning (positive transfer from past to present)
   (b) involves active student participation (while avoiding "guessing" games during prime-time-1),
   (c) is relevant to the learning objective.

2. *Learning Objective.* This is a clear statement of what the students are expected to accomplish during the learning episode, including the levels of difficulty and complexity, and should include

   (a) a specific statement of the learning,
   (b) the overt behavior that demonstrates whether the learning has occurred, and whether the appropriate level of complexity has been attained.

When the teacher states the learning objective explicitly at the beginning of the lesson, it is called an *expository* lesson—that is, the objective is now "exposed." Sometimes, we prefer to have the students discover the lesson objective on their own. This is obviously called a *discovery* lesson. Discovery lessons require more careful planning and guidance to ensure that the students actually get to the intended objective. If the learner doesn't know where the lesson is going, *any* place will do.

3. *Purpose.* This states *why* the students should accomplish the learning objective. Whenever possible, it should refer to how the new learning is related to the students' prior and future learnings to facilitate positive transfer and meaning.

4. *Input.* This is the information and the procedures (skills) that students will need to acquire in order to achieve the learning objective. It can take many forms, including reading, lecture, cooperative learning groups, audiovisual presentations, the Internet, and so on.

5. *Modeling.* Clear and correct models help students make sense of the new learning and establish meaning. Models must be given first by the teacher and be accurate, unambiguous, and noncontroversial. Nonexemplars could be included later to show contrast.

6. *Check for Understanding.* This refers to the strategies the teacher will use during the learning episode to verify that the students are accomplishing the learning objective. The check could be in the form of oral discussion, questioning, written quiz, think-pair-share, or any other overt format that yields the necessary data. Depending on the results of these checks, the teacher may decide to provide more opportunities for input, reteach, or move on to new material.

7. *Guided Practice.* During this time, the student is applying the new learning in the presence of the teacher who provides immediate and specific feedback on the accuracy of the learner's practice. Later, the teacher checks any corrections that the student made as a result of feedback.

8. *Closure.* This is the time when the mind of the learner can summarize for itself its perception of what has been learned. The teacher gives specific directions for what the learner should mentally process and provides adequate time to accomplish it. This is usually the last opportunity the learner has to attach sense and meaning to the new learning, both of which are critical requirements for retention. Daily closure activities can take many forms, such as using synergy strategies or journal writing. Closure activities for the end of a unit might include writing plays, singing songs, reciting poetry, playing quiz games, and so on.

> **Closure is usually the last opportunity the learner has to attach sense and meaning to new learning.**

9. *Independent Practice.* After the teacher believes that the learners have accomplished the objective at the correct level of difficulty and complexity, students try the new learning on their own to enhance retention and develop fluency.

> **Not every lesson needs every component. The teacher should consider each component and choose those that are relevant to the learning objective and teaching method.**

Important Note. Not every lesson needs to include every component. However, the teacher should consider each component and choose those that are relevant to the learning objective and teaching method. For example, when introducing a new major unit of study, the lesson may focus primarily on *objectives* (What do we hope to accomplish?) and *purpose* (Why are we studying this?). On the other hand, a review lesson before a major test might include more ways of *checking for understanding* and for *guided practice*.

Table 8.1 shows the lesson components that could be used with each teaching method. Table 8.2 shows the lesson components, their purpose, their relationship to the research, and an example from a lesson on teaching the characteristics of suffixes.

Twenty-One Questions to Ask During Lesson Planning

Table 8.3 contains some important questions that teachers should ask while planning lessons. The questions relate to information and strategies included in previous chapters. Following each question is the rationale for considering it and the chapter number where its main reference can be found.

Table 8.1	Lesson Components for Different Teaching Methods							
	Direct Teaching	**Demon-station**	**Concept Attain**	**Socratic Method**	**Coop. Learning**	**Simul. & Games**	**Indepen. Instruc.**	**Drill & Practice**
Antic. Set	X	X	X	X	X	X		
Lesson Objective	X	X	X		X	X		X
Purpose	X	X	X		X	X	X	X
Input	X		X	X	X		X	X
Modeling	X	X	X	X	X			X
Check for Under.	X	X	X	X	X	X	X	X
Guided Practice	X		X				X	X
Closure	X	X	X	X	X	X	X	X
Indepen. Practice	X					X	X	X

Table 8.2	Components to Consider in Designing Lessons		
Lesson Component	**Purpose**	**Relationship To Research**	**Example**
Anticipatory Set	Focuses students on the learning objective.	Establishes relevance and fosters positive transfer during prime-time-1.	"Think of what we learned yesterday about prefixes and be prepared to discuss them."
Learning Objective	Identifies what is to be learned by the end of the lesson.	Students know what they should learn and how they will know they have learned it.	"Today we will learn about suffixes, and you will make up words with them."
Purpose	Explains why it is important to accomplish this objective.	Knowing the purpose for learning something builds interest and establishes meaning.	"Learning about suffixes will help us understand more vocabulary and give us greater creativity in our writing."
Input	Gives students the information, sources, and skills they will need to accomplish the objective	Bloom's **remember** level. Helps identify critical attributes	"Suffixes are letters placed after words to change their meanings."

(Continued)

Lesson Component	Purpose	Relationship To Research	Example
Modeling	Shows the process or product of what students are learning.	Modeling enhances sense and meaning to help retention	"Examples are: *-less*, as in helpless; *-able*, as in drinkable; and *-ful*, as in doubtful."
Check for Understanding	Allows instructor to verify if students understand what they are learning.	Bloom's **understand** level.	"I'll ask some of you to tell me what you learned so far about the meaning and use of suffixes."
Guided Practice	Allows the students to try the new learning under teacher guidance.	Bloom's **apply** level. Practice provides for fast learning.	"Here are 10 words. Add an appropriate suffix to each and explain their new meanings."
Closure	Allows students time to mentally summarize and internalize the new learning.	Last chance to attach sense and meaning, thus improving retention.	"I'll be quiet now while you think about the attributes and uses of suffixes."
Independent Practice	Students try new learning on their own to develop fluency.	This practice helps make the new learning permanent.	"For homework, add suffixes to the words on page 121 to change their meanings."

Table 8.2   (Continued)

UNIT PLANNING

Teacher's Work Sample

Federal and state initiatives to ensure that teachers are highly qualified has prompted some teacher training institutions to develop designs that assist beginning teachers in planning instructional units. Called the Teacher Work Sample, the design can also be used for daily lessons, and some of its components parallel the modified Hunter model discussed earlier. One sample, developed by the Renaissance Partnership for Improving Teacher Quality, contains the following elements:

- **Contextual Factors.** The teacher lists information about the community, school, and characteristics of students, including their prior learning and learning styles.
- **Learning Goals.** The teacher sets significant and challenging learning objectives that are clear, appropriate for the specific student population, and consistent with national, state, and local standards.

Table 8.3 Questions to Ask When Planning Lessons		
Question	**Rationale**	**Chapter**
1. What tactics am I using to help students attach meaning to the learning?	Meaning helps retention.	2
2. How will I use humor in this lesson?	Humor is an excellent focus device and adds novelty.	2
3. Have I divided the learning episode into mini-lessons of about 20 minutes each?	Short lesson segments have proportionally less down-time than longer ones.	3
4. What motivation and novelty strategies am using?	Motivation and novelty increase interest and accountability.	1 & 2
5. Which type of rehearsal should be used with this learning, and when?	Rote and elaborative rehearsal serve different purposes.	3
6. Am I using the prime-times to the best advantage?	Maximum retention occurs during the prime-times.	3
7. What will the students be doing during down-time?	Minimum retention occurs during down-time.	3
8. Does my plan allow for enough wait-time when asking questions?	Wait-time is critical to allow for student recall to occur.	3
9. What chunking strategies are appropriate for this objective?	Chunking increases the number of items working memory can handle at one time.	3
10. What related prior learning should be included for distributed practice?	Distributed practice increases long-term retention.	3
11. How will I maximize positive transfer and minimize negative transfer?	Positive transfer assists learning; negative transfer interferes.	4
12. Have I identified the critical attributes of this concept?	Critical attributes help distinguish one concept from all others.	4
13. Are the concepts or skills too similar to each other?	Concepts and skills that are too similar should not be taught together.	4
14. How will I show students how they can use (transfer) this learning in the future?	The prospect of future transfer increases motivation and meaning.	4
15. Is it appropriate to use a metaphor with this objective?	Metaphors enhance transfer, hemispheric integration, and retention.	4
16. Have I included activities that are multisensory?	Using many senses increases retention.	5
17. Would a concept map help here?	Concept maps help hemispheric integration and retention.	5
18. Am I using strategies that promote imaging and imagining?	Imaging and imagining help establish meaning, promote novelty, and increase retention.	6
19. Would some music be appropriate? If so, what kind and when?	Some music assists processing and cooperative learning activities.	6
20. How will I move this objective up Bloom's Taxonomy?	The taxonomy's upper levels involve higher-order thinking and are more interesting.	7
21. What emotions (affective domain) need to be considered or avoided in learning this objective?	Emotions play a key role in student acceptance and retention of learning.	7

- **Assessment Plan.** The teacher indicates the technically sound multiple assessments to determine student learning before, during, and after instruction.
- **Design for Instruction.** The teacher designs the unit's lesson plans that use a variety of instructional methods, activities, assignments, and resources, including technology.
- **Instructional Decision-Making.** The teacher uses ongoing analysis of student progress to make instructional decisions, and ensure that any adjustments to instruction are consistent with the learning objectives.
- **Analysis of Student Learning.** The teacher uses assessment data to profile student learning by using graphs to compare the pre-assessment and assessment results for individuals and for the class.
- **Reflection and Self-Evaluation.** The teacher reflects on the instruction to determine what went well and why, what needs to be changed and why, and what implications there are for future decisions on teaching practice and assessment.

Teacher work samples are particularly helpful in assisting novice and veteran teachers in assessing their skills, refining their craft, and improving their classroom presentations. They also serve to measure the training outcomes of professional development initiatives and to validate new teaching practices.

MAINTAINING SKILLS FOR THE FUTURE

This book suggests strategies that teachers can try in order to enhance the effectiveness of the teaching-learning process. The strategies have been derived from the current research on how we learn. Teachers who try these strategies for the first time may need support and feedback on the effectiveness of their implementation. The school-based support system is very important to maintaining teacher interest and commitment, especially if the new strategies don't produce the desired results in the classroom right away.

The Building Principal's Role

Building principals and head teachers play a vital role in establishing a school climate and culture that are receptive to new instructional strategies and in maintaining the support systems necessary for continuing teacher development. Providing opportunities for teachers to master an expanded repertoire of research-based instructional techniques is an effective way for principals to foster collaboration, establish their role as an instructional leader, and enhance the teaching staff's pursuit of professional inquiry. Such opportunities can include peer coaching, in-building study groups, action research projects, and workshops that keep the staff abreast of continuing discoveries about the teaching-learning process (Sousa, 2003).

Types of Support Systems

Peer Coaching

This structure pairs two teachers who periodically observe each other in class. During the lesson, the observing teacher is looking for the use of a particular strategy or technique that was identified in a preobservation conference. After the lesson, the observing teacher provides feedback on the results of the implementation of the strategy. The non-threatening and supportive nature of this peer relationship encourages teachers to take risks and try new techniques that they might otherwise avoid for fear of failure or administrative scrutiny. Peer coaches undergo initial training in how to set the observation goal at the preconference and on different methods for collecting information during the observation.

Study Groups

Forming small groups of teachers and administrators to study a particular topic further is an effective means of expanding understanding and methods of applying new strategies. The group members seek out new research on the topic and exchange and discuss information, data, and experiences in the group setting. Each group focuses on one or two topics, such as wait-time, transfer, and retention techniques. Groups within a school or district can use cooperative learning techniques as a means of sharing information across groups.

Action Research

As discussed more fully in the Introduction, conducting small research studies in a class or school can provide teachers with the validation they may need to incorporate new strategies permanently into their repertoire. Action research gives the practitioner a chance to be a researcher and to investigate specific problems that affect teaching and learning.

For example, deliberately changing the length of the wait-time after posing questions yields data on how the amount and quality of student responses vary with the wait-time. If several teachers carry out this research and exchange data, they will have the evidence to support the continued use of longer wait-time as an effective strategy. Action research on the use of humor and music in the classroom can help teachers determine the value of these strategies on student performance. Teachers can then share their results with colleagues at faculty meetings or study group sessions. This format also advances the notion that teachers should be involved in research projects as part of their professional growth.

Workshops on New Research

Periodic workshops that focus on new research findings in the teaching and learning process are valuable for updating teachers' knowledge base. Areas such as the transfer and transformation of learnings, reflection, memory, and concept development are the targets of extensive research at this time and should be monitored to determine if new findings are appropriate for district and school workshops.

When educators encourage ongoing staff development activities, such as study groups and action research, they are recognizing that our understanding of the teaching-learning process is in continual change as the research yields more data on how the amazing brain learns. True professionals are committed to updating their knowledge base constantly, and they recognize individual professional development as a personal and lifelong responsibility that will enhance their effectiveness.

CONCLUSION

The potential contributions of neuroscience to educational practice continue to accumulate. The very fact that neuroscientists and educators are meeting and talking to each other regularly is evidence that we have crossed a new frontier in our profession. There are, of course, no magic answers that make the complex processes of teaching and learning successful all the time. Educators recognize that numerous variables affect this dynamic interaction, many of which are beyond the teacher's influence or control. What teachers *can* control is their own behavior. Although a few students can learn on their own, most of them rely heavily on the instructional talents of their teachers to learn information and skills. For them, the quality of their learning rarely exceeds the quality of teaching. My hope is that this book provides teachers with some new information, strategies, and insights that will increase their chances of success with more students.

> **The quality of learning rarely exceeds the quality of teaching**

HAPPY TEACHING AND LEARNING!

PRACTITIONER'S CORNER

Reflections on Lesson Design

Here's a sample lesson design using the information processing model in Chapter 2.

Objective: The learner will be able to describe verbally the major parts of the brain processing model in the text *How the Brain Learns*.

Anticipatory Set: "Take a moment to think about whether it is important for teachers to know how we believe the brain selects and processes information. Then discuss your thoughts with your partner."

Purpose: "The purpose of this lesson is to give you some of the latest research we have on how we think the brain processes information so that you can be more successful in choosing those teacher actions that are more likely to result in learning."

Input: The teacher describes major steps in the process, including uptake by senses, interplay of the perceptual register and short-term memory, working memory, long-term storage, the cognitive belief system, and self-concept. Emphasizes the importance of sense and meaning, as well as of past experiences, throughout the entire process.

Modeling: Teacher explains the four metaphors (venetian blinds, clipboard, work table, and filing cabinets). Uses examples of working memory capacity, uses hands as model, and shows the model brain.

Check for Understanding: Teacher has students fill in the function sheet after several parts of the model are covered, and has them use the synergy strategy to discuss with their partners.

Guided Practice: Teacher gives examples of sense and meaning differences, and of positive and negative self-concept differences, to determine the extent of application of the model.

Closure: "Take a few minutes to quietly summarize in your mind the major parts of the brain processing model, and be prepared to explain them."

Chapter 8—Putting It All Together

Key Points to Ponder

Jot down on this page key points, ideas, strategies, and resources you want to consider later. This sheet is your personal journal summary and will help to jog your memory.

Glossary

Action research. A systematic process for evaluating the effectiveness of classroom practices using the techniques of research.

Alphabetic principle. The understanding that spoken words can be broken down into phonemes, and that written letters represent the phonemes of spoken language.

Amygdala. The almond-shaped structure in the brain's limbic system that encodes emotional messages to long-term storage.

Angular gyrus. A brain structure that decodes visual information about words so they can be matched to their meanings.

Apoptosis. The genetically programmed process that destroys unneeded or unhealthy brain cells.

Associative learning. A learning situation whereby a response gets linked to a specific stimulus.

Axon. The neuron's long and unbranched fiber that carries impulses from the cell to the next neuron.

Brain stem. One of the major parts of the brain, it receives sensory input and monitors vital functions such as heartbeat, body temperature, and digestion.

Cerebellum. One of the major parts of the brain, it coordinates muscle movement.

Cerebrum. The largest of the major parts of the brain, it controls sensory interpretation, thinking, and memory.

Chunking. The ability of the brain to perceive a coherent group of items as a single item or chunk.

Circadian rhythm. The daily cycle of body functions, such as breathing and body temperature.

Closure. The teaching strategy that allows learners quiet time in class to mentally reprocess what they have learned during a lesson.

Cognitive belief system. The unique construct one uses to interpret how the world works, on the basis of experience.

Computerized tomography (CT, formerly CAT) scanner. An instrument that uses X-rays and computer processing to produce a detailed cross-section of brain structure.

Confabulation. The brain's replacement of a gap in long-term memory by a falsification which the individual believes to be correct.

Constructivism. A theory of learning stating that active learners use past experiences and chunking to construct sense and meaning from new learning, thereby building larger conceptual schemes.

Corpus callosum. The bridge of nerve fibers that connects the left and right cerebral hemispheres and allows communication between them.

Cortex. The thin but tough layer of cells covering the cerebrum that contains all the neurons used for cognitive and motor processing.

Critical attribute. A characteristic that makes one concept different from all others.

Declarative memory. Knowledge of events and facts to which we have conscious access.

Delayed sleep phase disorder. A chronic condition caused mainly by a shift in an adolescent's sleep cycle that results in difficulty falling asleep at night and waking up in the morning.

Dendrite. The branched extension from the cell body of a neuron that receives impulses from nearby neurons through synaptic contacts.

Distributed practice. The repetition of a skill over increasingly longer periods of time to improve performance.

Electroencephalograph (EEG). An instrument that charts fluctuations in the brain's electrical activity via electrodes attached to the scalp.

Emotional memory. The retention of the emotional components of an experience.

Endorphins. Opiate-like chemicals in the body that lessen pain and produce pleasant and euphoric feelings.

Engram. The permanent memory trace that results when brain tissue is anatomically altered by an experience.

Episodic memory. Knowledge of events in our personal history to which we have conscious access.

Flashbulb memory. A vivid memory of the circumstances surrounding a shocking or emotionally charged experience.

Frontal lobe. The front part of the brain that monitors higher-order thinking, directs problem solving, and regulates the excesses of the emotional (limbic) system.

Functional magnetic resonance imaging (fMRI). An instrument that measures blood flow to the brain to record areas of high and low neuronal activity.

Glial cells. Special "glue" cells in the brain that surround each neuron providing support, protection, and nourishment.

Gray matter. The thin but tough covering of the brain's cerebrum also known as the cerebral cortex.

Guided practice. The repetition of a skill in the presence of the teacher who can give immediate and specific feedback.

Hippocampus. A brain structure that compares new learning to past learning and encodes information from working memory to long-term storage.

Hypothalamus. A small brain structure at the base of the limbic area that regulates body functions in response to internal and external stimuli.

Imagery. The mental visualization of objects, events, and arrays.

Immediate memory. A temporary memory where information is processed briefly (in seconds) and subconsciously, then either blocked or passed on to working memory.

Independent practice. The repetition of a skill on one's own outside the presence of the teacher.

Laterality (also Hemisphericity). The notion that the two cerebral hemispheres are specialized and process information differently.

Limbic area. The structures at the base of the cerebrum that control emotions.

Long-term potentiation. The increase in synaptic strength and sensitivity that endures as a result of repeated, frequent firings across a synapse between two associated neurons. As of now, it is the accepted mechanism for explaining long-term storage.

Long-term storage. The areas of the cerebrum where memories are stored permanently.

Magnetic resonance imaging (MRI). An instrument that uses radio waves to disturb the alignment of the body's atoms in a magnetic field to produce computer-processed, high-contrast images of internal structures.

Massed practice. The repetition of a skill over short time intervals to gain initial competence.

Mnemonic. A word or phrase used as a device for remembering unrelated information, patterns, or rules.

Motivation. The influence of needs and desires on behavior.

Motor cortex. The narrow band across the top of the brain from ear to ear that controls movement.

Myelin. A fatty substance that surrounds and insulates a neuron's axon.

Neural efficiency. The ability of the brain to use fewer neurons to accomplish a repetitive task.

Neuron. The basic cell making up the brain and nervous system, consisting of a cell body, a long fiber (axon) which transmits impulses, and many shorter fibers (dendrites) which receive them.

Neuroplasticity. The brain's lifelong ability to reorganize neural networks as a result of new experiences.

Neurotransmitter. One of several dozen chemicals stored in axon sacs that transmit impulses from neuron to neuron across the synaptic gap.

Nonassociative learning. A learning whereby the individual responds unconsciously to a stimulus.

Nondeclarative memory. Knowledge of motor and cognitive skills to which we have no conscious access, such as riding a bicycle.

Perceptual representation system. A form of nondeclarative memory in which the structure and form of objects and words that can be prompted by prior experience.

Phonemes. The minimal units of sound in a language that combine to make syllables.

Phonemic awareness. The ability to hear, identify, and manipulate phonemes in spoken syllables and words.

Phonological awareness. In addition to phonemic awareness, it includes the ability to recognize that sentences are comprised of words, words are comprised of syllables, and syllables are comprised of onsets and rimes that can be broken down into phonemes.

Plasticity. The ability of the brain to change as a result of daily learning.

Positron emission tomography (PET) scanner. An instrument that traces the metabolism of radioactively tagged sugar in brain tissue producing a color image of cell activity.

Practice. The repetition of a skill to gain speed and accuracy.

Primacy-recency effect. The phenomenon whereby one tends to remember best that which comes first in a learning episode and second best that which comes last.

Prime-time. The time in a learning episode when information or a skill is more likely to be remembered.

Procedural memory. A form of nondeclarative memory that allows the learning of motor (riding a bicycle) and cognitive (learning to read) skills.

Prosody. The rhythm, cadence, accent patterns, and pitch of a language.

Psychological-cognitive cycle. One of the body's circadian rhythms that determines the degree of focus one has during cognitive processing.

Rate of learning. The amount of time it takes one to learn cognitive information with sufficient confidence that it will be consolidated into long-term memory.

Rate of retrieval. The amount of time it takes one to recall information from long-term memory to working memory.

Rehearsal. The reprocessing of information in working memory.

Retention. The preservation of a learning in long-term storage in such a way that it can be identified and recalled quickly and accurately.

Reticular activating system (RAS). The dense formation of neurons in the brain stem that controls major body functions and maintains the brain's alertness.

Self-concept. Our perception of who we are and how we fit into the world.

Semantic memory. Knowledge of facts and data that may not be related to any event.

Sensory memory. The short-lived (usually in milliseconds) retention of information, such as recalling what someone just said to us, although we were not paying attention to the speaker.

Specialization. The notion that certain brain regions are mainly dedicated to accomplishing specific tasks, such as Broca's area.

Suprachiasmatic nuclei. A tiny cluster of neurons (located just above where the optic nerves cross on their way to the visual cortex) that monitors the intensity of signals along the optic nerve to determine the intensity of external light and start the sleep cycle.

Synapse. The microscopic gap between the axon of one neuron and the dendrite of another.

Thalamus. A part of the limbic system that receives all incoming sensory information, except smell, and shunts it to other areas of the cortex for additional processing.

Transfer. The influence that past learning has on new learning, and the degree to which the new learning will be useful in the learner's future. Positive transfer aids, and negative transfer inhibits, the acquisition of new learning.

Wait-time. The period of teacher silence that follows the posing of a question before the first student is called to respond.

White matter. The support tissue that lies beneath the cerebrum's gray matter (cortex).

Window of opportunity. An important period during which the young brain responds to certain types of input to create or consolidate a neural network.

Working memory. The temporary memory wherein information is processed consciously.

References

Abeles, H. F., & Sanders, E. M. (2005). *Final assessment report: New Jersey Symphony Orchestra's Early Strings Program.* New York: Center for Arts Education Research, Columbia University.

Acebo, C., Wolfson, A., & Carskadon, M. (1997). Relations among self-reported sleep patterns, health, and injuries in adolescents. *Sleep Research, 27,* 149.

Amunts, K., Schlaug, G., Jancke, L., Steinmetz, H., Schleicher, A., Dabringhaus, A., & Zilles, K. (1997). Motor cortex and hand motor skills: Structural compliance in the human brain. *Human Brain Mapping, 5,* 206–215.

Anderson, L. W. (Ed.), Krathwohl, D. R. (Ed.), Airasian, P. W., Cruikshank, K. A., Mayer, R. E., Pintrich, P. R., Raths, J., & Wittrock, M. C. (2001). *A taxonomy for learning, teaching, and assessing: A revision of Bloom's Taxonomy of Educational Objectives* (Complete edition). New York: Longman.

Anvari, S. H., Trainor, L. J., Woodside, J., & Levy, B. A. (2002, October). Relations among musical skills, phonological processing, and early reading ability in preschool children. *Journal of Experimental Child Psychology, 83,* 111–130.

Baddeley, A. (1995). Working memory. In M. S. Gazzaniga (Ed.), *The cognitive neurosciences,* pp. 755–764. Cambridge, MA: MIT Press.

Banich, M. (1997). *Neuropsychology: The neural bases of mental function.* New York: Houghton Mifflin.

Baron-Cohen, S. (2003). *The essential difference: The truth about the male and female brain.* New York: Basic Books.

Barry, N., Taylor, J., & Walls, K. (2002). The role of the fine and performing arts in high school dropout prevention. In R. J. Deasy (Ed.), *Critical links: Learning in the arts and student academic and social development* (pp. 74–75). Washington, DC: Arts Education Partnership.

Bassok, M., & Holyoak, K.J. (1989). Interdomain transfer between isomorphic topics in algebra and physics. *Journal of Experimental Psychology: Learning, Memory and Cognition, 15,* 153–166.

Bateman, B. Warner, J. O., Hutchinson, E., Dean, T., Rowlandson, P., Gant, C., Grundy, J., Fitzgerald, C., & Stevenson, J. (2004). The effects of a double blind, placebo controlled artificial food colorings and benzoate preservative challenge on hyperactivity in a general population sample of preschool children. *Archives of Diseases in Childhood, 89,* 506–511.

Bates, E. (1999, July-August). Language and the infant brain. *Journal of Communication Disorders, 32,* 195–205.

Beatty, J. (2001). *The human brain: Essentials of behavioral neuroscience.* Thousand Oaks, CA: Sage Publications.

Begley, S. (2000, January 1). Rewiring your gray matter. *Newsweek,* 63–65.

Blanchette, I., & Dunbar, K. (2000). How analogies are generated: The roles of structural and superficial similarity. *Memory & Cognition, 28,* 108–124.

Blanchette, I. & Dunbar, K. (2002). Representational change and analogy: How analogical inferences alter target representations. *Journal of Experimental Psychology: Learning, Memory, and Cognition, 28,* 672–685.

Blood, A. J., Zatorre, R. J., Bermudez, P., & Evans, A. C. (1999, April). Emotional responses to pleasant and unpleasant music correlate with activity in paralimbic brain regions. *Nature Neuroscience, 2*, 382–387.

Bloom, B. S. (Ed.), Engelhart, M. D., Furst, E. J., Hill, W. H., & Krathwohl, D. R. (1956). *Taxonomy of educational objectives: The classification of educational goals. Handbook I: Cognitive domain*. New York: David McKay.

Bloom, B. S. (1976). *Human characteristics and school learning*. New York: McGraw-Hill.

Bor, D., Duncan, J., Wiseman, R. J., & Owen, A. M. (2003, January). Encoding strategies dissociate prefrontal activity from working memory demand. *Neuron, 37*, 361–367.

Bower, J. M., & Parsons, L. M. (2003, August). Rethinking the lesser brain. *Scientific American, 289*, 51–57.

Brannon, E. M. & van der Walle, G. (2001). Ordinal numerical knowledge in young children. *Cognitive Psychology, 43*, 53–81.

Bromley, K., Irwin-DeVitis, L., & Modlo, M. (1995). *Graphic organizers*. New York: Scholastic.

Brooks, J. G., & Brooks, M. G. (1999). *In search of understanding: The case for constructivist classrooms* (2nd ed.) Alexandria, VA: Association for Supervision and Curriculum Development.

Buckner, R. L., Kelley, W. M., & Petersen, S. E. (1999, April). Frontal cortex contributions to human memory formation. *Nature Neuroscience, 2*, 311–314.

Burton, J. M., Horowitz, R., & Abeles, H. (2000). Learning in and through the arts: The question of transfer. *Studies in Art Education, 41*, 228–257.

Butterworth, B. (1999). *What counts: How every brain is hardwired for math*. New York: Free Press.

Butzlaff, R. (2000, Fall). Can music be used to teach reading? *Journal of Aesthetic Education, 34*, 167–178.

Buzan, T. (1989). *Use both sides of your brain* (3rd ed.). New York: Penguin.

Buzzell, K. (1998). *The children of Cyclops: The influence of television viewing on the developing human brain*. San Francisco: Association of Waldorf Schools of North America.

Cahill, L. (2005, May). His brain, her brain. *Scientific American, 292*, 40–47.

Cahill, L., & McGaugh, J. (1998). Mechanisms of emotional arousal and lasting declarative memory. *Trends in Neuroscience, 21*, 294–299.

Calvin, W., & Ojemann, G. (1994). *Conversations with Neil's brain: The neural nature of thought and language*. Menlo Park, CA: Addison-Wesley.

Cardoso, S. H. (2000, Fall). Our ancient laughing brain. *Cerebrum, 2*, 15–30.

Carskadon, M. A., Acebo, C., Wolfson, A. R., Tzischinsky, O., & Darley, C. (1997). REM sleep on MSLTS in high school students is related to circadian phase. *Sleep Research, 26*, 705.

Carter, R. (1998). *Mapping the mind*. Los Angeles: University of California Press.

Carter, T., Hardy, C. A., & Hardy, J. C. (2001, December). Latin vocabulary acquisition: An experiment using information-processing techniques of chunking and imagery. *Journal of Instructional Psychology, 28*, 225–228.

Catterall, J., Chapleau, R., & Iwanga, J. (1999, Fall). Involvement in the arts and human development: Extending an analysis of general associations and introducing the special cases of intense involvement in music and in theater arts. *Monograph Series No. 11*. Washington, DC: Americans for the Arts.

Chapman, C. (1993). *If the shoe fits: Developing the multiple intelligences classroom*. Thousand Oaks, CA: Corwin Press.

Chapman, C., & King, R. (2000). *Test success in the brain compatible classroom*. Tucson, AZ: Zephyr.

Cheour, M., Ceponiene, R., Lehtokoski, A., Luuk, A., Allik, J., Alho, K., & Näätänen, R. (1998, September). Development of language-specific phoneme representations in the infant brain. *Nature Neuroscience, 1*, 351–353.

Chularut, P., & DeBacker, T. K. (2004, July). The influence of concept mapping on achievement, self-regulation, and self-efficacy in students of English as a second language. *Contemporary Educational Psychology, 29*, 248–263.

Chung, S-C., Tack, G-R., Lee, B., Eom, G-M., Lee, S-Y., & Sohn, J-H. (2004, December). The effect of 30% oxygen on visuospatial performance and brain activation: An fMRI study. *Brain and Cognition, 56*, 279–285.

Courchesne, E. (1999, March 23). An MRI study of autism: The cerebellum revisited. Letter in *Neurology, 52,* 1106–1107.

Cowan, N. (2001). The Magical Number 4 in Short-term Memory: A Reconsideration of Mental Storage Capacity. *Behavioral and Brain Sciences, 24.* Available online at www.bbsonline.org/documents

Cumming, J., & Hall, C. (2002, February). Deliberate imagery practice: The development of imagery skills in competitive athletes. *Journal of Sports Sciences, 20,* 137–145.

Dale, P. S., Simonoff, E., Bishop, D.V.M., Eley, T. C., Oliver, B., Price, T. S., Purcell, S., Stevenson, J., & Plomin, R. (1998, August). Genetic influence on language delay in two-year-old children. *Nature Neuroscience, 1,* 324–328.

Damasio, A. (1999). *The feeling of what happens: Body and emotion in the making of consciousness.* New York: Harcourt Brace.

Danesi, M. (1990). The contribution of neurolinguistics to second and foreign language theory and practice. *System, 3,* 373–396.

Davis, J. (1997). *Mapping the mind: The secrets of the human brain and how it works.* Secaucus, NJ: Birch Lane Press.

de Fockert, J. W., Rees, G., Frith, C. D., & Lavie, N. (2001). The role of working memory in visual selective attention. *Science, 291,* 1803–1806.

Dehaene, S. (1997). *The number sense: How the mind creates mathematics.* New York: Oxford University Press.

Dehaene, S., Spelke, E., Pinel, P., Stanescu, R., & Tsivkin, S. (1999, May 7). Sources of mathematical thinking: Behavioral and brain-imaging evidence. *Science, 284,* 970–974.

DeHouwer, A. (1999). *Two or more languages in early childhood: Some general points and practical recommendations.* Washington, DC: ERIC Clearinghouse on Languages and Linguistics.

Diamond, J. (1992). *The third chimpanzee: The evolution and future of the human animal.* New York: Harper Perennial.

Diamond, M., & Hopson, J. (1998). *Magic trees of the mind: How to nurture your child's intelligence, creativity, and healthy emotions from birth through adolescence.* New York: Dutton.

Droz, M., & Ellis, L. (1996). *Laughing while learning: Using humor in the classroom.* Longmont, CO: Sopris West.

Duggan, G. B., & Payne, S. J. (2001, December). Interleaving reading and acting while following procedural instructions. *Journal of Experimental Psychology: Applied, 7,* 297–307.

Eisner, E. (2002a, September). What the arts do for the young. *School Arts, 102,* 16–17.

Eisner, E. (2002b). *The arts and the creation of mind.* New Haven, CT: Yale University Press.

Ericsson, K. A. (2003, June). Exceptional memories: Made, not born. *Trends in Cognitive Sciences, 7,* 233–235.

Everhart, D. E., Shucard, J. L., Quatrin, T., & Shucard, D. W. (2001, July). Sex-related differences in event-related potentials, face recognition, and facial affect processing in prepubertal children. *Neuropsychology, 15,* 329–341.

Fagan, J., Prigot, J., Carroll, M., Pioli, L., Stein, A., & Franco, A. (1997, December). Auditory context and memory retrieval in young infants. *Child Development, 68,* 1057–1066.

Fields, R. D. (2005, February). Making memories stick. *Scientific American, 292,* 75–81.

Fiske, E. B. (Ed.). (1999). *Champions of change: The impact of the arts on learning.* Washington, DC: President's Committee on the Arts and the Humanities.

Fleck, D. E., Berch, D. B., Shear, P. K., & Strakowski, S. M. (2001, Spring). Directed forgetting in explicit and implicit memory: The role of encoding and retrieval mechanisms. *The Psychological Record, 51,* 207–221.

Fredrickson, B. L., & Branigan, C. (2005). Positive emotions broaden the scope of attention and thought-action repertoires. *Cognition and Emotion, 19,* 313–332.

Gallup Poll (2004a). *Most teens associate school with boredom, fatigue.* Available online at http://www.gallup.com/poll

Gallup Poll (2004b). *In teens own words: Which teachers motivate you?* Available online at http://www.gallup.com/poll

Gardner, H. (1993). *Frames of mind: The theory of multiple intelligences.* (Rev. Ed.) New York: Basic Books.

Gazzaniga, M. S. (1967, August). The split brain in man. *Scientific American, 207,* 24–29.

Gazzaniga, M. S. (1989). Organization of the human brain. *Science, 245,* 947–952.

Gazzaniga, M. S. (1998a). *The mind's past.* Berkeley: University of California Press.

Gazzaniga, M. S. (1998b, July). The split brain revisited. *Scientific American, 279,* 48–55.

Gazzaniga, M. S., Ivry, R. B., & Mangun, G. R. (2002). *Cognitive neuroscience: The biology of the mind,* (2nd Ed). New York: Norton.

Gobet, F., Lane, P. C. R., Croker, S., Cheng, P., Jones, G., Oliver, I., & Pine, J. M. (2001, June). Chunking mechanisms in human learning. *Trends in Cognitive Sciences, 5,* 236–243.

Goldberg, E. (2001). *The executive brain: Frontal lobes and the civilized mind.* New York: Oxford.

Goleman, D. (1995). *Emotional intelligence: Why it can matter more than I.Q.* New York: Bantam.

Graziano, A. B., Peterson, M., & Shaw, G. L. (1999, March 15). Enhanced learning of proportional math through music training and spatial-temporal training. *Neurological Research, 21,* 139–152.

Gur, R., Turetsky, B., Matsui, M., Yan, M., Bilker, W., Hughett, P., & Gur, R.E. (1999, May 15). Sex differences in brain gray and white matter in healthy young adults: Correlations with cognitive performance. *The Journal of Neuroscience, 19,* 4065–4072.

Gur, R. C., Alsop, D., Glahn, D., Petty, R., Swanson, C. L., Maldjian, J. A., Turetsky, B. I., Detre, J. A., Gee, J., & Gur, R. E. (2000, September). An fMRI study of sex differences in regional activation to a verbal and a spatial task. *Brain and Language, 74,* 157–170.

Guterl, F. (2003, Sept. 8). Overloaded? *Newsweek,* E4–E8.

Haier, R. J., Jung, R. E., Yeo, R. A., Head, K., & Alkire, M. T. (2004, September). Structural brain variation and general intelligence. *NeuroImage, 23,* 425–433.

Hallam, S. (2002). The effects of background music on studying. In R. J. Deasy (Ed.), *Critical links: Learning in the arts and student academic and social development* (pp. 74–75). Washington, DC: Arts Education Partnership.

Hannon, E. E., & Johnson, S. P. (2005, June). Infants use meter to categorize rhythms and melodies: Implications for musical structure learning. *Cognitive Psychology, 50,* 354–377.

Hart, L. (1983). *Human brain and human learning.* New York: Longman.

Harwood, C., Cumming, J., & Hall, C. (2003, September). Imagery use in elite youth sport participants: Reinforcing the applied significance of achievement goal theory. *Research Quarterly for Exercise and Sport, 74,* 292–300.

Hawkins, J. & Blakeslee, S. (2004). *On intelligence.* New York: Times Books.

Hedges, L., & Nowell, A. (1995). Sex differences in mental test scores: Variability and numbers of high scoring individuals. *Science, 269,* 41–45.

Hetland, L. (2000a, Fall). Listening to music enhances spatial-temporal reasoning: Evidence for the "Mozart Effect." *Journal of Aesthetic Education, 34,* 105–148.

Hetland, L. (2000b, Fall). Learning to make music enhance spatial reasoning. *Journal of Aesthetic Education, 34,* 179–238.

High School Survey of Student Engagement Project (HSSSE). (2005). *The 2004 high school student engagement survey.* Bloomington, IN: Indiana University. Available online at http://www.indiana.edu/~nsse/hssse/

Ho, Y-C., Cheung, M-C., & Chan, A. S., (2003, July). Music training improves verbal but not visual memory: Cross-sectional and longitudinal explorations in children. *Neuropsychology, 17,* 439–450.

Hunter, M. (2004). *Mastery teaching.* Thousand Oaks, CA: Corwin Press.

Hyerle, D. (1996). *Visual tools for constructing knowledge.* Alexandria, VA: Association for Supervision and Curriculum Development.

Hyerle, D. (2004). *Student successes with thinking maps: School-based research, results, and models for achievement using visual tools.* Thousand Oaks, CA: Corwin Press.

Iverson, P., Kuhl, P. K., Akahane-Yamada, R., Diesch, E., Tohkura, Y., Kettermann, A., & Siebert, C. (2003, February). A perceptual interference account of acquisition difficulties for non-native phonemes. *Cognition, 87,* B47–B57.

Jausovec, N., & Jausovec, K. (2000, April 3). EEG activity during the performance of complex mental problems. *International Journal of Psychophysiology, 36,* 73–88.

Johnson, J., & Newport, E. (1991). Critical period effects on universal properties of language: The status of subjacency in the acquisition of a second language. *Cognition, 39,* 215–258.

Kempermann, G., & Gage, F. (1999, May). New nerve cells for the adult brain. *Scientific American, 280,* 48–53.

Key, N. (1991). *Research methodologies for whole-brained integration at the secondary level.* Report No. SP 037894. Pueblo, CO: U.S. Government Document Service.

Kim, A-H., Vaughn, S., Wanzek, J., & Wei, S. (2004). Graphic organizers and their effects on the reading comprehension of students with LD: A synthesis of research. *Journal of Learning Disabilities, 37,* 105–118.

Kim, K., Relkin, N., Lee, K., & Hirsch, J. (1997). Distinct cortical areas associated with native and second languages. Letter to *Nature, 388,* 171–174.

Kimura, D. (1992, September). Sex differences in the brain. *Scientific American, 267,* 119–124.

Kimura, D. (1997). *Sex and cognition.* Cambridge, MA: MIT Press.

Knecht, S., Deppe, M., Drager, B., Bobe, L., Lohmann, H., Ringelstein, E., & Henningsen, H. (2000, January). Language lateralization in healthy right-handers. *Brain, 123,* 74–81.

Korol, D. L., & Gold, P. E. (1998). Glucose, memory, and aging. *American Journal of Clinical Nutrition, 67,* 764S–771S.

Kosslyn, S. M., Pascual-Leone, A., Felician, O., Camposano, S., Keenan, J. P., Thompson, W. L., Ganis, G., Sukel, K. E., & Alpert, N. M. (1999, April 2). The role of Area 17 in visual imagery: Convergent evidence from PET and rTMS. *Science, 284,* 167–170.

Kotulak, R. (1996). *Inside the brain: Revolutionary discoveries of how the mind works.* Kansas City, MO: Andrews McMeel.

Kripke, D. F., Youngstedt, S. D., & Elliot, J. A. (1997). Light brightness effects on melatonin duration. *Sleep Research, 26,* 726.

Kuhlmann, S., Kirschbaum, C., & Wolf, O. T. (2005, March). Effects of oral cortisol treatment in healthy young women on memory retrieval of negative and neutral words. *Neurobiology of Learning and Memory, 83,* 158–162.

Laviola, G., Adriani, W., Terranova, M. L., & Gerra, G. (1999). Psychobiological risk factors for vulnerability to psychostimulants in human adolescents and animal models. *Neuroscience Biobehavior Review, 23*(7), 993–1010.

LeBoutillier, N., & Marks, D. F. (2003, February). Mental imagery and creativity: A meta-analytic review study. *British Journal of Psychology, 94,* 29–44.

Leonard, J. (1999, May-June). The sorcerer's apprentice: Unlocking the secrets of the brain's basement. *Harvard Magazine,* 56–62.

Lieberman, B. (2005, June). Study narrows search for brain's memory site. *Brain in the News, 12,* 4.

Loftus, E. (1997, September). Creating false memories. *Scientific American, 277,* 51–55.

Loomans, D., & Kolberg, K. (1993). *The laughing classroom: Everyone's guide to teaching with humor and play.* New York: H. J. Kramer.

Luciana, M., Conklin, H. M., Hooper, C. J., & Yarger, R. S. (2005). The development of nonverbal working memory and executive control processes in adolescents. *Child Development, 76,* 697–712.

Lutchmaya, S., Baron-Cohen, S., & Raggatt, P. (2002). Fetal testosterone and vocabulary size in 18– and 24-month-old infants. *Infant Behavior and Development, 24,* 418–424.

Lynch, G. (2002). Memory enhancement: The search for mechanism-based drugs. *Nature Neuroscience, 5,* 1035–1038.

Maquire, E. A., Frith, C. D., & Morris, R. G. M. (1999, October). The functional neuroanatomy of comprehension and memory: The importance of prior knowledge. *Brain, 122,* 1839–1850.

Mazard, A., Laou, L., Joliot, M., & Mellet, E. (2005, August). Neural impact of the semantic content of visual mental images and visual percepts. *Cognitive Brain Research, 24,* 423–435.

Menon, V., & Levitin, D. J. (2005, October). The rewards of music listening: Response and physiological connectivity of the mesolimbic system. *NeuroImage, 28,* 175–184.

Merzenich, M. M., Jenkins, W. M., Johnston, P., Schreiner, C., Miller, S. L., & Tallal, P. (1996, January 5). Temporal processing deficits of language-learning impaired children ameliorated by training. *Science,* 271.

Mestre, J. (2002). *Transfer of learning: Issues and research agenda.* Arlington, VA: National Science Foundation.

Miller, G. A. (1956). The magical number seven, plus-or-minus two: Some limits on our capacity for processing information. *Psychological Review, 101,* 343–352.

Millichap, J. G., & Yee, M. M. (2003). The diet factor in pediatric and adolescent migraine. *Pediatric Neurology, 28,* 9–15.

Millman, R. P. (2005, June). Excessive sleepiness in adolescents and young adults: Causes, consequences, and treatment strategies. *Pediatrics, 115,* 1774–1786.

Moore, K. D. (2005). *Effective instructional strategies: From theory to practice.* Thousand Oaks, CA: Sage Publications.

Muftuler, L. T., Bodner, M., Shaw, G. L., & Nalcioglu, O. (1999). *fMRI of Mozart effect using auditory stimuli.* Abstract presented at the 7th meeting of the International Society for Magnetic Resonance in Medicine, Philadelphia.

Nakamura, S., Sadato, N., Oohashi, T., Nishina, E., Fuwamoto, Y., & Yonekura, Y. (1999, November 19). Analysis of music-brain interaction with simultaneous measurement of regional cerebral blood flow and electroencephalogram beta rhythm in human subjects. *Neuroscience Letters, 275,* 222–226.

National Center for Education Statistics. (NCES). (2003). *The nation's report card, 2003.* Washington, DC: Author.

National Governors Association (NGA). (2005). *2005 Rate Your Future Survey.* Washington, DC: Author. Available online at http://www.nga.org

National Reading Panel. (NRP). (2000). *Teaching children to read: An evidence-based assessment of the scientific research literature and its implications for reading instruction.* Washington, DC: National Institute of Child Health and Human Development.

Neubauer, A. C., Grabner, R. H., Fink, A., & Neuper, C. (2005). Intelligence and neural efficiency: Further evidence of the influence of task content and sex on the brain-IQ relationship. *Cognitive Brain Research, 25,* 217–225.

Neubauer, A. C., Grabner, R. H., Freudenthaler, H. H., Beckmann, J. F., & Guthke, J. (2004, May). Intelligence and individual differences in becoming neurally efficient. *Acta Psychologica, 116,* 55–74.

Njemanze, P. C. (2005, March). Cerebral lateralization and general intelligence: Gender differences in a transcranial Doppler study. *Brain and Language, 92,* 234–239.

Norton, A., Winner, E., Cronin, K., Overy, K., Lee, D. J., & Schlaug, G. (2005). Are there pre-existing neural, cognitive, or motoric markers for musical ability? *Brain and Cognition.*

Oberauer, K., & Kliegl, R. (2004, August). Simultaneous cognitive operations in working memory after dual-task practice. *Journal of Experimental Psychology: Human Perception and Performance, 30,* 689–707.

Oberman, L. M., Hubbard, E. M., McCleery, J. P., Altschuler, E. L., Ramachandran, V. S., & Pineda, J. A. (2005, July). EEG evidence for mirror neuron dysfunction in autism spectrum disorders. *Cognitive Brain Research, 24,* 190–198.

Ornstein, R., & Thompson, R. (1984). *The amazing brain.* Boston: Houghton Mifflin.

Parrott, C. A. (1986). Visual imagery training: Stimulating utilization of imaginal processes. *Journal of Mental Imagery, 10,* 47–64.

Parsons, L. M., & Osherson, D. (2001, October). New evidence for distinct right and left brain systems for deductive versus probabilistic reasoning. *Cerebral Cortex, 11,* 954–965.

Patterson, M. N. (1997). *Every body can learn.* Tucson, AZ: Zephyr.

Paus, T. (2005). Mapping brain maturation and cognitive development during adolescence. *Trends in Cognitive Sciences, 9,* 60–68.

Penhune, V. B., & Doyon, J. (2005, July). Cerebellum and M1 interaction during early learning of timed motor sequences. *NeuroImage, 26,* 801–812.

Perkins, D., & Salomon, G. (1988, September). Teaching for transfer. *Educational Leadership, 46,* 22–32.

Perani, D., & Abutalebi, J. (2005, April). The neural basis of first and second language processing. *Current Opinion in Neurobiology, 15,* 202–206.

Petrosini, L., Graziano, A., Mandolesi, L., Neri, P., Molinari, M., & Leggio, M. G. (2003, June). Watch how to do it! New advances in learning by observation. *Brain Research Reviews, 42,* 252–264.

Pinker, S. (1994). *The language instinct: How the mind creates language.* New York: Harper Perennial.

Poe, M. D., Burchinal, M. R., & Roberts, J. E. (2004). Early language and the development of children's reading skills. *Journal of School Psychology, 42,* 315–332.

Press, D. Z., Casement, M. D., Pascual-Leone, A., & Robertson, E. M. (2005). The time course of off-line motor sequence learning. *Cognitive Brain Research, 25,* 375–378.

Rabkin, N., & Redmond, R. (2004). *Putting the arts in the picture: Reforming education in the 21st century.* Chicago: Columbia College.

Raths, J. (2002, Autumn). Improving instruction. *Theory Into Practice, 41,* 233–237.

Rauscher, F. H., & Zupan, M. A. (2000). Classroom keyboard instruction improves kindergarten children's spatial-temporal performance: A field experiment. *Early Childhood Research Quarterly, 15,* 215–228.

Rauscher, F. H., Shaw, G. L., Levine, L. J., Wright, E. L., Dennis, W. R., & Newcomb, R. L. (1997). Music training causes long-term enhancement of preschool children's spatial-temporal reasoning. *Neurological Research, 19,* 2–8.

Reiss, D., Neiderheiser, J., Hetherington, E. M., & Plomin, R. (2000). *The relationship code: Deciphering genetic and social influences on adolescent development.* Cambridge, MA: Harvard University Press.

Restak, R. M. (2001). *The secret life of the brain.* Washington, DC: Dana Press.

Restak, R. M. (2003). *The new brain: How the modern age is rewiring your mind.* New York: Rodale.

Ringo, J. L., Doty, R. W., Demeter, S., & Simard, P. Y. (1994). Time is of the essence: A conjecture that hemispheric specialization arises from interhemispheric conduction delays. *Journal of the Cerebral Cortex, 4,* 331–343.

Roberts, P., & Kellough, D. (2003). *A guide for developing interdisciplinary thematic units* (3rd Ed.). Englewood Cliffs, NJ: Prentice Hall.

Rodier, P. (2000, February). The early origins of autism. *Scientific American, 282,* 56–63.

Roediger, H. L., III, & McDermott, K. B. (1995). Creating false memories: Remembering words not presented in lists. *Journal of Experimental Psychology: Learning, Memory, and Cognition, 21,* 803–814.

Root-Bernstein, R. S. (1997, July 11). Art for science's sake. *Chronicle of Higher Education,* B6.

Rose, S. (1992). *The making of memory.* New York: Doubleday.

Rose, S. (2005). *The future of the brain: The promise and perils of tomorrow's neuroscience.* New York: Oxford University Press.

Rowe, M. B. (1974). Wait-time and rewards as instructional variables: Their influence on language, logic, and fate control. *Journal of Research on Science Teaching, 2,* 81–94.

Russell, P. (1979). *The brain book.* New York: E. P. Dutton.

Schacter, D. L. (1996). *Searching for memory: The brain, mind, and the past.* New York: Basic Books.

Schacter, D. L. (2001). *The seven sins of memory.* New York: Houghton Mifflin.

Schafer, G. (2005). Infants can learn decontextualized words before their first birthday. *Child Development, 76,* 87–96.

Schank, R. C. (1990). *Tell me a story: Narrative and intelligence.* Evanston, IL: Northwestern University Press.

Schlaug, G., Jancke, L., Huang, Y. X., & Steinmetz, H. (1995). In-vivo evidence of structural brain asymmetry in musicians. *Science, 267,* 699–701.

Schmidt, S. R. (1995). Effects of humor on sentence memory. *Journal of Experimental Psychology: Learning, Memory and Cognition, 20,* 953–967.

Schmidt, S. R. (2002). The humour effect: Differential processing and privileged retrieval. *Memory, 10,* 127–138.

Schmithhorst, V. J., & Holland, S. K. (2004, January). The effect of musical training on the neural correlates of math processing: A functional magnetic resonance imaging study in humans. *Neuroscience Letters, 354,* 193–196.

Scholey, A. B., Moss, M. C., Neave, N., & Wesnes, K. (1999, November). Cognitive performance, hyperoxia, and heart rate following oxygen administration in healthy young adults. *Physiological Behavior, 67,* 783–789.

Scott-Simmons, D., Barker, J., & Cherry, N. (2003, May). Integrating research and story writng. *The Reading Teacher, 56,* 742–745.

Shadmehr, R., & Holcomb, H. H. (1997, August 8). Neural correlates of motor memory consolidation. *Science, 277,* 821–825.

Shallice, T. (1999, July). The origin of confabulations. *Nature Neuroscience, 2,* 588–590.

Shaywitz, S. E. (2003). *Overcoming dyslexia: A new and complete science-based program for reading problems at any level.* New York: Knopf.

Shaywitz, B. A., Shaywitz, S. E., & Gore, J. (1995). Sex differences in the functional organization of the brain for language. *Nature, 373,* 607–609.

Shaywitz, S. E., Shaywitz, B. A., Pugh, K. R., Fulbright, R. K., Constable, R. T., Mencl, W. E., Shankweiler, D. P., Liberman, A. M., Skudlarski, P., Fletcher, J. M., Katz, L., Marchione, K. E., Lacadie, C., Gatenby, C., & Gore, J. C. (1998, March 3). Functional disruption in the organization of the brain for reading in dyslexia. *Neurobiology, 5,* 2636–2641.

Shearer, B. (2004). Multiple intelligences theory after 20 years. *Teachers College Record, 106,* 2–16.

Silverberg, S., & Samuel, A. G. (2004, October). The effect of age of second language acquisition on the representation and processing of second language words. *Journal of Memory and Language, 51,* 381–398.

Smith, E. E., & Jonides, J. (1999, March 12). Storage and executive processes in the frontal lobes. *Science, 283,* 1657–1661.

Sousa, D. A. (1998a, May). Brain research can help principals reform secondary schools. *NASSP Bulletin, 82,* 21–28.

Sousa, D. A. (1998b, December 16). Is the fuss about brain research justified? *Education Week,* p. 52.

Sousa, D. A. (2003). *The leadership brain: How to lead today's schools more effectively.* Thousand Oaks, CA: Corwin Press.

Sousa, D. A. (2005). *How the brain learns to read.* Thousand Oaks, CA: Corwin Press.

Sowell, E. R., Thompson, P. M., Holmes, C. J., Jernigan, T. L., & Toga, A. W. (1999). In-vivo evidence for post-adolescent brain maturation in frontal and striatal regions. *Nature: Neuroscience, 2,* 859–861.

Spencer, S. J., Steele, C. M., & Quinn, D. M. (1999, January). Stereotype threat and women's math performance. *Journal of Experimental Social Psychology, 35,* 4–28.

Sperry, R. (1966). Brain bisection and consciousness. In Eccles, J. (Ed.), *How the self controls its brain.* New York: Springer-Verlag.

Springer, S. P., & Deutsch, G. (1998). *Left brain/right brain* (5th ed.). New York: W. H. Freeman.

Squire, L. R., & Kandel, E. R. (1999). *Memory: From mind to molecules.* New York: W. H. Freeman.

Stahl, R. J. (1985). *Cognitive information processes and processing within a uniprocess superstructure/ microstructure framework: A practical information-based model.* Unpublished manuscript, University of Arizona, Tucson.

Stein, H. (1987, July-August). Visualized notetaking: Left-right brain theory applied in the classroom. *The Social Studies.*

Steinberg, L. (2005). Cognitive and effective development in adolescence. *Trends in Cognitive Sciences, 9,* 69–74.

Sternberg, R. J., Ferrari, M., Clinkenbeard, P. R., & Grigorenko, E. L. (1996). Identification, instruction, and assessment of gifted children: A construct validation of a triarchic model. *Gifted Child Quarterly, 40,* 129–137.

Sternberg, R. J., Grigorenko, E. L., Jarvin, L., Clinkenbeard, P., Ferrari, M., & Torfi, B. (2000, Spring). The effectiveness of triarchic teaching and assessment. *National Research Center on the Gifted and Talented Newsletter,* 3–8.

Tallal, P., Miller, S. L., Bedi, G., Byma, G., Wang, X., Nagarajan, S., Schreiner, C., Jenkins, W. M., & Merzenich, M. M. (1996, January 5). Fast-element enhanced speech improves language comprehension in language-learning impaired children. *Science, 271,* 81–84.

Terry, W. S. (2005). Serial position effects in recall of television commercials. *Journal of General Psychology, 132,* 151–163.

Thomas, E. (1972, April). The variation of memory with time for information appearing during a lecture. *Studies in Adult Education,* 57–62.

Thomas, L. (1979). *The Medusa and the snail.* New York: Viking Press.

Tuma, R. S. (2005, July-August). An eye on shut-eye. *Brain Work, 15,* p. 6.

United States Department of Education. (USDOE). (2000). *Elementary and secondary survey, 2000.* Washington, DC: Author.

Van Petten, C., & Bloom, P. (1999, February). Speech boundaries, syntax, and the brain. *Nature Neuroscience, 2,* 103–104.

Vaughn, K. (2000, Fall). Music and mathematics: Modest support for the oft-claimed relationship. *Journal of Aesthetic Education, 34,* 149–166.

Vaughn, K., & Winner, E. (2000, Fall). SAT scores of students who study the arts: What we can and cannot conclude about the association. *Journal of Aesthetic Education, 34,* 77–89.

Wagner, A. D., Schacter, D. L., Rotte, M., Koutstaal, W., Maril, A., Dale, A. M., Rosen, B. R., & Buckner, R. L. (1998, August 21). Building memories: Remembering and forgetting of verbal experiences as predicted by brain activity. *Science, 281,* 1188–1191.

Walker, M. P., Stickgold, R., Alsop, D., Gaab, N., & Schlaug, G. (2005). Sleep-dependent motor memory plasticity in the human brain. *Neuroscience, 133,* 911–917.

Weinberger, N. M. (2004, November). Music and the brain. *Scientific American, 291,* 89–95.

Weisman, D. H., & Banich, M. T. (2000). The cerebral hemispheres cooperate to perform complex but not simple tasks. *Neuropsychology, 14,* 41–59.

West, C. K., Farmer, J. A., & Wolff, P. M. (1991). *Instructional design: Implications from cognitive science.* Englewood, Cliffs, NJ: Prentice-Hall.

Wigfield, A., & Eccles, J. S. (2002). Students' motivation during the middle school years. In J. Aronson (Ed.), *Improving academic development: Impact of psychological factors in education.* New York: Academic Press.

Witney, A. G. (2004, November). Internal models for bi-manual tasks. *Human Movement Science, 23,* 747–770.

Wixted, J. T. (2004). The psychology and neuroscience of forgetting. *Annual Review of Psychology, 55,* 235–269.

Wolfson, A., & Carskadon, M. (1998). Sleep schedules and daytime functioning in adolescents. *Child Development, 69,* 875–887.

Wulf, G., Shea, C. H., & Matschiner, S. (1998). Frequent feedback enhances complex motor skill learning. *Journal of Motor Behavior, 30,* 180–192.

Zimmerman, F. J., & Christakis, D. A. (2005, July). Children's television viewing and cognitive outcomes: A longitudinal analysis of national data. *Archives of Pediatrics and Adolescent Medicine, 159,* 619–625.

Resources

Books

Berninger, V., & Richards, T. (2002). *Brain literacy for educators and psychologists.* San Diego, CA: Academic Press.

Calvin, W. (2004). *A brief history of the mind: From apes to intellect and beyond.* New York: Oxford University Press.

Damasio, A. (2003). *Looking for Spinoza: Joy, sorrow and the feeling brain.* New York: Harcourt Brace.

Edelman, G. (2004). *Wider than the sky: The phenomenal gift of consciousness.* New Haven, CT: Yale University Press.

Juslin, P. N., & Sloboda, J. A. (2001). *Music and emotion: Theory and research.* New York: Oxford University Press.

Pinker, S. (2002). *The blank slate: The modern denial of human nature.* New York: Viking.

Ridley, M. (2003). *Nature via nurture: Genes, experience, and what makes us human.* New York: Harper Collins.

Strauch, B. (2003). *The primal teen: What the new discoveries about the teenage brain tell us about our kids.* New York: Doubleday.

Sylwester, R. (2005). *How to explain a brain: An educator's handbook of brain terms and cognitive processes.* Thousand Oaks, CA: Corwin Press.

Internet Sites

Brain Connection

www.brainconnection.com

Brainland: The Neuroscience Information Center

www.brainland.com

Although this site is designed for professionals in neuroscience, educators interested in brain research will find a lot of interesting information.

The Center for Applied Linguistics

www.cal.org

This is a private, non-profit organization that uses the findings of linguistics and related sciences in identifying and addressing language-related problems. CAL carries out a wide range of activities including research, teacher education, analysis and dissemination of information, design and development of instructional materials, technical assistance, and program evaluation.

The Center for Arts Education

www.cae-nyc.org

This Center is committed to restoring, stimulating, and sustaining quality arts education as an essential part of every child's education. It identifies, funds, and supports exemplary partnerships and programs that demonstrate how the arts contribute to learning and student achievement. Although the Center mainly supports New York City's schools, its Web site has useful information about arts programs and resources.

Dana Alliance for Brain Initiatives

www.dana.org

Earobics Literacy Launch

Cognitive Concepts, Inc.
www.earobic.com

A research-based supplemental reading program for students in pre-kindergarten through grade 3. A combination of computer technology, multimedia tools, and print materials support components in phonological awareness, vocabulary, fluency, phonics, and reading comprehension.

Education Resources Information Center (ERIC)

www.eric.ed.gov

Fast ForWord Reading Language Program

Scientific Learning Corporation
www.scientificlearning.com

A scientifically based computer program that is designed for helping beginning readers develop phonemic awareness, letter-sound correspondences, fluent word recognition, vocabulary, and an appreciation of literature. Programs for older struggling readers are also available.

Inspiration Software, Inc.

http://inspiration.com

This company produces software that helps students construct all types of visual organizers for improving comprehension and building thinking skills. *Kidspiration* is designed for grades K through 5, and *Inspiration* is for grade 6 and higher. Demonstration versions can be downloaded from the site.

National Institutes of Health

www.nih.gov

National Network for Early Language Learning (NNELL)

www.nnell.org

This is an organization for educators involved in teaching foreign languages to children. The organization facilitates cooperation among organizations directly concerned with early language learning; facilitates communication among teachers, teacher educators, parents, program administrators, and policymakers; and disseminates information and guidelines to assist in developing programs of excellence.

Neuroscience for Kids

http://faculty.washington.edu/chudler/neurok.html

The Society for Neuroscience

www.sfn.org

Educators will find useful information in *Brain Briefings* and *Brain Backgrounders.*

Thematic Units Sites:

Lesson Plans for K-12 Teachers: http://library.csus.edu/guides/rogenmoserd/educ/lesson.htm
A to Z Teacher Stuff/Themes: http://atozteacherstuff.com/Themes/
CA Dept. of Education/Recommended Literature: http://www.cde.ca.gov/ci/rl/ll/
Lessonplanz.com Thematic Units: http://lessonplanz.com/Lesson_Plans/Thematic_Units/
Teacher Guide.com Thematic Units: http://www.theteachersguide.com/Thematicunits.html

U.S. Department of Education

www.ed.gov

Whole Brain Atlas

www.med.harvard.edu/AANLIB/home.html

Hundreds of different types of brain scans.

Index

Page numbers in **boldface** are **Practitioner's Corners.**

**CORWIN
PRESS**

The Corwin Press logo—a raven striding across an open book—represents the union of courage and learning. Corwin Press is committed to improving education for all learners by publishing books and other professional development resources for those serving the field of PreK–12 education. By providing practical, hands-on materials, Corwin Press continues to carry out the promise of its motto: **"Helping Educators Do Their Work Better."**